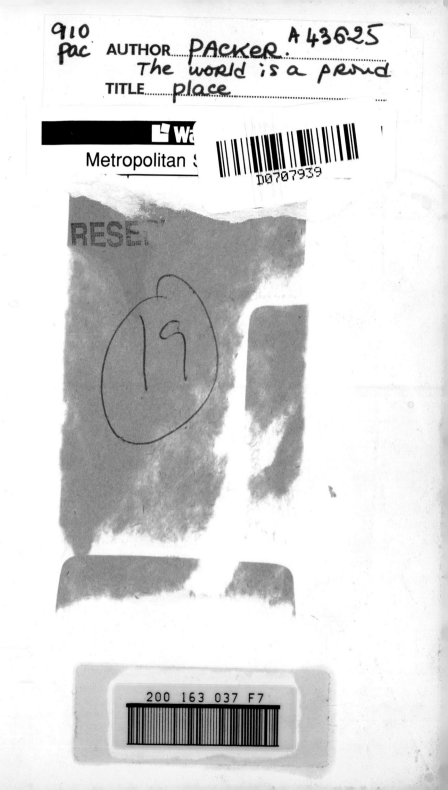

THE WORLD IS A PROUD PLACE

Also by Joy Packer

Autobiography

PACK AND FOLLOW
GREY MISTRESS
APES AND IVORY
HOME FROM SEA

Novels

VALLEY OF THE VINES
NOR THE MOON BY NIGHT
THE HIGH ROOF
THE GLASS BARRIER
THE MAN IN THE MEWS

JOY PACKER

The World
is a Proud Place

EYRE & SPOTTISWOODE · LONDON

First published 1966
by Eyre & Spottiswoode (Publishers) Ltd
167 Fleet Street, EC4
© *1966 by Joy Packer*
Printed in Great Britain by
Cox & Wyman Ltd, Reading

For Elspeth
who shared so much

Contents

Contents

Illustrations

9

Acknowledgments

The right to reproduce the following plates is gratefully acknowledged: Australian News and Information Bureau, 4; *Barrier Daily Truth*, 3a; Joy Cooke, 1a, 1b, 2b and 5a; John Fairfax and Sons (Australia) Ltd., 6b; Hawaii Visitors Bureau, 10a; Infoplan, 10b, 12a and 12b; Beryl Keirnander, 8b; Helen Lefroy, 2a; New South Wales Government Tourist Bureau, 9; Elspeth Rhodes, 3b, 5b and 7b; United States Travel Bureau, 7a, 8a, 11a and 11b; Western Australia Government Tourist Bureau, 6a.

Acknowledgments and thanks are due to the following authors and publishers for permission to quote copyright material:

to Victor de Kock and Allen & Unwin Ltd. (Those in Bondage); to the Australian National Travel Association and Ure Smith Pty., Ltd. (Walkabout's Australia); Mary Durack and Constable and Co. Ltd. (Kings in Grass Castles); Alan Moorehead and Hamish Hamilton Ltd. (Cooper's Creek); Lawrence G. Green and Howard Timmins Pty., Ltd. (Karoo).

PART ONE

The Proud Place

The world is a proud place, peopled with men of positive quality, with heroes and demi-gods standing round us, who will not let us sleep.

EMERSON

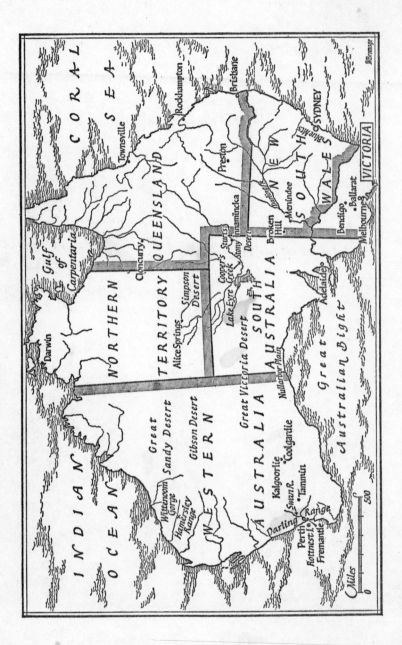

CHAPTER ONE

Indian Ocean Prelude

The little Dutch cargo boat, *Straat Cumberland*, looked tiny that February afternoon in Cape Town docks. She was loading wool and timber and a smelly cargo of fishmeal. The snow-white cruise ship, *Brasil*, with her small smart green funnel and patrician air, was disdainful in the neighbouring berth. On the other side a Union Castle fruit ship embarked peaches and grapes.

'For Covent Garden,' I said to the friends who were seeing me off. 'Oranges, bananas, avocados, pineapples – all on their way to grey old England. What a lucky land we are!'

There'd be blizzards in Europe now, while here in South Africa we basked in summer's warmth. In Australia too the sun would be shining. By nine o'clock tonight I'd be on my way to Fremantle, the port for Perth, Western Australia, where my son, Piet, and his wife and four boys had settled over two years ago. In a lifetime of travel in the continents of Africa, Europe and Asia I had never yet set foot in Australia or America.

It didn't take long to explore the twelve passenger accommodation. I had a nice cabin and shower; there was a small lounge with seascape windows, and the deck space outside was equipped with steamer-chairs; the dining-room was below, and the ship was air-conditioned. The officers were Dutch and the crew Chinese, recruited in Hong Kong.

A family of playful seals, Pa, Ma and the baby, disported themselves in the basin, full of doggy charm. The gulls mewed about us, their wing-tips gold in the sunset. The first wisps of cloud hovered over Table Mountain. Soon the snowy cloth would pour over her granite bastion and the white-horses would prance in the bay. By then we'd be out at sea.

Night fell, the giraffe-necked cranes ceased their groaning labours; my friends bade me good-bye and left.

Down on the well deck the Chinese seamen leaned over the rail. When not on duty they wore pyjamas day or night. They wolf-whistled and postured for the benefit of a handsome coloured tart. Her gay upturned face was hard as the smooth brown skin of a passion-fruit as she laughed back at them. The gangway creaked out of sight, the escorting tug bustled about her business and the *Brasil* preceded us out of harbour like a duchess wearing a little green cap from a Christmas cracker. We passed between the flashing harbour lights and the swish of our tug faded. The glittering encrusted pattern of Cape Town danced with life as the endless flow of traffic shuttled along the pale green ribbons of the great arteries to the north. The Twelve Apostles came into view with chains of coloured lights about their ankles and the lonely beam of Slangkop Lighthouse raked the dark ocean.

The raucous gulls were silent now and the Chinese pyjama-boys had melted into their quarters. There was a change in our rhythm as the Cape rollers lifted and rocked our vessel gently. The moon swam into the herring sky and threw her wavering silver path across the sea. You could wade in light from *Straat Cumberland* all the way to the horizon.

Next day I settled in.

Wong, my cabin-steward, brought me tea at seven o'clock. He was lightly built with the smooth small-featured celestial face which makes it impossible to tell the age of any Chinaman. Actually he was twenty-six.

'Good morning,' he said with a bright smile. 'How are you this morning?'

'Very well. How are you?'

'I am well. Littie bit lough last night.'

'She rolled a bit.'

He put the tray on the stool by my bunk and poured the tea with a narrow oriental hand.

'Milk? Shoo-gah?'

'Yes, sugar one spoon.'

Wong was amiable, well-mannered and easily amused. The pocket of his white jacket always bulged with a much thumbed

English-Chinese dictionary which he studied diligently whenever he was not engaged in his manifold duties. He had escaped from Red China into Hong Kong where he had signed on in *Straat Cumberland*.

'My father and mother still in Led China,' he said sorrowfully. 'But I go to see my cushin in Shudney.'

We had many conversations about this cousin in Sydney, who was studying to be a doctor.

'Takee long time – four, five years to be doctor,' Wong said.

'Four, five years only the beginning. Seven, eight years and then learn all the time.'

This was his second voyage. Both Sydney and the cousin had entranced him and it grieved him that Australia's 'all white' policy forbade him or his relation to settle permanently in that land of promise and prosperity. Except in the case of students, the Australian quota does not allow Asiatics more than a year in the country, so a good deal of stowing away goes on between Hong Kong and Sydney, and the crew help their compatriots. There was the dramatic case of the British ship carrying three Asiatic stowaways. The Sydney police were wise to it and searched the crew's quarters. The ship's carpenter quickly knocked up a panel over a wall recess and walled in the stowaways until the police had gone. When the panel was removed all three were found suffocated. The crew lost their heads, wrapped the bodies in sheets and flung them overboard, where they floated in the harbour in shrouds stamped with the vessel's name!

Straat Cumberland was based on Sydney. She plied between Australia, the Far East and the African coast. The Captain, who was married to an Australian, had his home in Sydney, the big jolly Chief Engineer and his South African wife and children lived near Durban, and the Chief Officer's family was in Holland.

All the officers spoke good English, especially the Captain. In his years at sea he had literally carried the biblical African cargoes of 'gold and silver and ivory and apes and peacocks'. Well, possibly not peacocks, but ostriches, to say nothing of rhinos, gazelles, giraffes, elephants and the little rhesus monkeys so often used for scientific experiments.

'The monkeys get flu,' he said. 'They sit shivering miserably, looking like homesick children. We dose them with sulphur and they usually recover. They are really trusting and sweet-natured and one gets very fond of them.'

The First Officer joined in. 'We're circus hands. I even had to give injections to a rhino once. He hardly noticed.'

Dutch ships' officers take a hospital course for several weeks and can cope with accidents and emergencies – even confinements – whether their patients happen to be monkeys, rhinos or human beings.

Three days out from Cape Town we docked in the humid summer heat of beautiful Durban, where I was met by Elspeth Rhodes who had flown to Natal to see her ageing mother.

Elspeth lives in London, and it was there, a few months earlier, that we had planned the journey that was to take us round the world.

It was one of those unpremeditated decisions that can make life so exciting. She had come to see me in the mews cottage where I was spending the summer. Her husband and mine had been close friends from the age of twelve, when they had been term-mates at Dartmouth; and when Elspeth had married Philip Rhodes during the war the family friendship had become, if possible, even closer. Then Philip had died in Kenya where they had bought a dairy farm after the war.

'It's too bad Piet and Glen and their boys are so far away,' she said. 'You must miss them terribly.'

'I do. But I'm going to Perth next year to see them.'

'How splendid! Aren't you lucky! I've never been to Australia.'

That was when it struck me – the wonderful idea.

'Why don't you meet me there?'

She looked up, startled.

'Do!' I urged. 'Why not?'

'And return to England by America. I've never seen America either – and I dote on Americans.'

'I hadn't thought about America – or coming to England again next year.'

'Why not?' She threw my question back at me, her dark eyes brimming as they do when she laughs. 'We could go from Perth to Sydney and across the Pacific—'

'Stopping at Hawaii!'

'Stepping ashore in America at San Francisco – and we could see the Grand Canyon and fly to the Deep South – New Orleans—'

'And visit Frances Hoare-Smith in Virginia.'

'Then New York and across the Atlantic in a Queen.'

We gasped. We studied an atlas and considered our bank accounts. The milk cheque from the farm she still owned in Kenya was good.

'But how can I do all this?' she said. 'I have to go and see my old Mum in Durban next year.'

'Then we can meet in Durban and start from there.'

'If we do that, it's round the world!'

That was how it all began. So now Elspeth was spending a month with her old Mum in Durban while I dawdled across the Indian Ocean by sea. By making the crossing by air she could meet me in Perth soon after my arrival there.

We had a day together, and, when she came to see me off, *Straat Cumberland* was loading the last of a consignment of coffee.

'See you in Perth,' I said as she went down the gangway. She turned and smiled and waved a long slender hand.

The rest of our passengers had joined us in Durban. We were a mixed bag.

Mr and Mrs Thiel inhaled the aroma of coffee nostalgically. It was strong in the hot sun.

'That's part of the life we're leaving behind,' said Mrs Thiel. 'I was brought up on a coffee plantation in Uganda.'

Her husband had been in Government service in East Africa but his job had recently been given to an African.

'Fair enough. Africanization. Part of the show,' he said. 'But there's nothing more in East Africa for us. We're going to try our luck in Australia.'

Dr Sweeteapple, a well-known Durban surgeon who had originally hailed from Adelaide, was taking his wife to Australia on a prolonged holiday. Dr McLaren, who had been visiting a nephew in Natal, was likewise from Adelaide, though of an earlier vintage. Mrs Childers was the widow of an Australian, and her son, Hugh, was going to complete his education at Melbourne University. Miss Perry and Miss Calderwood were retired London school-teachers. They were born explorers enjoying the study of history and geography at first hand. The other two who made up our temporary family were Jerry Gifford, a Cockney commercial traveller who sold clothing in the Outback, and Mrs Guttig, the widow of a Dutch sea-captain who had escaped with his ship and his wife when Holland was overrun by the Nazis. Mrs Guttig was probably the most seasoned sailor of us all and had even sailed in her husband's ship throughout the war years when every convoy was an enemy target.

'I had no home any more, and no children. My man's ship was my home, so I stayed with him.'

Lourenço Marques was our last African port of call. The capital of the Portuguese East African Province of Mozambique, it is a modern sophisticated city of splendid boulevards of yellow cassias and scarlet flamboyants, with many restaurants spilling over the sidewalks to help account for its famed 'continental atmosphere'.

In Mozambique and Angola, Portugal still clings to the African remnants of her once great colonial empire. Her medieval mariners had been the first to round the Cape and blaze the Indian Ocean trail to the spice islands and treasure houses of the East. Her civilizing influence has been far-reaching, but now her hold is slipping.

That night most of us dined ashore on a palm-fringed terrace by the sea. The languorous tropical night was fragrant with flowers and the spicy aroma of our giant prawns piri-piri. The Dao white wine was fresh and a little sharp.

'It's extraordinary,' remarked Dr Sweeteapple, 'how colonial has become a dirty word. Yet without colonialism Africa would have remained the Dark Continent indefinitely.'

Indeed, colonial expansion brought many blessings – some questionable – to the natives of remote and backward parts of the world. It brought trade, Christianity, medical science, an awareness of money, and a desire for firearms and hard liquor to a great many savage parts of the earth. But in Africa it engendered an undying desire for revenge. For three centuries the world's most profitable African trade was slaves – from the West Coast to the plantations of the New World, and from the East Coast to North Africa and the Middle East. Europeans, Arabs and

African Chiefs were all in the lucrative tragic game up to their ears. Then the world trend towards Liberty, Equality and Fraternity put an end to this evil traffic, and, as a cynical result, Europe's penetration of Africa deepened. The great mercantile powers piously moved into the Dark Continent (which still had untold wealth to yield) to enforce the abolition of slavery. At the turn of the last century the scramble for Africa was at its height. Today's scramble out is just as interesting in its own fashion, with a long legacy of black hate to speed it on its dangerous way.

At dawn we sailed on a new course, south-east across the Indian Ocean for a fortnight without landfall.

We lived in the vacuum of our little world apart and soon shook down into a communal existence. Shook with a vengeance! Off Madagascar cyclone Giselle tossed our vessel to and fro with wild abandon, and, when Giselle had gone her wanton way, Henrietta followed with equal violence.

I had incorrectly expected the voyage to be steamy hot, but the weather settled down and became perfect. Fresh, calm and sunny with a sapphire sea, air-conditioning off and windows open. The chief steward produced quoits and a ping-pong set, and a canvas swimming-pool was rigged on the iron deck by the after-holds.

Our amusements were simple. We shared each others' books and 'toys'. Dr McLaren produced a lovely carved red and white chess set and taught Miss Calderwood and Jerry Gifford the finer intricacies of the game. In the evenings we played cards and Scrabble, and once young Hugh ran off his Merseybeat tapes. They met with a slightly mixed reception. The school-teachers entertained us with a show of coloured slides taken on their last holiday through Italy and the Isles of Greece, punctuated with an interesting commentary and some fashionably eccentric effects when slides were shown upside-down or sideways-on. The Captain, who was sociable and excellent company, often joined his passengers.

'We haven't seen a ship since leaving Lourenço Marques,' complained Mrs Childers one evening when we were having sundowners. 'Nothing but sea.'

'This is a big empty ocean,' said the Captain, 'and we have it to ourselves. We're not likely to see another ship till we're near Fremantle. Not many birds either, except an albatross or two.'

Miss Perry uttered an exclamation. 'Why, look! The sea is positively boiling over there!'

The Captain followed her gaze. 'Must be a shoal.'

Then we saw them. A school of leaping dolphins, making for the shimmering patch of water that indicated the shoal's feeding ground. The dolphins were exciting, like a herd of springbok in the veld. There is such gaiety in the act of leaping, such life and elasticity, that one's spirit leaps to match it. Springbok, impala, porpoises. These we knew. Soon there would be kangaroos and wallabies!

Although, as the Captain predicted, we didn't sight so much as a whiff of smoke till we reached Western Australia, ghost sails in plenty must have haunted our 'big empty ocean'.

Nearly five centuries ago the Portuguese expeditions of Prince Henry the Navigator were rounding the Cape in search of an eastern seaway to the wealth of the Indies, China and Japan. Spain was on the verge of discovering a western passage via the Americas, and Britain, Holland and France were wondering how to horn in. In 1577 the most exciting sailor in the world did just that. Sir Francis Drake encircled the globe in the legendary *Golden Hind*, about the size of a modern racing yawl, and, in the course of a three-year voyage, elevated piracy to its most profitable and glamorous heights. He swooped into the Pacific through the icy [mountainous] Magellan Straits and 'arrived terrible and unannounced, like a falcon from the blue' right into Spain's hitherto undisputed sphere of influence. He plundered and petrified the entire Pacific coast of the Americas, seeking and looting the Spanish galleons wherever they might be found, and returned to Plymouth via the Cape of Good Hope, carrying a fortune in treasure trove for his Queen and changing the balance of sea-power for ever more.

Surely on nights when the moon mist lay on the sea, the sails of the *Golden Hind* filled again for those who could see her!

By the seventeenth century the Dutch mariners were plying regularly between Amsterdam and Batavia and were the first to land on the mysterious uncharted country known as Terra Australis Incognita.

In 1642 Captain Abel Janszoon Tasman found his way from Batavia to the island south-east of Australia which he explored and named Van Diemen's Land after the Governor of the Dutch East Indies, but today the island commemorates her discoverer with the name Tasmania. Tasman then sailed up the east coast and actually took possession of the country in the name of the Government of the Netherlands, but his sailors' tales of its wildness and the 'fabulous giants' inhabiting the territory were so discouraging that Holland did not interest herself further. As for Western Australia, the navigator, Pelsaert, sent gloomy reports home to the Netherlands about this desolate land fit only for weird bounding beasts that sit up and pray. The gentle inquisitive kangaroo appeared sinister to his crew and the aborigines were hostile. The fact, of course, was that the wilderness of Terra Australis Incognita had nothing to offer traders. At that time nobody wanted to colonize new lands, they only wanted to trade, preferably with the civilized wealthy Far East.

The first English navigator to sight the new continent was William Dampier in 1688. His account of what little he saw of Western Australia was as unfavourable as Pelsaert's; but nevertheless he was sent off in the *Roebuck* the following year to learn a bit more about this unpromising land, and also to hunt for the wreck of a Dutch treasure ship that had been lost twelve years previously.

Dampier failed to salvage any treasure, but he charted and claimed the beautiful Swan River, which is the glory of modern Perth, and explored the adjacent island of Rottnest before sailing up the east coast, thus blazing a trail for that tireless circumnavigator of the globe, Captain James Cook, whose explorations and voyages spread his name from end to end of the world and earned him, among other things, the title of 'Father of Australia'. It was Cook, in 1770, who literally and figuratively put New Zealand and Australia on the map, claiming for Britain the lands that were to become her most satisfactory colonies and later her faithful allies within the Commonwealth of Nations. (Holland's original claim had lapsed through 'non-use'.)

Captain Cook knew the Cape route well. He refitted his ships at the Cape and revictualled there with the fresh vegetables and fruits that saved his crews from a horrible death by scurvy. He had sailed from the Cape, south to the Antarctic Circle – as present day whalers still do – seeking the fabled 'temperate southern continent', and declared rightly that no such desirable land-mass existed. On board the *Resolution*, among the grinding icebergs and the perils of the pack, he wrote: 'I can be bold enough to say that no man will venture farther than I have done; and that the lands which may be to the south will never be explored.'

Perhaps his astonished spirit witnessed the crossing of Antarctica by Hillary and Fuchs! And it could be that the good ships, *Endeavour*, *Resolution* and *Discovery* passed us in the dark of the night, phantom sails billowing in the wind, bound for Captain Cook's distant northern home, his admiring countrymen and his proud but long-suffering wife.

During our long lazy voyage I had resumed my intermittent habit of keeping a Writer's Notebook, jotting down impressions and ideas. On the night before our first landfall in Australia I made a note.

March 1964.

We have had a calm happy voyage, getting along well together and learning from each other. From our little Chinese steward too, Wong, who works so hard with such a pleasant smile. Tomorrow Fremantle! I can't really believe it yet!

CHAPTER TWO

Perth, a City Apart

We docked early and went through the immigration and health formalities in the lounge. As I put my passport back in my bag and turned to go I stepped straight into the arms of my son. A small boy was with him.

I had said good-bye to Piet in tragic circumstances eighteen months ago and it was two and a half years since I had seen his family. Now the early morning sun shone brilliantly on the shores of this new land where they had made their home and our meeting was full of happiness. I would have recognized the sparkling brown eyes of my youngest grandson anywhere but the lapse of time had turned the toddler into a little boy of four.

Old Dr McLaren appeared and was introduced. Majestic and immaculate, he gently refused the left hand Willie, somewhat overcome, had proffered.

'Other hand, my boy. That's it! Always the right.'

Willie was docile and solemn. It was a totally misleading impression.

'Willie's been given the morning off to meet you,' Piet explained. 'The other boys are at school and I have to work. Glen'll be here any time now to take you home; meanwhile we'll get you through the customs.'

The porter who took charge of my luggage made himself known to Piet and they shook hands. When I fumbled in my bag a quick aside deterred me. 'Not in Western Australia, Mom!' So I learned that here every man was adequately paid for his job and took pride in his work. I refrained from affronting the dignity of labour, but the rule of no tipping does not apply everywhere in Australia and a sensitive assessment of the situation is called for.

I spent my first days in Australia with my family.

Their home in Peppermint Grove, between the port of Fremantle and the city of Perth, was an attractive single-storeyed house with a wide L-shaped verandah and a garden ablaze with bougainvillaea, cassia, moon-flowers and other shrubs reminiscent of South Africa. The red and yellow hibiscus, single and double, were as fine as any I have ever seen. The rose-beds were Piet's delight and he performed delicate little grafting operations on them with varying success. A frangipani tree in full bloom drenched the summer air with its exotic perfume mingled with the sweetness of jasmine.

There was a kitchen-garden at the back, with a work-shed and a lawn where Willie had made his 'cubby' – an abode run up out of old bits of wood and tin, like any Bantu *pondokkie*. He crawled in an out of this, and, when it fell on him like a house of cards, he thought it a wonderful joke. Tony's guinea-pigs in their hutch were his next-door neighbours. When they had 'mowed' one patch of grass the hutch was moved to another. A drake and his two wives stalked round the borders in single file; whenever they were thirsty they went to the tap and quacked and somebody turned it on for them. They showered and ruffled their plumage under the lawn sprinklers.

'They eat the snails,' Glen explained. 'Very useful.'

'Mightn't someone steal them for the pot?'

Glen laughed. 'Not likely. Here you can leave your front door unlocked and your key in your car. Anyway, our ducks are too tough for cooking!'

At the bottom of their tree-lined road was the Yacht Club and the beautiful Swan River – blue as the sea, wide as a fjord, and the focal point of their lives, for yachting is Perth's favourite recreation.

I was surprised to find that my older grandsons, Ronnie, Chris, and Tony, then aged thirteen, eleven and nine, had developed a pronounced though erratic sense of responsibility not yet shared by their small brother, Willie. The Australian way of life, where domestic help is rare, demands that everybody should give a hand, including the children. But Australian women take work and play in their stride. They enjoy life and find time to help others too.

When Elspeth Rhodes flew in from South Africa – a long tiring flight with stops at Mauritius and the Cocos Islands – she and I settled in at the Ocean Beach Hotel, North Cottesloe, commonly known as the O.B.H. It was on the sea-front, only five minutes by car from Peppermint Grove, and the day after her arrival we went into Perth and hired a Holden. When we asked if this car were reliable, we were told, 'You can drive her from here to Adelaide without a care.' Adelaide, Perth's nearest important city, is 1,800 miles across the desolate waste of the Nullarbor Plain, so that assurance had to be good enough for us!

We soon lost our hearts to Perth. It is a city apart, dreamy, out on a limb, patient with strangers, sometimes melancholy and inclined to think of itself as the neglected capital of 'the Cinderella State', remote and lonely, isolated by a hinterland of grim deserts and forgotten by the rest of Australia. It has a few skyscrapers, many modern buildings, a fine University and wide up hill, down dale streets between the heights of King's Park and the Swan River. Its suburbs, with their grass sidewalks and lovely gardens, meander along the river bank towards the sea or inland to the Darling Range. Ultra-modern bungalows share half an acre with sedate old-fashioned colonial houses and the latter are often cleverly converted to accommodate different generations of the same family without undue sharing of amenities. Or, as often happens, parents present part of their own once spacious grounds to a married son or daughter to enable the young couple to build a cottage on it, for both land and building are expensive and the cost of living is high. But then so are wages. The lack of domestic help has created a sort of tribal interdependence, with the old and the young keeping a protective eye on each other. Flat-life has not really taken on. Children need a garden, 'somewhere they can play', and young Australia thinks on family lines.

For the next two months Elspeth and I lived pleasantly between the Ocean Beach Hotel and the house in Peppermint Grove. Our terms were bed and breakfast. Our sitting-room was oddly dominated by a large white refrigerator, and how we cared to stock it was our own affair. Another convenient innovation was the tea tray for two with an electric hot water jug. Every day the little tea-bags and paper packets of sugar were replenished and a milk bottle was put in the fridge. We could brew when and how we pleased. My bedroom upstairs (the O.B.H. was no skyscraper, there was only a downstairs and an upstairs) had enormous west-facing seascape windows overlooking Cottesloe Beach, and when I woke I had only to turn my head on the pillow and feel that I was down there on that wonderful long white beach. Every morning, soon after sunrise, a dozen or more husky men would rush across the sand and plunge into the waves. Whatever the weather, they began the day with their morning dip.

'They never miss, winter or summer,' said Ettie, the part-time maid who did my room. She was married with a school-age family and lived in Fremantle.

'It's a wonderfully empty beach,' I said.

Ettie smiled. 'There's so much of it, and the surfers prefer the other end. But, in the holidays, it's always packed with picnic parties, parents and kids.'

'What about sharks?'

She shrugged her shoulders. 'Not here. They don't seem interested.'

I was, at that time, still working on *The Man in the Mews*, the novel due to be published in the autumn. I'd hired a typewriter and was often at work while Ettie swept and dusted.

'I'm under your feet,' I apologized. But she reassured me.

'You're not in my way, any road. You just go ahead.'

If the weather was fine, Glen usually brought Willie to the beach with a sandwich lunch. There were scores of smooth pretty shells to fill his tin pail. They were patterned like heather-mixture tweeds in soft browns and golds and misty mauves. The older boys only came home from school in the afternoon.

We often lunched at a little Italian restaurant on the seashore where we could watch the lunch-hour surfers, for this was the section of the long beach where the rollers were best. It was truly dramatic. The performers were mostly men and they used finned foam-and-fibreglass boards. Australians are natural 'water babies' and surfing is their most spectacular individual outdoor cult. Lying flat, they paddle their board out over the lines of breaking surf and then turn for the run in. Still lying flat, they breast a promising swell, scooping furiously with their hands as the great jade wall of water balloons to incredible heights, its thin crest of flying foam preceding the thunderous burst. Before that crucial moment, the surfer kneels, then stands and comes swooping triumphantly shorewards, propelled by the wild white power of the breaking wave. There are as many different riding stances as there are shots at tennis and the *surfies* have a name for all of them, including the 'wipe out' when the rider loses to the wave and disappears. At the end of the run, when the roller has spent its strength, the surfer slides from his board into a tumult of spray which tosses the board vertically into the air. He retrieves it and the exciting game of man and wave is resumed.

This sport has taken on in South Africa recently. It has become a fever and a cult with its own language and fanatic disciples. While we have our seasonal south-easters – the trade winds that can blow for days at a stretch or rise without warning – Western Australia, backed by her burning deserts, cools the coastal summer air with a regular afternoon breeze. This thermal wind dictates the order of favourite holiday pursuits. Swim in the mornings and sail in the afternoons.

Saturday is the great day for the Yacht Clubs, so on our first Saturday Elspeth and I went along to Peppermint Grove about noon. We found Glen preparing a salad, Chris in the work-shed with Willie and the Australian sheep-dog, Bluey, while Tony was occupied with the task of persuading a reluctant guinea-pig to make friends with a new mate.

'This is Pickles. His last wife swelled up and died,' explained Tony. 'He's lost without her, so I've got Martha for him.'

But the bereaved beast treated the trembling Martha much as Henry VIII treated Anne of Cleves – the 'Flemish mare' – with disdain amounting to aversion, an attitude which Tony assured us would pass, and his experience of the subject was considerable. They were cuddlesome little creatures and made a subdued snuffling noise when we held them in our laps. 'Their way of purring,' Tony told us. 'Shows they're pleased.'

'Piet and Ron have gone to buy pies for lunch,' said Glen. 'They'll be back in a minute.'

After we had done justice to the salad and pies we went to the Yacht Club among the trees of the river bank.

The Swan River, between the Perth Narrows Bridge and the Fremantle Bridge, is more like a lake, and, on a Saturday afternoon, when many types of yachts from different clubs are competing in the various sailing races, the blue water looks as if a flock of brilliant butterflies had alighted on its sparkling surface. It was choppy in the stiff breeze as we watched Chris and Ron set off in their Pelican. Tony usually crewed with his father and one or two friends in the family boat, *Winnibelle*, and Willie, in his little yellow life-jacket, went along as mascot.

As the Pelican heeled in a strong gust I turned to Glen: 'Aren't the boys rather young to manage that boat on such a squally day?'

She laughed. 'There are seven and eight-year-olds sailing those Pelicans! Anyway, they wear life-jackets. It's compulsory, and if they capsize, they right the boat and carry on.'

Perth schoolboys are taught to swim and sail at an early age, which encourages them to become self-reliant and quick thinking. I have seldom seen finer looking youngsters than the bronzed boys and girls we saw that afternoon.

When we got home that evening Ron produced a torn spinnaker for his mother. 'Something to mend, Ma.'

'I'll do it,' offered Elspeth. 'If someone can find a patch.'

Chris produced blue sail-silk, and we marvelled at its strong light texture.

'Like parachute silk in the war,' I said. 'You remember, Elspeth – those captured enemy parachutes.'

The boys glanced up, momentarily interested, but World War Two meant nothing to them, parachutes were no novelty and human invasions were as commonplace as raiding an orchard for somebody else's windfalls. They belonged to the Space Age and their imaginations were conditioned to embrace the fantastic and incredible. Not long after their arrival in Perth they had been among thousands to queue for a glimpse of the capsule in which the American astronaut, Major Glenn, had orbited the earth. Perth had been one of the cities visible to him on his voyage through Outer Space. All night the lights of that remote Australian city had blazed a message of cheer and encouragement to the lone human pioneer probing the awesome mysteries, terrors and wonders of the firmament; so Perth had been included in the terrestial tour which followed the capsule's space voyage.

Elspeth patched the blue spinnaker that same evening, her dark head with its sheen of pewter bent gleaming under a standard-lamp while I watched television.

'You're very prompt,' I said. 'Doing it at once.'

'I loathe people who promise to do jobs and don't get on with them.'

Glen groaned when she saw the patch next day.

'How can I ever live up to that? It's flawless!'

The family was amazed and enraptured. Ron, who loves everything to do with sailing and assembles and inspects his equipment with hawk-eyed care, paid Elspeth the supreme compliment.

'The sailmaker couldn't do better!'

She glowed.

Television is as much a part of the home in Perth as it is in England. We often saw my grandsons, sprawled on the floor of the dining-room, with one eye on their homework and the other on the television set. The visitors' TV set at the O.B.H. was placed at the top of the stairs in a corner of the comfortably furnished landing. We passed it whenever we went to or from our rooms. One evening we saw Dan, the hotel handyman, and a small boy watching the screen, obviously absorbed. So, very soon, were we. We were back in Africa, on trek with Laurens van der Post in the Kalahari Desert. With him we studied the little Bushman hunters of that arid land. We followed their lives and their customs and saw for ourselves their poisoned arrows, their dances, their feasts and their conservation of water in ostrich eggs.

'The abos are like that,' said Dan, when the programme was over. 'They have their secret waterholes too. They can find water in places where a white man would die of thirst.'

He'd recently come from Queensland, where he'd been boring for water, helping to establish the artesian water system that has transformed the thirst-land.

We saw many familiar English and American TV features in our remote part of the great Australian Continent, and of course the ubiquitous Westerns, with exciting stories of the Wells Fargo coaches in the early lawless days of California. There were educational films too, sponsored by Australian universities and schools.

Australia, land of vast distances, is acutely conscious of the value of radio in education. I was to learn more about this later in the Outback, where I was given every opportunity to study the School of the Air, and the Royal Flying Doctor Service, two of Australia's remarkable contributions to the education and health of those who live in the vast isolation of the bush or the desert.

CHAPTER THREE

Rottnest, Isle of the Past

The day Elspeth saw *Winnibelle*, with the wind in her high heeling sail and her gunwale nearly flush with the water, she turned to me and said:

'That's for you, not for me.'

We had arranged to spend the following week-end at Rottnest Island, sailing across with the family in *Winnibelle*. Rottnest is the small unsophisticated island where, they say, Perth goes to 'get rid of its inhibitions'.

I looked across the water churned by white-horses. 'If you don't fancy sailing you can go in the ferry.'

All ferries are anathema to Elspeth. 'The shilling sick! No thank you.'

When my friend jibbed she was immovable, so I gave in. Elspeth feared no foe but she had a horror of making an ass of herself. Piet saved the situation.

'You can fly. It's only twelve minutes' flight. Rather nice to see Rottnest from the air, anyway.'

So we settled for that. We'd fly over together and I'd return in *Winnibelle* with my family, while Elspeth came back by plane.

'You'll be there ahead of us,' said Ron. And Chris, blue eyes innocent, added, 'Don't go to the hotel. Ma has booked us in at the gaol.'

We said we were not surprised, considering the company we were keeping. Piet grinned.

'A bus meets the plane. Ask the driver to put you down at the Hostel.'

So, on a brilliant blue morning without a breath of wind, we circled over the island with its salt-pans, its cliffs and pretty coves, and the little harbour built by convicts over a century ago to link the salt-works with the Mainland. Under those rocky cliffs lie the wrecks of old sailing vessels of the Indies fleet, treasure ships such as Captain Dampier was commissioned to seek three centuries ago. Even recently attempts have been made to examine and salvage what may be priceless cargoes, but the savage surf protects its drowned wealth.

There are no cars on Rottnest Island. You use your legs or hire a bicycle. The bus is the exception. At strategic points we saw the gun emplacements of the last war, when the island was used as a military base.

'It could be Robben Island,' I said to Elspeth, as we rattled along in the bus with a number of fellow passengers in shorts or slacks.

Robben Island in Table Bay was once a gaol too. It was also a leper colony and later, in World War Two, it became a South African Naval base. It is now once more a gaol where political prisoners are confined with time and leisure in which to reflect upon past errors and future prospects. Like Rottnest, it derived its Dutch name from its first inhabitants, *robben* – the seals.

Rottnest too, was christened by a Dutch mariner, but the 'rats' after which it was called were not rats at all. They were quokkas, a curious little marsupial with its roots in antiquity. The island is now a sanctuary for these nocturnal 'kangaroo-rats' who have become practically extinct on the Mainland. Some ten thousand of them live on the island, which is also the home of over a hundred and thirty species of birds – peacocks, plovers, quails and pheasants being the main land types. Mutton-birds lay their eggs in holes in the ground, just to add a hazard for the unwary walker.

The bus dumped us outside the Hostel, and, when we had checked in at the office, we discovered that our rooms were indeed in the old gaol across the road. The 'cells', big enough to accommodate three beds and a chest of drawers, were built round a large grass quadrangle, one section of which was used for showers.

A gaol – any gaol – is rather a spooky place. Even when it is converted out of all recognition, hallowed by holiday-makers and their children in an unconventional unspoilt island of great charm, it retains a faint flavour of old grim associations.

Australia's early convicts were unique. They were the basis of civilized British settlement in a remote undeveloped possession of the mother country, who, at that time, couldn't care less about her distant acquisition.

Certain Pacific tribes once had the custom of laying the cornerstones of their temples upon the bodies of slaves buried upright and alive. Only the human sacrifice and support could give the edifice its strength and spirit. Something rather similar happened to Australia. The doomed and the reluctant left their bones beneath the cornerstones of the Continent into which they breathed the first European life.

When Britain lost her American colonies in 1782 she lost also certain convenient dumping grounds for felons condemned to transportation, the terrible sentence that covered not only shocking crimes but political intrigue and petty theft. In an age of the press gang, of hunger and inhumanity a man might steal a loaf of bread for his starving family and suffer the penalty of having his hand chopped off or of being transported to some penal settlement across the ocean – two oceans in the case of Australia. Even such slight civic offences as slaughtering butcher's meat without a licence was punishable by this most dreaded sentence!

Botany Bay on the east coast was the first European settlement of any kind in Australia. More convict immigrants followed. So did private enterprise. American loyalists, who felt unable to remain under the flag of the new independent United States, sailed for the distant Australian Continent already rumoured to be rich with possibilities. The convicts seldom saw their homeland again. When they had served their term in the labour gangs they were emancipated, but they stayed. The worst offenders were re-deported to convenient islands such as Norfolk Island in the Pacific.

In 1837 Rottnest received a convict labour gang from Perth to work the salt-pans and build the necessary pier and causeway. At first they lived like the quokkas in dark places. They were cave-dwellers, confined in their rocky habitations by harsh guards, but thirty years later they were transferred to the agreeable cloistered gaol which was used as such till 1907, after which the convicts were no longer required and Rottnest came into its own as a haven of peaceful recreation.

Long before that – in the middle of the nineteenth century – deportation had become a thing of the past, and Australia had gained many thousands of stalwart Irish and English immigrants swept out of their own countries by the want and unemployment following upon the potato famine and the industrial revolution.

If Captain Cook was the 'father of Australia', the god-father of that southern continent – the smallest on the globe, approximately the same size as the United States – was Midshipman Matthew Flinders of H.M.S. *Reliance*, the man-of-war which brought Governor Hunter to Sydney at the end of the eighteenth century.

In those days little was really known of Terra Australis Incognita. Not even its shape was firmly established. Was it attached to the Asian land-mass to the north? Was it divided by undiscovered straits? Was there a sort of Caspian Sea at the centre? For Flinders and his shipmate, Surgeon George Bass, speculation wasn't good enough. These friends, both from Lincolnshire, were driven by the true explorer's insatiable curiosity. They had to find out the answers. The Royal Navy has grown and thrived on individual action, and the initiative of Midshipman Flinders and Surgeon Bass in Australian waters contributed considerably to the world's knowledge of that unexplored continent. Moreover, they set out in craft that would make the members of Perth's modern Yacht Clubs shake their heads.

George Bass had brought out in the *Reliance* his own boat with an eight foot keel and a five foot beam, and in this he and Flinders explored the George River. Later, in a borrowed whaler, the two friends sailed through the Bass Strait, reached 'the monstrous swell' of the open ocean and circumnavigated Tasmania, proving it to be a separate island. Bass was lost soon afterwards in a trading voyage to South America, but Flinders persevered with his explorations. In 1803 he sailed right round Australia, accurately charting the coast and establishing the continent's island shape.

In view of the fact that New Holland (as Western Australia was still called) and New South Wales were now proved to be part of one and the same huge country, Matthew Flinders suggested that the whole continent be given one name – Australia. After a good deal of argument the young man's proposal was adopted and

Terra Australis Incognita was re-christened. The coastline was no longer a mystery, the shape and size of the continent was known, but the interior remained a formidable death-dealing challenge to those dauntless men who were mesmerized by the great question mark of the centre.

Elspeth and I left our few weekend belongings in the erstwhile gaol and wandered down to the pier constructed by those first occupants of our hostel. Any time now we expected to sight *Winnibelle* crossing from the mainland to the island.

Nowhere in Rottnest was any distance from anywhere else. The Hostel on the one side and the hotel on the other bracketed the general store where you could hire a bicycle, the baker where you could buy the most delicious home-made bread, and the fish-monger and bait-bar where a board announced: 'Fresh fish, craytails, kippers, ice blocks, octopus bait, scaley mackerel, mulies and white bait.' This 'shopping centre' was beautifully shaded by enormous spreading Moreton Bay figs and tall Norfolk Island pines. Crows lived in the trees and filled the air with their laments. 'Ah-ha-ha, ah-ha-ha,' they cried, with the broad 'a' of the land they lived in.

We explored the little beach, and the row of summer bungalows, and then joined the other lazy holiday visitors drinking beer in the hotel garden from which we could keep an eye on the sea. Beer is Australia's national drink and the great continent is littered with empty beer-cans. It is good beer too, light and refreshing, and doesn't seem to put on weight. Or perhaps Australians don't run to fat. The men are, on the whole, rangy hatchet-featured types, men of few words. The women, who are also beer-drinkers, have good figures and plenty of vivacious charm.

'There's *Winnibelle*!' said Elspeth, who is long-sighted.

Far away the tall mast had come into view, pencil thin. It was so still that *Winnibelle* depended on her engine alone. We went down to the jetty to meet the family, who came ashore with bundles, bags and bathing-towels.

'Where's Bluey?' I asked.

'We farmed him out with the guinea-pigs,' said Tony. 'No dogs allowed here. They'd chase the quokkas.'

'I haven't seen a quokka yet.'

'Wait till after dark!' said Chris.

That afternoon Piet and I and the three older boys sailed round to a lovely peaceful cove where we dropped anchor and bathed from *Winnibelle*. Glen and Elspeth hired bikes and joined us there, Willie on Glen's carrier. But they lost their way and had to scramble down to the beach through thick bush. Willie, who had no shoes with him, complained that it gave his bare feet 'hell'. He spoke with great feeling and indignation, but when he was offered a passage home in *Winnibelle* he gritted his teeth and refused.

But, if Willie braved the bush barefoot, it was more than he was allowed to do in the dining-room of the Hostel. Life on Rottnest was informal, but a little notice outside the dining-room required visitors to wear shoes for meals. A substantial hot dinner was served by two friendly young waitresses and coffee could be fetched at the coffee bar; there was a TV set in the lounge for anyone who cared to look in.

The twilight deepened and Glen went across to the quad to settle Willie for the night. He could hardly keep his eyes open. Ron and Chris were playing some game at the Hostel and Piet was chatting with an acquaintance.

'Now, Grandma,' said Tony. 'This is the time. Come, Mrs Rhodes!' We sauntered with him to a spot near a house on stilts.

'They live in there, under the floor – in the foundations. You can see by their droppings.'

Here and there a bird called and the sea murmured softly, but the dense leaves of the Moreton Bay figs were quiet, their shadows thickening in the gathering gloom. It was then, in that eerie light between the dying day and nightfall, that we became aware of the strange life stirring about us. Small fantastic creatures were moving in the dusk, emerging from their underground dwellings, to graze in the cool hours of darkness. Survivals of the dim past, the stunted marsupials had come out to feed.

'Quokkas aren't fierce,' whispered Tony. 'Only inquisitive.'

As we approached one it sat straight up, its strong back legs hinged as if it rested on skis, its heavy balancing tail straight along the ground behind it, its short forepaws drooping over its chest like tiny praying hands.

'I think there's a baby in her pouch,' said Tony. 'She has that fat look.'

A young cat had prowled out to snake round our ankles. Suddenly it darted playfully towards the quokka with a *miaow* – an invitation to play. But the quokka grunted nervously. They were much of a size. The cat put out a tentative paw, the quokka squeaked and turned tail, hopping off into the night with the extraordinary agility we were later to see in its most impressive form.

When we returned to the quad the gates were barred.

'To keep the quokkas out,' said Tony, opening them. 'They do no harm but they make a mess.'

Later, when the boys were all in bed, we strolled over to the hotel where the Saturday night's dance was in full swing. We took our drinks on to the lawn, and watched the enthusiastic stompers, and after a while, the moon came up and we strolled slowly back to the erstwhile prison, where all was peace and the sound sleep of children.

Outside, in the moonlight dappled by spreading trees, the small nocturnal grazers nibbled the dewy grass, shadowy shapes from a forgotten millennium, the last of their kind. No other ghosts stirred that summer night.

CHAPTER FOUR

Merino Stud

Although we had no intention of driving our Holden across the
sandy waste of the Nullarbor Plain to Adelaide, we thought it
would be fun to go as far as Kalgoorlie.

Some of our new friends looked astonished. 'Nearly four
hundred miles and only a mining town at the end of it!'

That was all right, we said. Four hundred miles was less than a
day's run and we wanted to see Western Australia's Golden Mile.

So away we went. We wouldn't do the outward bound journey
all at a stretch, as we were stopping off half-way to spend the
night at Hagley with Frank and Joy Cooke. Joy was coming on to
Kalgoorlie with us just for the ride. Hagley, the Cooke property –
a famous Merino Stud – is near Tammin, the heart of Western
Australia's wheat belt.

Frank Cooke combined the growing of wheat with his stud.
From him we learnt the distinctions between Australian land
owners. In South Africa the word 'farm' covers everything,
from wine-farming to sheep, cattle, grain, or the lot all produced
on the same farm. But in Australia the word 'farm' implies a
fairly small holding. Agriculture in this empty continent is both
on a grander and more specialized scale. Land under one ownership – whether individual, family or syndicate, freehold or leasehold – may be anything up to one or 2 million acres. I had always
thought of my own country as being the land of wide open spaces
– and so it is – but Australia, with her vast Outback, thinks even
bigger. The Hagley property, with over 30,000 acres only 250
miles from Perth, seemed to the Cookes and their friends a mere
stone's throw from the capital city.

Land may be freehold or government leasehold, but since the
lease is usually 'in perpetuity', the owner will not be turned off

his territory unless he grossly misuses it by neglect or failure to produce a reasonable number of beasts. In many cases the 'reasonable living area' is judged to be one beast to twenty acres. It depends, of course, upon the quality and amount of grazing land. The great Australian cattle kings can own ranches of over a million acres, as can the big sheep-breeders. The love and understanding of raising sheep and cattle is bred into certain families and Australia has its hereditary aristocracy of the Outback. Wool, beef and wheat still form the core of the country's economy.

We set off from Perth early on a misty morning. There had been rain the night before, but the Australian highways are bitumen and, so long as you stay on the 'black', you can make good time.

Once clear of Perth and its industrial suburbs we began to ascend the gentle gradient of the Darling Range. From soft parchment savannah, wooded with many varieties of eucalyptus and quaint 'blackboy' palms like fuzzy-wuzzy warriors, we looked back upon the Swan Valley.

'It's their valley of the vines,' said Elspeth. 'Rather heavenly.'

The vineyards, spreading between the foothills and the shining river, were tinged with autumn gold; the city, reflected in its wide placid water-front, was ethereal mother-of-pearl under a cloud-laden sky. This was the classic pattern of Australian settlement – the cities on the coast, the agricultural belt to supply them, and then, further inland, wool, beef and minerals.

Elspeth was entranced by the parklands through which we drove. This gentle countryside reminded her of Kenya and her own dairy-farm with its thousand acres of arable land.

'Frank Cooke would probably reckon my Green Hill to be about the size of a paddock,' she chuckled. 'Oh, look at those gorgeous red pohls!'

Here and there, many miles apart, we'd see simple homesteads like up-country farmhouses in South Africa, tin-roofed, surrounded by gums and the inevitable windmills. Sometimes a flock of 'twenty-eights' – green and gold parrots – rose into the air with their raucous cries of 'twennyay! twennyay!' and now and again we'd slow up in wonder at the majesty of a grove of ghost-gums, their long smooth trunks and silvery branches pale as the

39

legendary limbs of dryads. I could never have imagined so great a variety of gums as those that shade the hot Australian scene. We met very little along the road, only an occasional lorry or a powerful car with the gleaming bars of a kangaroo-fender above the front bumper. Most of the heavy traffic moves at night, especially the great refrigerated meat-vans that go direct from Outback stockyards to city markets.

We now had a constant companion, an endless python travelling with us over hill and dale. The pipe-line from the Darling Range to Kalgoorlie. One is never able to forget that Australia is a thirst-land. The golden city of Kalgoorlie depends for its water supply upon a source 350 miles distant. Pumping stations along the route keep the water flowing and supply tributaries from the main pipe. C. Y. O'Connor, the Perth engineer responsible for this great project in 1903, had worked out that it would take three weeks before the first water pumped from the Mundaring Dam could reach its destination. The pumps were set in action and Western Australia waited. Three weeks passed. Still no water for Kalgoorlie. Every day after that seemed like a year to the engineer. One, two, three, four, five days of agonizing doubt and anxiety went by, weighing him down with the burden of responsibility and the dread of a disastrous failure on a grand scale. On the night of the sixth day he shot himself. On the morning of the seventh the life-giving water flowed.

We turned off the 'black' on to the 'dirt' at the agricultural junction of Tammin and within a few miles we were at Hagley in good time for lunch.

Frank and Joy Cooke have a delightful home and four children, three little girls and a boy. Sometimes Joy has help in the house, sometimes not, but in any case she does the cooking and that status symbol of the Australian woman – a good kitchen – is, in her case, way up in the Rolls Royce class. The Kalgoorlie pipeline supplies the Tammin area with water and in midsummer, when the thermometer soars, the swimming-pool in the garden is a family delight. It is also the rendezvous of a multitude of highly vocal wild birds, and the children have their 'cubby' near it under the trees – a secret 'house' tucked away among the palms behind a tall bamboo thicket.

When we arrived we found the baby, Kate, very sorry for herself with a bung eye. The little bushflies are Australia's plague and are particularly attracted by the wide shining eyes of children. A bite results in swelling and inflammation. Henry and 'Umpty' were playing in their 'cubby' and Joanna, the seven-year-old, was at school in Tammin.

'She goes in the school bus and doesn't get back till the early afternoon,' Joy explained. 'They have quite a tour as the bus does a round of the outlying properties to pick up the pupils. The children rather enjoy it. They regard it as a sort of extra playtime.'

Every school-bus is yellow and green and only an ambulance shares its pride of importance. No vehicle is allowed to pass it when it is stationary in case some child should dart out and meet with an accident. Children within the school-bus circuit must attend the school as it is necessary to have a certain number of pupils to justify the existence of both school and transport. Australia has unique educational problems owing to her vast, sparsely populated inland and she meets them with enlightened determination.

Owing to her geographical position Western Australia is peculiarly cut off from the rest of the world – by a waste of water to the west and south and a hinterland of deserts to the north and east. I have heard my Perth friends groan, 'You can travel thousands of miles in this continent and only meet another Australian at journey's end!' So they take holidays in New Zealand, Singapore or South Africa.

Before he took over the management of Hagley, Frank Cooke was sent on an extended tour by his father, in the course of which he studied South African methods of farming. It was then, on a 'blind date', that he met Joy and instantly decided that she was adorning the wrong continent.

Joy was then working in the photographic department of Satour (South African tourism) where her professional skill had received enthusiastic recognition. She has the valuable gift of using a picture to suggest a whole way of life, and, thanks to her experience in the studios of the famous Court Photographer, Marcus Adams, she could catch and interpret a child's mood with artistic sensitivity. When Frank met Joy she had never been to

Australia but she was about to embark on a tour of New Zealand
to exhibit her South African work and take pictures of New
Zealand and its people. Her Maori studies held Elspeth and me
spellbound when we saw them, and several of her pictures had
won gold medals and high awards. On her return journey to
South Africa she held an exhibition in Perth. Frank, who has an
irresistible grin and an inflexible will masked by an easy-going
attitude to matters of slight importance, saw to it that he was in
Perth at the time. The sequel was inevitable.

Not long after their marriage and the birth of their first children
Frank's father retired to Perth and passed the ownership of
Hagley to his son.

That afternoon Frank took Elspeth and me round the property.

It could have been the highveld. There was the tawny earth,
the swathes of bush and the high blue sky with its own white
flocks running before a cool rain-scented wind. Where the corn
had been cut Frank examined the earth for new germination – the
sweet grass that would feed his sheep. The tiny green shoots had
begun to break through the soil. Much of the land had already
been ploughed, for the ploughing is done immediately after rain,
but it is light surface ploughing. The deeper soil is salt. The
natural water too is brackish, but the Kalgoorlie pipe-line supplies
the Tammin wheat belt with sweet, fresh water.

The slim emerald 'twenty-eights' flew with the car when we
were among the gums, and sometimes we were joined by clouds
of exquisite rosellas, the small brilliant parrots with red breasts
who live near homesteads. Or a colony of pearl-grey and rose-red
galahs would rise, shrieking, from a dead tree or a television
aerial, which looked like a windmill without blades.

Although Hagley was mechanized, there were still stables with
horses in them and kennels where the lively little kelpie sheep-dogs
lived when they were not out on the job. And the cleanest pigsties
I have ever seen housed the big white pigs that yield the best
bacon.

The fenced paddocks were enormous – about 200 acres – and
the sheep and the rams of various qualities were carefully segrega-

ted. The ewes mate in the spring and lamb in the autumn and the shearing teams come round soon after the lambing season.

Frank showed us his pedigree rams of different values, priced anywhere between £50 and £1,000 each. He pointed out their quality – the 'open face' and strong legs. When a merino is wearing its woollen coat those frail-looking legs have a heavy weight to carry! The finest rams were in a cool stilted shed with a slatted floor through which manure slipped to await collection as fertilizer.

'Do you export these magnificent fellows?' I asked.

'No,' said Frank. 'Our Government doesn't allow the export of Merino rams. As a matter of fact, our first merinoes were imported from your country.'

South African sheep for Australia date back to the very beginning of the colonization of New South Wales. In 1787, when Captain Phillip was dispatched to Botany Bay with a large convoy of men and supplies, his ships called in at the Cape to replenish their stores and continued their voyage the richer by seeds and livestock, including cattle and the first flock of sheep ever to land on Australian soil. After that there was a valuable interchange of sheep between South Africa and Australia.

Our own South African sheep-breeding goes back over three centuries. In his book, *Karoo*, Lawrence Green writes:

Sheep from the best flocks in Holland were sent to the Cape in Van Riebeeck's day, some of them only to be killed by leopards ... Spanish rams arrived as far back as 1689 to raise the grade of wool. Before the end of the seventeenth century, ships were carrying Cape wool to Holland. One writer noted: 'It was very remarkable that the wool of the Fatherland sheep, sent to the Cape, improved so perceptibly by the change of climate' ... The first serious attempt to breed sheep on a scientific basis appears to have been made by Colonel Gordon, who was in the Dutch Company's service in 1790. He procured a number of rams of the fine-woolled sheep of the Escurial breed which had been presented to the Netherlands Government by the King of Spain. . . . They were crossed with the hairy native sheep, producing an animal with a rough, lustreless but abundant fleece. Some of Colonel Gordon's sheep went on later to Australia. These were among the original progenitors of Australia's millions of sheep. Some years after receiving Colonel Gordon's sheep, Australia contributed to South Africa's flocks by sending a number of Saxon rams from Mr Alexander Reley's estates in New South Wales. They arrived in the barque *Leda* in excellent condition, and a committee of experts decided that they were of greatly superior quality to anything yet imported into the Cape Colony. The wool combined weight and softness, strength, elasticity and closeness of pile. As a result, further large shipments of Saxon and Merino rams were ordered.

Where South African sheep-farmers have the jackal and the leopard to combat – to say nothing of the fierce lammervanger eagle, which preys on baby lambs – Australia has the fox and the dingo. Strong wire fences keep the vermin of one state from invading neighbouring territory. The yellow dingoes hunt in packs like wild dogs and the foxes tear out the throats of their victims. Rabbits too are a menace, their burrows creating natural snares for the brittle-legged sheep. In an attempt to stamp them out a number were caught and injected with myxomatosis and returned to the bush, where they infected millions of other rabbits. Though hordes died of the disease, the survivors have produced a strain resistant to myxomatosis, so the pest-control scientists will have to think again.

'I've been told,' I said to Frank, 'that some sheep-breeders shoot parrots, put strychnine in their crops and bury them in the ground with their tail feathers sticking out, and the foxes dig them up and eat them and die.'

Frank's engaging smile broke all over his face. 'Ah, well, if you've nothing else to do. We just buy meat, bait it and lay a trail in the usual way.'

All the time we were driving over the wide tawny landscape I had a curious feeling that something essential was missing from the scene. There were tall eucalypts on the skyline, wheat fields, salt-pans, ploughed earth, pasturage where the flocks grazed contentedly. What was it? Suddenly I knew. There were no shepherds! No old coloured man or Bantu with his dog and his crook went along with the sheep, a hurt one or a lamb slung over his shoulders. There were no walled kraals to which they were guided at nightfall to protect them from the fierce marauders of the veld. I had expected to see aborigines. But there were none. The Australian wool industry is so highly mechanized that the minimum of labour is required. A couple of station-hands and a jackaroo – a young apprentice – manage stations grazing many thousands of sheep.

The aborigines live in their own reserves, and, if you wish to go into their 'homelands', you must get a permit from the Government to do so. They appear to be generally regarded as 'unemployable'. They are temperamentally unreliable. When they are fed up with work they wander off into the bush to 'go walkabout', returning when it suits them, or not at all. The early Hottentots of the Cape had similar nomadic habits, which have been charmingly described by Victor de Kock in his little classic, *Those in Bondage*.

These happy care-free people neither knew nor wished to know the meaning of the word toil. So long as they could slumber in front of their huts all day long and dance and feast in the bright moonlight nights, their cup of happiness was full.

The Cape Hottentot no longer exists. He has died out or been absorbed. And the Australian aboriginal too belongs to a declining race. It is the black man of very different stock and calibre who is the dominant dark race in the world today. He is the true Negro, the descendant of warriors, and although he may not care about toil any more than the Hottentots, abos or the rest of us, he is capable of it, physically strong, mentally alert and quick to learn. And the medical science of his white friends and erstwhile masters has saved him from the plagues that once decimated his people.

When we returned to the house that evening the children were in their pyjamas and dressing-gowns, eating their supper in charge of a young friend who was helping out for a few weeks.

'There's no hurry for us,' said Joy. 'We'll eat when we're ready.'

I bathed in the children's bathroom, still warm from their ablutions, the steamy air touchingly innocent with its soft emollient smell of baby soap and powder.

Joy, dressed in a becoming house-gown, grilled tender fillets of beef for dinner and produced a delectable sweet made of the famous Tasmanian apples.

That night I asked Elspeth how Hagley compared with her farm in Kenya. She thought for a bit.

'You can't really compare them. This is splendid and magnificently run and it's a lovely house. But, in its own way, Green Hill is less isolated. More civilized.'

'More civilized! And you went through all that Mau Mau horror!'

'There was that, for a time,' she admitted. 'But you still had a cook and a boy – and a dog and a gun. And it was very sociable. People drove over to dinner – in evening dress through the forest – and brought their children with strict injunctions not to wet Auntie's bed, and you played bridge till one in the morning. Then everybody went home with their guns and their children. It wasn't really as lonely as this.'

As was often the case, she astonished me. Yet her outlook was not – for her – astonishing. Elspeth lived with all sorts of nebulous fears, but real danger she could ignore. To go into a room full of strangers was more nerve-racking for her than to enter the Aberdare Forest in the days when terror reigned in the White Highlands that are white no more.

CHAPTER FIVE

Golden Mile and Desert Lands

Joy woke us with coffee at daybreak next morning and by sunrise we were on the road.

We were kidnapping her for the week-end. Frank, who had to stay and get on with the ploughing, was well able to hold the fort. She had prepared a breakfast hamper and when the sun was up we called a halt and picnicked beside our serpentine friend, the pipe-line. The country was open and flat with a moorland look. Once a pair of emus hurriedly crossed the road, but, apart from bird life, there was little to break the monotony of our journey. At long intervals we'd see a truck drivers' lay-by with coffee drive-in and shower advertised in bold white paint on a heavy tyre strategically fixed to the trunk of a gum tree at the side of the highway. We encountered few cars in the two hundred miles between Tammin and Kalgoorlie, but one at precisely the right moment. The sinister boomp-boomp-boomp of a flat had brought us to a standstill.

Elspeth began to pull on her gloves.

'Looks as if we'll have to change the wheel ourselves.'

She opened the boot and we heaved out our suitcases to get at the jack.

'Wait!' Joy stood, listening intently. 'Believe it or not, there's something coming!'

A fast-travelling saloon car braked as it passed us and drew up in the grass verge ahead. A cheerful sunburnt young man got out.

'Want some help? Obviously, yes.'

The traveller did not bother with our jack. In a flash he had his own kit out and the wheel was changed. He slapped our Holden on the rump.

'She'll right! Away you go!'

47

We left him stowing his tool-case, and a few minutes later he whizzed past us with a cheerful wave of the hand.

We reached Kalgoorlie before noon and drove up the broad main street to the Palace Hotel.

Kalgoorlie, Western Australia's Golden Mile with a young population of about 30,000, is an open city in the middle of the bush, an important junction for road, rail and air which caters for thirsty travellers with no less than thirty-two licensed hotels. Its streets are wide to allow for the passage of a thousand sheep or a camel-train, just as the main streets of our South African towns were originally designed to permit a wagon with a span of sixteen oxen to turn in comfort.

I had half expected to find in the Golden Mile an echo of our South African Golden City. But Johannesburg with its sky-scrapers, gardens, luxurious homes and crowded Bantu locations, trailing its satellite mining towns some fifty miles along the Reef, bears little resemblance to Kalgoorlie. Western Australia's Golden Mile, which in the past seventy years has produced more than 77 million tons of ore and 33 million ozs of gold, is more like our Diamond City of Kimberley which retains an atmosphere of the colonial past and a great deal of provincial charm.

Our hotel was Victorian and personal and its owners were Kalgoorlie born and bred. A small notice near the reception desk informed us that dinner was from six to seven and requested that 'Ladies will please wear frocks in the dining room except for breakfast when travelling'.

The Golden Mile, first discovered by Patrick Hannan in the blazing June of 1893, still yields its rich harvest though drilling goes deeper and deeper. One shaft goes down over a mile. In Johannesburg tourists can arrange to go underground but in Australia only the surface workings are open to visitors. This was frankly a relief to me as the echoing galleries and claustro-phobic sweating tunnels with their rumbling miniature railways terrify me. That afternoon the three of us went round the Lake View and Star Mine with the official guide and his small con-ducted party. The sun beat down remorselessly and we could get a faint idea of what the heat of Kalgoorlie would be like in mid-summer when the thermometer keeps steadily over the 'century'.

48

Only a few weeks earlier an immigrant miner with his wife and baby had arrived in Kalgoorlie straight from Europe's icy winter into a temperature of 120 degrees. Within twelve hours he had left the job and removed his family to the cooler sea air of Perth. The story made local headlines and was received with exasperated dismay. The heatwave passed, the miner changed his mind and returned to Kalgoorlie and people said, 'Now they'll acclimatize and it'll come good.' So it did. But a considerable amount of adaptability is needed in the new settler. It is not merely a question of climate but of language, custom and the bush, the feeling of being dumped down in the wilderness. Kalgoorlie is vital and gay with parks and playgrounds, scores of sports and social clubs, an Olympic swimming-pool, a cheerful community and a growing culture borrowed from Adelaide and Perth. To Australians it does not seem in the least isolated. It may be in the middle of nowhere but it is on the way to everywhere and there are excellent communications. After all, you only have to hop into a plane to go where you like.

No part of the world owes more to the advent of the aeroplane than Australia – not even America – and no country is more air-minded. When man grew wings Australia was finally and firmly established on the map as a new powerful force in global affairs. Air travel has given her quick contacts beyond her oceans, has linked State with State, has revolutionized station life in the Outback and has made possible the survey of one of the harshest lands on earth.

A century ago settlers in Western Australia were the most isolated in the continent, one might almost say in the world. There was no Kalgoorlie then, only Perth's uninhabited hinterland. Even the Overland Telegraph, laid in 1872, made no attempt to link Western Australia with the other States. It ran north and south between Darwin and Adelaide.

Australia's history of the nineteenth century is largely composed of inland exploration and attempts to cross the continent. Of these crossings the most deadly was east to west. Part of the trail was blazed in the eighteen twenties, thirties and forties by men like Captain Charles Sturt; Major Thomas Mitchell, the Surveyor-General of New South Wales; E. J. Eyre; and L. Leichhardt, the

German botanist who tried to cross from Queensland to Perth in 1848. His entire expedition vanished without trace. A few years later, McDouall Stuart got as far as the centre, followed almost immediately by Burke and Wills who crossed from Melbourne to the Gulf of Carpentaria and perished on the return journey.

Western Australia remained remote, conducting her own probes into the north-west. But in 1872 that fanatical explorer, Ernest Giles, followed the newly laid telegraph from Adelaide to the South Australian border where he branched out into the dreaded east-west crossing. He was a stubborn strong-willed Englishman with experience of the bush and the desert, and his epic journeys are admirably described by Kathleen E. Graves in *Walkabout's Australia*.

Ernest Giles, whose explorations took him so near Kalgoorlie's hidden gold, was chiefly concerned with finding fertile areas for new settlement and a good stock route from east to west. Like all those early explorers, he dreamed of discovering a freshwater lake system or an inland sea in the centre, but his hopes invariably disappeared in mirage. Kathleen Graves quotes frequently from the explorer's journal and gives her reader an idea of the way in which glimpses of rare beauty haunted him so that every time he was forced to turn back he knew that he must soon try again, inspired by the memory of spring nights encamped by some creek with the air 'cool and dewy and laden with the scent of shrubs and flowers, the odour of almonds', or an oasis 'so richly grassed, so beautifully decked with ferns, that it seemed like suddenly escaping from purgatory into paradise. . . . It is happiness most ecstatic to know that I am the first white man ever to behold it.'

In all his journeys Giles was aware of hostile natives resenting any intrusion on the precious water. When nothing else stirred in a desolate scene smoke on the far horizon would tell of tribe communing with tribe to report his party's progress in the Stone Age language of the aboriginals who often raided the party, armed with long spears. 'They were painted and feathered in a most alarming manner. As soon as they saw us they were off like emus, running along as close to the ground as is possible for any human creature to do.'

Time and again he was forced to give up, yet in 1873 he set off once more on the east-west trail with a young man called Alfred Gibson as second in command of his party. Poor Gibson got lost and died alone in the dreadful desert which bears his name, and, after fearful ordeals, Giles and his remaining followers were compelled to turn back. Two years later, nothing daunted, he led an expedition, financed by Sir Thomas Elder, to cross the sterile Nullarbor Plain westwards, this time with camels. The party nearly perished of thirst but accomplished their aim. Kathleen Graves writes:

> They made a triumphant entry into Perth . . . riding in on their camels like an Eastern caravan, the city decked with flags and bunting. Addresses of welcome, banquets, balls, dinners and receptions by the populace followed. But Giles notes in his journal that in the two thousand five hundred terrible miles traversed he had found no area suitable for settlement. . . . After only eight weeks of resting he left Perth in January 1876 with two white men of his party, the Afghan (camel-man) and a native boy, taking the way north.

So, driven once again by the inexorable compulsion to cross the centre, he followed the trail of the Westralian explorer, Sir John Forrest, who had recently surveyed the rivers of the north-west. On the lower reaches of the Murchison, Giles's tiny expedition left the last human outpost and pressed north-east, plagued by flies, heat and thirst. By the end of May he found himself facing a terrible unknown desert. Half blinded by ophthalmia he nevertheless made up his mind to take his little party on past the point of no return. His journal tells of this appalling trek. 'The solitary caravan with its slow as eternity motion, presents the only living object . . . and the nights I pass in this frightful region are more dreadful than the days, for night is the time for care; then the pale spectre of despair comes to our lonely tent.'

I have noticed that many explorers, like Scott in Antarctica, Stanley and Mary Kingsley in Africa, Giles and Wills in Australia – to quote only a few – write their poignant journals to the bitter end, describing wonderfully the lonely altars on which they offer up their lives and those of their companions, as if they were poets and lovers pursuing the inescapable lure of a predestined fate, sustained by an unrecognized death-wish.

Yet, so mighty is the spirit of man, so indestructible the human will, that Giles and his comrades finally accomplished that appalling coast to coast crossing! Kathleen Graves ends the strangely inconclusive success story:

> His mission accomplished, his urge assuaged, Giles disappeared from the story of Australian exploration. Since he passed through that country, only an occasional prospector searching for a mythical gold reef has wandered into it; and a survey of it has been made from the air. In the Rawlinson Ranges a weather station now bears his name.

At so great a price in suffering and effort he had found the limited water of the Rawlinsons, but no central Eden with rivers flowing east and west. The cruel trail of heat and thirst could not even serve as a future stock route.

Less than twenty years later, Hannan and his contemporaries struck the 'mythical gold'. There it was – the rich reward of the unflagging prospector out for gain and not for glory! It had lain, undiscovered, between the territories Giles had explored – between the 'solemn stillness' of the Nullarbor Plain and that desertland 'so desolate that it is horrifying even to describe'.

Kalgoorlie's week-end highlight is the Saturday afternoon Race Meeting to which we went with our kind host, the proprietor of our hotel.

The course was delightfully landscaped, with gardens and lawns round the grandstand, and the meeting was opened by the band playing 'God Save the Queen' and huntsmen in pink coats leading in the fine Australian-bred horses. Racing is in Australia's blood and Country Meetings are social occasions for the entire family. Children played under the trees while their fathers studied form and their mothers chatted and eyed each other's outfits which were well worth a second glance.

'Pure Ascot!' said Elspeth. 'Splendid hats!'

That evening Frank Cooke's agent, Mr Bert Mettan, and his wife fetched us to see if we could find a two-up game in progress. I'd heard of this famous miners' gamble and wanted to see it, but Bert was dubious.

'I doubt if we'll get anywhere. It's illegal and they're tough on it here. It's the way the men throw their earnings down the drain. A miner will go to the two-up game with his pay packet in his pocket and driving his own car, and quite likely he'll come back with neither. The women won't stand for it, they've set their faces against two-up.'

We drove out into the bush and every now and again Bert followed mysterious but significant signs on trees or at the side of the road, like clues in a treasure hunt, and after a while a dirt track led us to a clearing where a corrugated iron fence surrounded a rough arena. He shook his head as he pulled up.

'Nothing doing. Sorry. But I expected it to be that way.'

So we had to be content to get out and view the empty scene of the big gamble which depends on the spin of a couple of coins – heads, tails, or two-up. But it was easy to imagine the furtive gathering of vehicles in the bush and the hundred or more tough miners intent upon the gleam and fall of the coins; money passing fast or on the nod; men made or ruined in an hour; the aftermath of empty beer cans, cigarette ends, car tracks and footprints in the thick dust; and, at home, a wife stony-faced and reproachful, silent, win or lose.

Kalgoorlie is Western Australia's biggest Flying Doctor base, so at eight next morning, before we left on our return journey, Bert Mettan took us to hear the morning session of this superbly organized Service which has grown up with the needs of a nation of graziers, cattle-men, planters, miners and the lonely outposts of the bush. In New South Wales I was to see this remarkable system in operation from every angle and was to fly with the Doctor many hundreds of miles but it was the base on the windy hill outside Kalgoorlie that was my introduction to the Outback's 'mantle of safety'.

The Flying Doctor radio network covers an area of a million square miles in Outback Australia and the same radio service operates the School of the Air, which makes isolated children members of a real, vital school of their own, although the pupils may be separated from each other and the schoolroom by hundreds of miles! In the case of emergency or accident the radio operator gets in touch with the doctor, wherever he may be, and connects him with the station in trouble. The doctor will advise on immediate treatment and then call up his pilot. Within minutes he will be on his way in the three-engined Drover that is always standing by, and within hours the patient will be receiving attention, and, if necessary, brought to hospital. Every Outback station homestead has its transceiving set and its airstrip.

The house of Kalgoorlie's radio operator was adjacent to the army-type hut in which the radio system was installed. When we arrived that dry bright morning with the wind murmuring through the bush, Charles Prideaux, the radio operator, was about to open the morning session.

'Come along in and sit down,' he said. 'I'm just going to take the telegrams and messages, but, of course, if there's an emergency call for the doctor, an alarm bell rings and breaks through any other business.'

He had curly grey hair and a young weather-beaten face and limped a bit from a war wound. He had been a radio operator in the Royal Australian Navy and I could imagine him calm and confidence-inspiring in any circumstances. Even over the air he could make the anxious caller feel safe.

He put on his ear-phones and settled down at his desk in front of the radio panel. He began to call in the various stations in rotation, dissecting the human voices out of the crackle of static that, to me, would have scrambled any message. All the stations on the Flying Doctor's network are entitled to use it for the dispatch of messages and telegrams. We could hear the messages and Charlie often gave us the background.

'That was a truck broken down three hundred miles from here in the Nullarbor. A broken crankshaft. He needs a spare part sent out as soon as possible.'

Once he looked perturbed. 'I can't get you, Mrs Harris. You've got the flattest battery in all the world, or else twisted aerial wires. It's pretty woeful, but give it another go in half an hour. Have a look at those wires and then I'll come back to you.'

The messages streamed through – machinery needed, supplies required for medical chests, or just plans being made with friends in town. There were consultations with the doctor who was in telephonic communication with the base.

'Right, Tom, I'll connect you with the doctor. Over.'

The new voice came in and we heard the conversation.

'It's an open network,' grinned Charlie. 'Like a party line. No secrets.'

Tom, the patient, was afflicted with boils, poor man. He had been bitten by a spider and attributed his boils to the bite. The doctor thought the spider was probably not to blame. He gave his prescription. Every item could be found in the medical chest supplied by the service.

'Item B 72. Take one capsule six hourly and two good washes a day with item C 34. That's the soap to disinfect the areas where the streptococci are most active. Got that, Tom? Over.'

Tom repeated the instructions and then Charlie, who had been making notes, ran over the items once more with him to make sure. 'Hope you'll be right soon, Tom. Over.'

'Thank you very much, Charlie. Cheerio for now. Over.'

'He's in a construction camp a hundred miles away,' Charlie told us. 'This next, coming in now, is a cattle station about four hundred miles out from here. . . . Good morning, Mrs Banks, how is it with you? Over.'

It was her baby son Mrs Banks was worried about. Charlie put her through to the doctor who prescribed powder 71 three times a day and no solid food. 'There's a lot of enteritis about, Mrs Banks. Got the idea? Over.'

'I've got the idea, Doctor.' She repeated the instructions.

'Good,' came the answer. 'And call me back tomorrow if you're worried. Cheerio for now, Mrs Banks. Over.'

'Pity it's Sunday,' said Charlie, when the session was finished. 'You'd have been interested in the School of the Air. The kids are bright as buttons. Last Christmas holidays they had their annual picnic get-together here in Kalgoorlie and they performed a play for us. They'd rehearsed the whole thing over the air and it was quite something. Imagine rehearsals with the cast hundreds of miles apart, not even knowing what the other performers look like till they meet on the stage!'

Bit by bit, I was beginning to understand this total war against the insidious foe – isolation.

We said good-bye to Charlie and the Mettans and took the highway to Coolgardie. Unlike Johannesburg, Kalgoorlie has sad spectres at her garden gate. Her neighbouring ghost towns haunt her with their grim reminders of glittering promises turned to ashes. There are many such in Australia, places with memorable names like Ballarat and Bendigo, north of Melbourne, that, a century ago, had brought the first great Australian gold rush and tripled the population of Victoria overnight.

Coolgardie, twenty-five miles from Kalgoorlie, was contemporary with the early strikes of the Witwatersrand. This shadow of a town once had 33,000 inhabitants and magnificent public buildings. Now her population is six hundred and her buildings are derelict. Joy and Elspeth took pictures of a baroque ruin in the wide main road and presently an old man, wearing his Sunday best, emerged and greeted us. He waved a lordly hand at the erstwhile mansion.

'This was a fine hotel once. As you can see. Now there's just a shell with me and my cobber batching it upstairs.'

With a proprietorial air he ushered us into the huge ballroom of fifty years ago. The chandeliers and the shutters were gone, the boards were bare and warped. The wind whistled through broken panes and the only furniture was a trestle-table, a few wooden chairs and some upturned boxes.

'Ready for our card game tonight.' He was like an old soldier who flaunts an empty sleeve and a peg-leg with proud defiance. Presently he directed us to the Denver City Hotel.

'It's run by a descendant of the first owner. In the bar you can see the photos of Coolgardie as she was in her heyday – the naughty nineties, as they say.'

The large clean bar, closed to the public as it was Sunday morning, smelt of Saturday night – yeasty, sour and rather smoky. The walls were hung with faded photographs of dashing, heavily moustached characters in wide-brimmed hats and moleskin trousers, and prospectors dry-blowing the gold. In that waterless land, before the pipe-line, they hadn't enough water to wash themselves, let alone the gold, and they had to 'winnow' it. We saw pictures of camel-caravans loaded high with supplies and water barrels for the pioneers. The camel-trains of the Australian goldfields took the place of the ox-wagons and donkey-teams of South Africa. A camel-team was usually a round dozen, and, instead of a black boy to crack the whip and shout insults at his sixteen horned friends, the camel-man in charge was a hawk-faced Afghan. Apart from that, the scene might well have been the Rand of the same exciting period. The bush, the sky, the wide horizons and the heat of the day glared out of faded prints, and in the masterful hirsute faces were stamped the hopes of tough fortune-hunters the world over. Some had won, some had lost, others had vanished from the Australian scene. Many, however, had remained, prospecting for minerals, with or without success; drifting from strikes that had petered out to tend cattle and sheep in the Outback; or to plant bananas, or grow beans, wheat or timber. But, whether they worked in the mines or on the land, or in construction gangs, or in the towns, they played their own special part in the development of a new country and a new nation.

We left Coolgardie to her ghosts and her card games in the early afternoon and set off once more on the highway to Perth. Near the Tammin-Hagley cross-roads we dropped Joy at the Greek fruit-store-café where Frank met her.

The long road uncoiled. Daylight faded on the Darling Range and night fell. The lights of Perth welcomed us from the hills, their reflections in the river wavering like windy banners and ribbons of drowned flame. Mist swirled up from the water in phantom veils and the scent of the ocean was on the breeze. Back at the O.B.H. the night watchman took our bags up to our rooms.

We made ourselves some tea, ate the last of our sandwiches and went yawning to bed, tired but content.

I fell asleep with the song of the sea in my ears – the pounding surf, deep and strong, answering the pull of the harvest moon. Who would exchange such a powerful symphony for the music of the night breeze blowing thinly through the bush or whispering in the dry leaves of the gums? I would never wish to live very far from the sea.

CHAPTER SIX

Lands of Opportunity

One of the people in Perth I was most anxious to meet was Mary Durack (Mrs Durack-Miller) whose magnificent Australian family saga, *Kings in Grass Castles*, had absorbed me throughout the lazy restful voyage in *Straat Cumberland*. In that book she described the pioneering history of her Irish-born progenitors in the young continent they had helped to develop, especially the important Kimberley district of north-western Australia, now famous for its cattle, sheep and rice.

Her grandfather, Patrick Durack, was the central character of the book and again and again, as I was reading, I thought: this could be South Africa and Patrick Durack could be my own Marais grandfather whose destiny was also shaped by the growth and promise of a young country. Mary Durack brought Australia and its personalities of the nineteenth century to vivid life with all their great endeavours, disappointments and achievements. Family parties trekked into the little known hinterland of drought, flood, burning sun and often hostile natives. The men were horse-breeders and pastoralists, seeking ever wider and better grazing for their herds.

In 1875 Alexander Forrest of Perth, true to his family's tradition, set out on a journey of exploration to survey the huge north-western Kimberley area with its great rivers and grassy plains. His accounts were enthusiastic and he told of 'a cattle-man's paradise' with fine grazing-lands for sheep nearer the coast. It was in the path of the monsoon, however, and flood and fever were snags to be endured or overcome. Fired by his report and personal encouragement, the Duracks and Emmanuels of Queensland launched a private expedition to inspect the territory for themselves, and by 1896 the Duracks were moving 7,500 head of breeding cattle on the hoof 3,000 'drovers' miles' overland to the new country. That northern trek from east to west took two years and half the cattle perished before they reached their destination. The total cost of the operation was £70,000. The names along the stock-route suggest a few of the hardships the overlanders and their mobs had to face. Drought Camp, Pleuro Camp, Wet Season Camp, Fever Camp. Some of the overlanders were murdered by hostile aborigines, who, in turn, were decimated by the white infiltration. A certain number of the more intelligent aborigines were later employed as stockmen, and their descendants still are, while other survivors found their way into the reserves of the Northern Territory to be educated by missions and form a considerable part of the Flying Doctor practice.

In time the overlanders made good. They put down roots, sent for their families, built homes, and lived an arduous dangerous frontier life, building up the great meat industries that are so important to the economy of present day Australia.

These incredibly long treks of Australia's overlanders with their flocks and their mobs had much in common with the family treks, great and small, that opened the rich hinterland of South Africa, though, in Australia's case, there was one vital drive missing – the compulsion to build an independent nation in a new land. No part of the Australian Continent had been acquired by treaty from a foreign power, as the Cape was ceded to Great Britain; nor by conquest, as the two Boer Republics of the Transvaal and Orange Free State were forced into Britain's Colonial Empire after the long anguish of the Boer War. Australia was, from the first, a single incipient nation, however divided the early colonists might be.

It is not so much the spirit of adventure that drives people to emigrate to new countries as disaster or dissatisfaction at home. If it hadn't been for the tragedy of the Irish potato famine the Durack family might still have been in the Emerald Isle. But they had to starve or emigrate. One day, I believe, just such a choice may face the people of the world. Our descendants may have to decide whether to stay and starve on earth or pioneer the infinite outback of space in search of a new planet in which man may survive.

When the first Duracks arrived in Sydney in 1849 under an assisted immigration scheme, Australian stockmen had already found a path through the Great Dividing Range. Mary Durack writes:

> When a pass was found at last and the explorers gazed enraptured on the vast sweep of the rich Australian prairies there appeared the first symptoms of a land fever that was to burn in men's blood, driving them into the remotest and most forbidding wilderness . . . the landtakers, with their herds and assigned servants, were over the hills and far away, past the reach of the law. Breathlessly the authorities set about the establishment of nineteen counties where, it was declared, settlement must be contained. . . . Fast as they worked, the pioneers on their indomitable westward march were even faster, pushing out the boundaries of settlement in a policy of their own. Undaunted by the government challenge that no police protection would be provided outside the authorized limits they made their own rules, fighting out the battles of their boundaries with rifles, stockwhips and stirrup irons.

Those words might just as well have been written about the early days in South Africa. The Boer trekkers too had taken their flocks and herds and wagons and servants across the mighty barrier ranges, where many had been massacred by hostile tribes. They too had made their own rules and cut themselves off from the distant government of the Cape and the still more remote law-givers of London.

Kim and Pat Rose arranged for me to meet Mary Durack-Miller.

'Nothing could be easier,' said Pat. 'You and Elspeth must come to lunch with us – quite informally – and I'll get Mary and her sister, Elizabeth, to come along.'

The Rose family, like the Duracks, were closely connected with the growth and development of the frontier region north of the 26th parallel. Kim's father had gone to the Kimberley with Alexander Forrest and the early explorers of Western Australia, while the Duracks, of course, had come from the other side of the Continent, Brisbane.

'Those Queenslanders,' said Kim. 'What ace stockmen they were! That three thousand mile trek with their cattle was an epic. They taught us Westerners to handle mobs. But now it's all different up there. The mob on the hoof and the swagman belong to the past. Cattle are trucked to the ports or the slaughter-houses and Air Beef looks after the rest.'

Kim is tall, grey-haired and fine-featured with the bright blue eyes one associates with men of the sea and the open air. Pat, his wife, has the same brilliant blue eyes in a thin tanned little face illumined by great sweetness and charm. They had lived nearly forty years in the Kimberley, building up a first-rate sheep station, and they both loved that savage frontier land.

'When I took Pat up there as a bride she couldn't boil water let alone an egg, and before long she was the best cook in the country and could turn her hand to anything.' He looked at his wife with pride. In the days of her youth Australian girls of the cities were raised in greater luxury than now and housewives did not have to do their own chores.

The Durack sisters joined us soon after twelve o'clock and we sat in the garden and drank cold beer. They are both famous women in their own country, Mary, the author, and Elizabeth, the artist. Curiously enough, I had been aware of Elizabeth's work before I learned of Mary's. In the London mews, where I had spent my last English summer and to which I was returning, there was a charming cottage belonging to a couple who knew Australia well. In fact, the wife was Australian-born. When I first went into their home I was struck by the pictures in their attractive lounge. Impressionist brush-work breathed the moods of a primitive lonely land and its people.

'They're wonderful!' I exclaimed. 'They grip you! Those wild faces – there's a sort of abandon about them.'

'They're Australian aborigines,' said my hostess.

'Who's the artist?'

'Elizabeth Durack. It's not easy to get her pictures any more. They're mostly in galleries or museums.'

Now, when I met this gifted artist, I found that she had the same elusive quality as her work, a fey, on-the-verge-of-flight look, with her platinum hair and willowy figure, while her sister Mary had her small feet more firmly on the ground. Mary's smile, spontaneous and quick, warmed her lively intelligent eyes with the humour which shines through her books. Her husband was the co-founder of the MacRobertson-Miller air service operating between Perth and Darwin, and serving the outposts and mission stations of Western Australia and the north. They have six children.

The day was bright and fresh and we ate our cold buffet lunch under a shady umbrella-shaped tree. A sprinkler played on the lawn that was bordered by dahlias and the lovely roses of Perth. A little white fence hemmed in a neat kitchen-garden. The lettuces we ate were home-grown. It was easy to talk in that happy informal atmosphere, and Elspeth and I were eager to hear all that we could about the early days of Western Australia.

'Our parents had a lot to contend with in the Kimberley,' said Kim. 'Ticks and floods and cattle sickness and the frantic search for markets. All those cattle and sheep and nowhere to sell them! For those who could hang on, it came good. But not all could hang on.'

There was a sad little silence. The hard-won Durack empire had not been able to 'hang on'.

'And now,' said Mary, 'there are markets in the Far East and cattle are sold to Borneo and Japan, and live sheep go to the Philippines to be killed in the Moslem way.'

Pat went into the house for some coloured snapshots to show us. A soft grey-green landscape, an opaque grey-green river.

'One of our children fell into the water just about here,' she said. 'We couldn't see a trace of her except her little starched sun-bonnet wilting. You can't see what's under the surface. You have to guess.'

'Did you dare swim in that river?'

'Oh, yes, why not?'

'What about crocs?'

She laughed. 'Heaps of those. But they're the fish-eating type. You don't often meet a man-eater.'

Bearing in mind our own fearful South African crocodiles

with their great jaws and serrated dentures, I wouldn't care to chance any saurian's nice nature or eating habits!

We weren't allowed to have it all our own way conversationally. Our hosts soon got us talking too. They wanted to know about Kenya from Elspeth. And they made me talk about South Africa with its curious parallels to Australian pioneering. They were astonished to find that I was an eleventh generation South African on my mother's side and third on my Danish and German father's. They had not realized how early the Cape had been colonized.

'In 1652! And when did your ancestors go there?' they asked me.

'Thirty years later.'

'What made them go?'

'Religious persecution at home. My first ancestors in South Africa were French Huguenots who escaped to Protestant Holland after the revocation of the Edict of Nantes. The Dutch East India Company wanted grape-growers and wine-makers and offered the Huguenot refugees grants of land in its new colony.'

'Did they do well?'

'Very. Some of the loveliest old Cape homesteads were built by the Huguenots who intermarried with the Dutch colonists. My grandfather's birthplace, "Nectar", is still a traditional example. But he was born in 1838, a difficult year for the Cape and one of fate for the hinterland.'

Mary turned to Elizabeth. 'Joy's grandfather must have been contemporary with our's.'

'Within a few years,' I said. 'And his life followed the same type of pattern.'

I told them how the emancipation of the slaves had broken the wine farmers of the Cape which was then a British Colony, and about the Boer cattlemen of the frontier who were full of grievances against London. Compensation for slaves could only be collected in London and no farmer could afford the time or the money to go there, so they sold their vouchers to touts for a song and their farms for wagon wheels and the exodus of a people with their flocks and herds began. The Boers – Australia would translate the word as pastoralists – trekked north and came into conflict with the warrior Kaffir tribes coming south, and after terrible conflicts and hardships they established the new Boer Republics of the Transvaal and the Orange Free State. When my grandfather was a lad of fifteen he left 'Nectar' with a saddle horse and five gold sovereigns to seek his fortune in the new country. For a time he stayed in the frontier town of Graaff-Reinet and became a transport rider, convoying wagon-trains with consignments of English goods from the coast inland through country often aflame with Kaffir wars. On one of these treks he met my grandmother, the daughter of Irish and English 1820 settlers, and they married and went on up to the new Transvaal Republic where he was given a grant to set up a trading store outside Pretoria. The store was soon a sort of club and meeting place for geologists and prospectors, and one day the thrilling word 'gold' sent my grandfather and a prospector friend on a mad ride across wild country to stake the claim that was to make their fortunes. Their claim was at the eastern end of the reef that was to change the course of South African history and lead inevitably to the Boer War, and on, through tragedy, into prosperity.

'That's how it is in a new country,' said Mary. 'Anything can happen! There's always a fortune over the next hill – mineral ore, luscious pasturage, and pests and battles too. But in pushing forward the frontiers of their own lives, the pioneers help develop and settle their country.'

Certainly the achievements of the Duracks and their friends in crossing Australia from the east to the north-west in their determination to reach the 'cattleman's paradise' of sweet grazing and permanent water blazed a 3,000-mile stock route for generations to come. Initiative and zest thrive in unopened territory which is so strong a challenge to the young and adventurous spirit.

A few evenings later we went to an after dinner party at Mary's home and had drinks and sandwiches under the huge trees of her almost tropical garden.

We made the acquaintance of her attractive blonde daughter

1a Tailing lambs in transportable pens at Hagley

1b The school bus dropping children at Hagley

2a A homestead in the Murchison sheep-rearing district north of Perth

2b A scene in the outback near Hagley

who was a qualified pilot and nurse and assistant to Dr H. G. Dicks, head of the Western Australian Section of the Royal Flying Doctor Service. Only the night before, a lumberjack in the timber forests of the south had been badly injured and it was imperative to get him to hospital in Perth without delay. Although the Flying Doctor Drovers are not yet equipped for night flying and there was no flare-path on the airstrip, Dr Dicks and his young co-pilot nurse took off while every vehicle in or near the lumber camp converged upon it with headlights blazing to guide the mercy plane. The mission was safely accomplished and the man saved. It was an unusual operation, but then Dr Dicks is an unusual person, fearless and determined. He had been one of the first Flying Doctors of the war years, when that remarkable service was still in its infancy. He was then based on the West coast which had suffered severe bombing by the Japanese. In 1945 there was a time when he found himself at the Port Hedland base, combining the duties of Flying Doctor, pilot, engineer, magistrate, mining warden and superintendent of the hospital! By 1959 he was Federal Vice-President of the Service, one of its most experienced organizers and administrators.

'I'm hoping Julie will show up,' said Mary. 'She's due in to-night.'

Her oldest daughter, Julie, was an air hostess in her father's MacRobertson-Miller line and she was then on the north-west run, a bumpy rather stormy passage at that time of year when cyclones were still apt to hit the coast and flood the airstrips. She arrived about ten-thirty, neat and dashing in her fawn uniform and jaunty forage cap. She was fair with an open face that could go deadpan or flash with sparkling humour, and I soon discovered that she had immense humanity for one so young.

'It's getting cold out here,' said Mary. 'Let's go in.'

The wind had risen, and she led us through the large rambling house and up some outside stairs into the self-contained annexe where she can hide from the world and write in peace. It was a spacious study-cabin with kitchenette and bathroom. Her reference library was near an enviably large desk in front of a window looking on to the shifting green tapestry of leaves.

'It's so quiet,' I said. 'A wonderful work-room!'

'Yes, but the kookaburras laugh in those trees at sunrise and you have to wake up and laugh with them!' The squat raucous kookaburras are birds who live near human habitations and become very tame.

Julie entertained us with stories of the strange passengers she had encountered in the course of her Outback flights. She loves people, whether they are pot-black aborigines, old tattooed grannies, young juvenile delinquents, or even mild lunatics. She had considerable experience of the aborigines of the Northern Territory. One trip they brought a native passenger to a mental home.

'He had a policeman with him because he was apt to become violent. He thought he was an elephant and we had to feed him bananas most of the trip. When I asked him what had become of his trunk, he said he'd got it tangled up in the branches when he was working timber in the jungle, so he'd lost it. We had to fill in a form for him, and when I asked him what his religion was, he said, "Whatever religion an elephant has." When he wanted to go to the wash-place the policeman had to go along with him. It's pretty small in those planes – hardly enough room for that big policeman, let alone an elephant!'

'Did he get better?' we asked.

'Ah, yes,' said Julie. 'He's an interesting fellow. Last time he flew with us he was a crocodile.'

She also took a team of aborigines from the Islands to Perth to perform their traditional dances at a festival. They were a great success and the return journey amused Julie. Outward bound they wore very little.

'They were soot-black – but *black* – and they carried their spears. I have to make a few notes after each trip. Wear and tear. And I had to write "Head-rests torn by spears". They had pipes too and they wanted "rotma-rotma, missus" – Rothman's cigarettes – and they stuffed their pipes with them, but the return journey was a very different story – only a fortnight later. They were dressed and carried umbrellas instead of spears, and they wanted "bens an' edges" – Benson & Hedges – and they smoked them in the usual fashion. Believe me, those boys learned fast!'

'Did their dance tour go well?'

'Terrific. Of course, they're marvellous at taking off the animals. You see them being kangaroos, and they *are*! The turn of the head, the attitude of the front paws, the back legs apart, the listening, everything.'

When Julie knew that we longed to see an Outback cattle station – preferably in the Kimberley – she was anxious to help, but it was rather like suggesting a flight from London to the Arctic Circle. It could be done and the MacRobertson-Miller airways could give us quite a tour, but it would use up all of a week, and the cyclone season was not yet over. It would also be an expensive jaunt. So, in the end, we settled for a compromise. We'd go to Wittenoom, over a thousand miles into the Outback, and Julie would see what she could arrange about the cattle station.

We were delighted to leave our plans in her hands.

CHAPTER SEVEN

Iron Core of the Outback

Wittenoom Gorge is a little asbestos mining town well to the west of Alice Springs, the tourist resort of the Inland. I may as well admit straight away that, as far as tourism was concerned, Elspeth and I left undone most of those things which we ought to have done, and, when we felt a bit guilty about our sins of omission, we looked at one another and said, 'Next time!'

So we did not obey the handbook which told us to: 'See romantic Alice Springs – capital of the "Red Heart" and relax and wander through the Centre of the Great Continent.' Neither did we 'join the aborigines from Hermannsburg Mission singing around the camp fires four or five days from Alice Springs' – a mere step by Australian standards! Nor did we 'explore the caves of Red Ayers Rock with their native paintings and see the aboriginal ceremonial sites'. Perhaps we're a bit sore that we didn't, but the well-trodden tracks were not for us that year.

Julie had arranged for us to meet Langley Hancock, a very remarkable pastoralist-prospector who would give us a real picture of the 'vacuum of the North-West' and its magnetic future. He was to fetch us at Wittenoom in his Cessna aircraft on the morning after our arrival and we were to spend a day at his cattle station, Hamersley. Elspeth was a trifle tight-lipped at the prospect of the Cessna. She was dying to see the cattle station but she felt about small planes much as she did about yachts and ferries, and I had an uncomfortable foreboding that, when it came to the point, she might toss her glossy head and shy, especially when Mrs White in the O.B.H. Reception Office raised her eyebrows and said, 'Flying to Wittenoom Gorge, are you? Boompety-boomp, boompety-boomp!'

'Mrs Rhodes has her tablets,' I said hastily. 'She'll be all right.'
Elspeth rolled a dark indignant eye at me.

'If it's boompety-boomp from here to Wittenoom, what'll it
be in that small Cessna?'

We left the hotel at 4 a.m. in our Holden, which could await
our return in the airport car park. We were due to fly at five –
an unearthly hour – but before sun-up is the best time for flying
in Australia. Less boompety-boomp.

There were no porters to take our bags at the airport, and
this, I think, is the great weakness in Australia's half-hearted
attempt to encourage tourism. You can look round in vain for
fetchers and carriers in that independent continent. But there are
plenty of thoughtful fellow passengers who help, if need be,
purely out of kindness.

At four-thirty the airport begins to come alive. Floor polishers
appear, working rapidly over the black and white linoleum of
the big modern central hall, the waitresses heat up the coffee
machines in the pleasant little Coffee Bar. It was cold in that hour
of pale stars, but the waitress said, 'Really, the coldest time is
six o'clock – sunrise.' It was still dark when our flight was called.
We filed past the artificial pond that is the home of some black
swans, the emblem of Perth, now seldom to be found on the
Swan River, and took our places in the MMA 'Fokker Friendship', which was fully booked. The air hostess, Julie's friend and
colleague, gave us a smiling welcome, the engine throbbed
and roared, the lights of the flare-path streamed away like comets
and we were looking down upon the sleeping city. I wondered
how it had appeared to Major Glenn from the limitless height
of space.

The sunrise that morning had a fierce improbable quality, with
feverish bands of violet and jade slashed across a sulphur background. In the west the cool silver thread of the Moore River
was woven into the thin grey-green spinifex, sword-cruel to the
feet of horses or humans. We came down at Mount Magnet,
where a windsock blew in a stiff breeze and a couple of tin shanties
and a windmill flashed in the hot immensity of the ochre desert.
Something else flashed too. A little aircraft about the size of a
bushfly was poised on the red earth.

'That,' said Elspeth, pointing with a long nervous finger, 'is a Cessna. That's for you!'

'And for you – if you want to see a cattle station.'

We came down once more at Meekatharra, a small Flying Doctor and School of the Air base, and then we were on the last lap of our flight into the Outback.

The shape and colour of the empty scene changed as the long horseshoe of the mineral-bearing Hamersley Range wrinkled the flat rose-pink earth, deepening salmon hues to ruby, pouring violet and indigo into chasms and canyons of erosion, and casting love-in-a-mist veils over peaks reaching for the high blue sky.

'It's the back of the moon in technicolor,' I said to Elspeth, but she was dozing. Her anti-nausea tablets always made her sleepy. In aeroplanes she was content to become a deaf-mute.

At last we were circling over Wittenoom, a pattern of tin-roofed prefab bungalows tossed into the middle of nowhere, criss-crossed with dirt roads and pointed up with the spire of a little church. There was a school, a small hospital and a homely pub shaded by palms and pepper-trees, which was clearly the heart of the matter. Now we were north of the 26th parallel in the sparsely populated undeveloped North-West territory, frontier country half the size of Europe well known to be fabulously rich with untapped minerals.

We were met by Mr Shean, the Clerk of the Tablelands Shire, and his boxer dog, which instantly recognized in Elspeth a true lover of his breed. The back of Mr Shean's bush-shirt was covered with tiny black flies, the plague of the Outback, but he didn't seem to notice them, and within seconds Elspeth and I were in the same condition.

'Well now,' said Mr Shean, when he had driven us to the hotel, booked us in, and ordered 'schooners', thirst-quenching beers. 'Lang Hancock is flying in for breakfast tomorrow at seven here at the hotel, and he'll fly you out to Hamersley, his cattle station.'

I stole a glance at my friend's non-committal face and wondered.

'So I thought perhaps today, after lunch, you'd like to go out to the Blue Asbestos Mine and then this evening we can look around the town. There's not much to see, but there's no point in my driving you all the way to Dale Gorge when you'll be seeing the Hamersley Canyon tomorrow. The one's as good as the other.'

About a thousand people live in Wittenoom, many of them 'new Australians' with experience of mining in their countries of origin – Yugoslavia, Holland, Greece, Italy, Hungary, to quote a few.

In summer the thermometer tops 'the century' day after day and, when the great heat breaks, the cyclone floods turn the gorges into raging torrents and the plain into a marsh.

Mr Shean drove us out to the mine soon after lunch. No wonder they called the Inland the 'Red Heart'! Red dust-devils waltzed over the spinifex and lost themselves in groves of cool ghost-gums, moonpale in coppery creeks. The mine and the asbestos mill scarred the sun-baked rock wall of a deep valley. A delightful engineer, called Philip, acted as our guide. We put on helmets and followed him into a Hades of noise – the mill. He was in love with life – with his work, with Wittenoom, with the mine, and no doubt there was some lucky girl somewhere who could take Outback Australia in her stride.

Machinery terrifies me, and it was Elspeth who trod the clanging galleries unafraid and mounted little wooden ladders to look down robot throats swallowing deafening tons of ore on its way through a fearful digestive process that would finally isolate the valuable blue asbestos fibre and its by-products.

'I wouldn't go into the middle of that ghastly din for anything,' I bellowed at Elspeth above the roar of machinery. 'It makes me giddy to think of it.' She gave me one of her telling looks.

'Then you'll know how I feel about other things – Cessnas and small boats.'

Trucks reversed to the very edge of a precipice and tipped their loads of waste into the abyss. Those blue pebbles could be used to pave whole cities if there were easy transportation. That was always the problem in this huge land – how to convey raw material thousands of miles from its source to the factory.

'It's wonderful safe mining,' enthused Philip. 'Horizontal tunnels. No shafts down into the depths. Of course you can't always stand up straight in tunnels!'

71

He had taken off his helmet and he ran his hand through his thick hair. He glanced down at Elspeth's little camera slung round her neck.

'You keen on photography?'

'I'm a beginner. This one's foolproof.'

'I know. It makes all its own arrangements. I'm keen too. The colours on these rocks at sunset – I can't tell you what they're like! They glow like jewels, fluorescent. Often in the evenings, when you go for a walk or a ride, you see the 'roos – such gentle animals, but slow to learn. And birds! You've never seen such birds.'

One of us said something about the heat. He laughed.

'Sure, it's hot. We topped a hundred and seventeen for three weeks one summer. But it's dry. Healthy.'

I gazed at the mountains with their curious rocky collars, sheer impregnable cliffs guarding the summits.

'We have the same formations in South Africa,' I said. 'We call them kranzes – crowns. The Karoo is very like this in parts. And in Basutoland the chiefs used to throw their enemies over those rock walls and leave the rest of the job to the vultures.'

'They're natural fortifications,' he said. 'Nobody could ever scale them. You have to find a pass, and two men can hold a pass.'

The air was cooler now as we thanked him for his trouble, and Mr Shean drove us back to the untidy dusty little township with its raw-looking homes and attempts at gardens. Children played on pocket handkerchief lawns of mangy summer grass, and young housewives watered tired borders. A very large percentage of them appeared to be on the brink of adding to their families. I remarked on this, and Mr Shean smiled.

'There's not much else to do here. Not even television, there'd be too much static with these ore-bearing mountains. I believe Wittenoom has the highest average birth-rate in Australia!'

He took us into his own home. It was like all the others, simple and labour-saving. He showed us a water-cooled fan in the outer kitchen wall.

'Outback air-conditioning. The air is filtered and cooled by the water. In the great heat the women get a sort of psychosis, and just sit and read and sew by the fan, as if they were hypnotized, hardly stirring except to look after the kids.'

I could well imagine them sheltering from the hot glaring hours, waiting for the tender touch of twilight on eyes and skin, the relief and refreshment of darkness and stars.

Dinner in our little hotel was excellent, served by a young Italian waitress, and afterwards we went out on to the lawn under the palms and pepper-trees.

In the bar the men were playing darts. We could see their shadows on the frosted glass of the window, the lifted arm drawn back and the quick throw. It might have been the silhouette of a cobra's head striking.

Mrs Johnson, the manager's wife, chatted to us for a few minutes.

'Our Ladies' Dart Club will be assembling any time now. The men all come here to play in their bar, so we wives have organized our own club in our section of the bar.'

She was merry and full of pep and obviously enjoyed the come and go of the planes and variety of her guests.

'We get all sorts – commercials, prospectors, drovers, graziers and, of course, shearers. One night I suddenly had to make up two dozen beds for a team turned up out of the blue.'

The shearing teams are an essential feature of station life. Though the modern equipment is mechanized the men are indispensable. Shearing goes on all the year round and the teams go from one station to the next, working hard and fast to keep to their programmes. D. H. Williamson gives a lively impression of their work.

The shearing shed and the buildings near it . . . are alive with men, and there are brown floods of sheep surging round the yards. There are cars and sulkies parked in the shade, there are shirts and corduroy trousers drying on lines slung between the trees, there is the growl of machinery by day, and at night the music of mouth-organs, banjos and men singing. Open fires light the undersides of the grey gums' branches while bearded old-timers crush their youthful competitors with tales twice as strange and far more cunningly told. . . .

The World is a Proud Place

There is no scene in all the world to be likened to an Australian shearing shed in full swing. . . . The overhead gear begins to whirr, a whistle shrills . . . and every shearer has disappeared into the catching pens. The first man emerges with a sheep, and the swish of the overhead shafting is reinforced by the clatter of the first handpiece as it is pulled into gear.

Stooping men are lined along the board. Their arms swing evenly under the urge of speed. . . . A shout of 'Wool away!' brings a roustabout scampering. He carries the fleece to the wool room and with a dexterous cast spreads it on the wool-rolling table as neatly as a woman spreads a blanket on a bed. The wool-rollers trim away all the heavily burred and stained edges of the fleece, which are thrown on to the piece-pickers' table to be sorted into first and second pieces. When the fleece is skirted and rolled with the shorn side out it finds its way onto the classer's table and from there into the bin nearest suited to its quality. . . .

Board-boys run a shuttle service between the tables and the shearing stands; the tar-boy, alternately mooning and starting up in terror, hurries towards a blasphemous shearer, smothers a cut sheep in tar, and returns to his meditation. . . .

The sun has become hotter, and the iron roof does little to damp its ardour. The cook with a kerosene-tin bucket of tea and a basin of rock-cakes is a welcome visitor, and a few minutes later the whistle for 'smoko' sounds.

The folk song of the shearers fills in the gaps.

> . . . They say that they can shear each day
> Their hundred pretty handy,
> But eighty sheep is no child's play
> If the wool is close and sandy.
>
> When the sheds are all cut out
> They get their bit of paper;
> To the nearest pub they run,
> They cut a dashing caper.
> They call for liquor plenty

And they're happy while they're drinking
But where to go when the money's done,
It's little they are thinking.

They're sleeping on verandahs
And they're lounging on the sofas;
For to finish up their spree
They're ordered off as loafers
They've got no friends, their money's gone,
And at their disappearing,
They give three cheers for the river bends [camps]
And jog along till shearing.

When we left the moonlit lawn and went up to bed I found the chambermaid combing out her hair in the washroom adjoining the baths and showers. She was in her dressing-gown. I asked her where she came from.

'Italy,' she said.

'I know your country. It's beautiful.'

'Not so bad – but not my country now.'

'Do you like it here?'

She laughed and tossed her heavy black mane.

'I like it okay. Everywhere the same. What you want is good work, good pay and no sick.'

As far as 'no sick' was concerned, Elspeth and the chambermaid were of one mind. So when Lang Hancock appeared for breakfast I took him aside and explained the situation.

'My friend is nervous of small planes because she is inclined to be airsick. Is it a long flight?'

'It needn't be,' he said kindly. 'It's really up to you. I could fly you right round the iron ore deposits of the Hamersley – that might take several hours – or we could cut it short. Say half an hour to the homestead with a slight detour to show you Turner River, the heart of it. Then we could drive to Hamersley Canyon by car this afternoon.'

We settled for the second alternative.

Although his family home is in Perth, Langley Hancock spends much of his time at Hamersley, for he is an Australian bushman to his bone marrow. But he is a bushman with an eye to the future, that rare creature, an intensely practical visionary.

The Economic and Financial Survey of Australia 1960–61 described him as follows:

Mr Langley Hancock, who could claim to have discovered more mineral deposits than any other living Australian, has spent most of his life north of the Tropic of Capricorn. His grandfather established Ashburton Downs station. Much later, Langley Hancock, in partnership with his father, owned Mulga Downs sheep station and Hamersley cattle station, both million-acre properties, which he now controls. He is a director of several mining and exploration companies. Recently, he formed an affiliation with Rio Tinto Mining Company of Australia. For almost twenty years, he has piloted his own light aircraft, and is a licensed ground engineer authorized by the Department of Civil Aviation to issue 'Safety Certificates' covering the air-worthiness of both his aeroplanes. When necessity drives, he invents small pieces of equipment for mining or treating ores, and has them fabricated from such scrap metal as is available in the remote areas in which he lives and works.

Lang's Cessna was poised, insect-tiny on the vast plain. As we strolled towards it Elspeth gave it one mettlesome look, but she did not flinch.

'I'm getting in the back,' she said. 'And nobody need talk to me over their shoulder!'

The little four-seater Cessnas are much used Outback because, among other things, they are light and easy to handle and their wings afford shade when on the ground. Even such limited shade is important in desert lands.

We took off and Elspeth closed her eyes. I sat beside Lang at the controls, and, looking down at the Red Heart, I was reminded of a flight in a tiny Post Office plane over the Namib desert of South-West Africa – the endless pink waste creased by wind-rumpled ranges and dry river-beds with homesteads hundreds of miles apart, yet the karakul flocks flourished in that arid land and the harsh inaccessible mountains were veined with wealth too difficult to mine or transport.

'Nature hides her wealth where you can't get at it,' said Lang. 'Right here she's hidden about five thousand million tons of the best iron ore in the world.'

Although he is a pastoralist, he is first and foremost a mining man, and his vision of the future in 'the mighty vacuum' is of mineral production on a grand scale, of towns and ports and railways where now there is only bush. It was he who originally discovered the blue asbestos of Wittenoom Gorge and brought in the Colonial Sugar Refining company with a capital of £4 million and a work force big enough to create the township in which we had spent the night. He is a tall well-knit man with a thick thatch of dark hair just beginning to grey, a pugnacious jaw and eyes that can be merry and kind or flash irritably behind his spectacles when he talks of bureaucrats who hamstring men of action. He is known as the 'flying prospector', but he has explored and prospected the vast mountainous area of the Hamersleys on foot, on horseback, with camels and with Land Rovers as well as aeroplanes.

Wittenoom was far away when he said, 'Now I'm going to fly low into Turner Gorge. Tell your friend to have her camera ready for a shot of iron unlimited.'

As he banked and turned, I saw, over my shoulder, a pair of large agonized eyes and a slender hand outstretched with the camera.

'Take it, Joy. The wing's in the way.' I knew that poor Elspeth dared not look out and down.

Lang swooped lovingly into the gorge, almost near enough to brush the dark ironclad bastion glinting in the sun. As we climbed and flattened out once more he gazed at the horn of mountains curved round the empty plain.

'Here, in the Pilbara, we have the most highly mineralized area in the world. Out of eighty commercial minerals seventy-eight are to be found here. It's our Aladdin's cave of Western Australia.'

'Who does all this belong to? Who owns this land?'

'I do,' he said. 'Two million acres of it – the iron heart. It's leasehold, of course, so the Government has a big interest and control.'

He had been fighting his battles with Canberra for many years – the battle for security of tenure, for the right of private enterprise to develop the mineral resources of the North-West, and for a tax free 'frontier territory' beyond the 26th parallel.

'Encourage investment, then plough back,' he said. 'Make the companies re-invest forty per cent of their profits in the tax free north and let them get on with their job unrestricted. We have the raw materials, but we need foreign capital. Sheep and cattle create negligible human settlement. Even if the big leaseholds are split up it wouldn't increase the population substantially, whereas mines create towns and a settled population.'

Lang is a man who deals in facts and figures. It was he who made me realize his country's greatest danger. Red China and Indonesia look longingly at Australia's undeveloped north. There is plenty to tempt their interest. Oil, minerals, grazing, rice, sugar, whaling, pearling. It would make a wonderfully rich outlet for their surplus populations. Ever since World War Two Australia has been the world's greatest importer of human material while China is the world's most prolific producer of the same commodity. In ten years' time it is estimated that Australia's immigration schemes will bring her total population up to 15 million, and it is chastening to reflect that this figure is roughly the same as *one year's* natural population growth in Red China!

'There's the homestead,' said Lang, as we circled over the sandy plain covered with spinifex and mulga trees.

It was the usual rather large Colonial one-storeyed house with a wide stoep sheltered by trees. A short distance away there were sheds, a hangar to take the two Cessnas and a bachelor bungalow.

Lang's manager met us as we landed. He was a young man with experience of engineering and he had his flying licence. It was characteristic of the owner of Hamersley and Mulga Downs that he should put a man with a knowledge of machinery in charge, a man who could repair windmills and look after the maintenance of vehicles and aircraft.

'My manager must be able to fly over the place,' Lang said.

'He must observe which windmills aren't working and see that they do, and so on. The stockmen know their own business. They're bred to it, but I don't expect them to be mechanics.'

The manager and his family lived in the big house, and, when he was at Hamersley, the owner occupied the bungalow but took his meals with them. Good meals too, for the manager's young wife was also an excellent cook. She had a 'gin' to help her, the wife of a half-breed stockman. In a corner of the large dining room where we all had lunch was the Flying Doctor transceiving set, an essential in any isolated station, and in the equally spacious kitchen were two of the most imposing refrigerators I have ever seen. Out in the shady garden was a 'cool-shed' for anyone who felt inclined to rest or snooze between water-cooled walls with the soporific hum of the fan in the peaceful half-dark.

That bright afternoon we travelled many miles with Lang, who put his car over the big clumps of spiky pale-green spinifex as if it were a horse taking a hurdle. He showed us the stock-yards, and the shed where the cattle were branded or slaughtered and transported direct by freezer-truck to Wittenoom or 1,370 miles to Perth.

I had expected to see great herds milling around on this huge cattle station, but, like aborigines, the cattle seemed hard to find. A few odd scattered mobs of shorthorns were huddled together in the shade of windmill waterpoints some fifteen or twenty miles apart where the gums and acacias were best and the vivid raucous bird life of parrots and cockatoos was richest. Only when there is a muster for some purpose of branding, slaughtering or trans-port can one get an idea of cattle on the move. The day of the old trekking drover is done, mourned by many, such as Ernestine Hill who writes so beautifully of her country and countrymen. She evokes the camp scene.

As the shadows grow long, the beasts are stringing, ready for rest. . . . The head drover rides ahead to put them on camp. A creek pool or billabong with a clear grassy flat beside it is the picture he has in his mind's eye. A good drover knows by heart the waterholes of Australia. . . . There is no more beau-tiful or impressive scene in the Australian bush than a drover's night camp, so long as the tranquillity lasts. Only a Rembrandt could paint it – the red glow of the firelight, men's faces, contented and thoughtful, the feathery grey of the trees above, and a night horse tethered; beyond, the shadowy herd, and a shadowy rider circling.

The watch is set. . . . No sound breaks the stillness save the singing of the watch. Tenor or tin-pot, baritone or wheelbarrow-tone, every man in a drover's camp must be prepared to sing a cowboy's lullaby to reassure his charges, lest the thud of his horse's hoofs, or the crack of a twig, or his ghostly form in the darkness should start a stampede. Cattle at night are the most nervous beasts that ever came out of the Garden of Eden, blindly racing to drown in the rivers, or lose themselves in the scrub. Only 'music hath charms' to make them forget their fears . . .

Ten miles a day, and a station a week, a running river of red and white, the herd drifts slowly down. A thousand cattle in one mob are a magnificent sight. Stages depend on the state of the track, the grass, the water, the weather. . . .

To his family a drover was a sailor at sea, who might never come home again. The northward journeys made the epic stories, the stocking up of the Territory and Kimberley from Western Queensland and New South Wales by such men as Nat Buchanan, Patrick and Michael Durack, and the MacDonalds of Fossil Downs – three thousand miles and three years on the trail through 'bad nigger country', across a route unknown. Those heroes followed the explorers. . . .

Cattle have always been the first step forward in the settlement of Australia. They open the country, eat down the rank grasses and pave the way for sheep. Closer settlement follows. So wheat lands and gardens are planted, and towns are built, with railways and roads and schools, and happy living.

Those words could all have been written equally well of South Africa and the frontier Boers, the cattlemen who always came into conflict with those other cattlemen advancing south – the Kaffirs. The aborigines of Australia were not cattlemen, but they became so, learning quickly and naturally to ride and handle

3a 'Old Arthur' recovering
in hospital

3b Noopi the Lamb

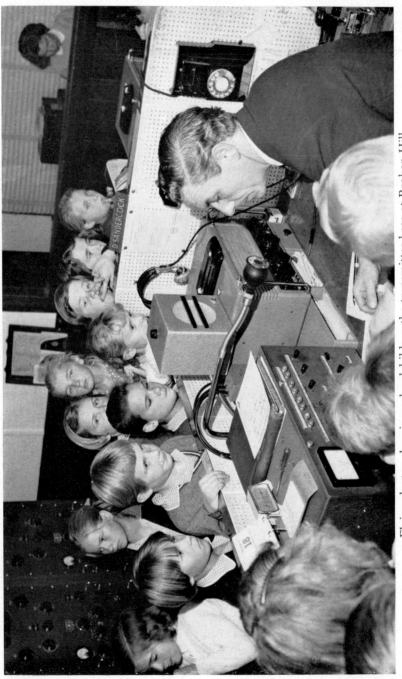

4 Flying doctor showing schoolchildren the transmitter base at Broken Hill

mobs. In the Northern Territory and the Kimberley they still have a place in the sun as ringers and station hands.

Ernestine Hill adds her 1964 postscript to the scenes she has described so well.

Since the coming of the aeroplane Australia has become an open book where he who runs across the sky ... will see cattle-freighters in the blue above, road-trains on the ant-roads far below, double-decker semi-trailers skimming the great plains and bounding the rivers and creeks where the drovers of old time waited weeks, months, sometimes years, for the floods to go down or for a fall of rain. They do not travel so far now – to the model meatworks in a dozen towns and depots that they will reach in not much more than the day, those fillet steaks and sirloin roasts to be presently snap-frozen in plastic wraps for the housewives' shopping baskets. But not all the drovers' routes are yet deserted. Quite a few are faithful to the trails, with stud cattle for delivery or inter-station trade. The long distance drovers are all gone, the 'great ones' with the big mobs that we used to meet ... on the stones of the Birdsville Track at night – still as statues, their eyes glowing like lamps and mesmerized at a ringer singing 'Till the Sands of the Desert Grow Cold'.

Lang bounced us across the bush to the lip of the deep Hamersley Gorge, a raw red erosion wound with a glade in its depths delicately clothed by trees and grasses. There were only the roughest trails in this country raying off from the various airstrips that served the two million acres of Hamersley and Mulga Downs. Here and there beacons punctuated the empty landscape.

'The signposts to the future,' said Lang. 'They indicate the course the iron ore railroad will follow on its journey several hundred miles to the deep water port that will be constructed to take the freighters waiting to carry millions of tons of Hamersley ore.'

His eyes gleamed as he spoke of the dream on the verge of coming true. He did not see what we did – the grey-green scrub dotted with weird red anthills standing fifteen or twenty feet high like fantastic totems carved by vanished aborigines to the vanishing kangaroos. He saw the shining rails, the camps and mining towns, a busy port on the Indian Ocean coast and the untold mineral wealth of Western Australia's frontier country being conveyed to different parts of the globe. His own land was the fount of his country's coming prosperity, the lure for new settlement and foreign capital. We looked at the same scene but to each of us it offered a different delight.

Elspeth and I were thrilled and enchanted to see our first kangaroos in their natural setting.

Like the giraffes of South African game sanctuaries, the free kangaroos are unforgettable, especially if they are in a hurry. Giraffes, cantering through the thorn-bush with their long necks swaying like masts at tree-top height, are unique; and so are the bounding 'roos with their seven-league boots, their heavy pot-hook tails and their little praying hands tucked close against their chests as they go hopping over the spinifex. Lang often stopped the car to let us watch them. They were usually in small family parties, and when we halted they frequently did the same, for they are inquisitive creatures. The big red males stood six foot high and could cover twenty-five to thirty feet in one hop, but the average leap at normal speed is more like ten feet. The does, smaller and bluish, are even swifter than the bucks, and the youngsters can hop almost as far and as fast as their parents. It was fascinating to watch them.

'They can travel easily at thirty miles per hour,' said Lang. 'I've paced them with the car. They have a strong maternal instinct. If the mother with a joey in her pouch is hunted she goes on till she's exhausted, then she throws out the joey and draws off the pursuers herself.'

He obviously hated the idea of these gentle harmless creatures being hunted, but they breed fast and they are greedy grazers and crop the sweet Mitchell grass to the detriment of the cattle and sheep, so from time to time it is essential to allow the ' 'roo shooters' to come in for a couple of days to thin them out. The shooters get a good price for pet-meat and hides.

There is a legend that once a female has bred, she can continue to do so without male assistance! This arises from the fact that the unborn infant spends most of its incubation period in the pouch, which is also the milk bar. When it is only an inch long the foetus crawls up into the pouch, there to continue its growth. If it fails to make the grade another takes its place and so on for a certain period. It is very funny to watch a baby 'roo leap into Mum's pouch when he's alarmed. He dives in head first, his awkward limbs sticking out stiffly in all directions like a badly packed parcel.

I shall never forget my delight in the kangaroos; nor will I forget a cloud of white cockatoos settling on a ghost-gum as if that lovely tree had suddenly blossomed into bridal flower.

As he flew us back to Wittenoom to connect up with our 'Fokker Friendship', Lang talked of the future when he reckoned Pilbara would supply at least 25 per cent of Japan's total iron ore. More perhaps.

'Japan – the most industrialized nation in Asia – depends on iron ore for her life,' he said. 'She has no mineral resources of her own, yet her steel industries are phenomenal.'

I have read since that:

One major Japanese yard last year launched 1,307,777 tons of shipping against Britain's total of around a million tons. The Japanese shipyard, Mitsubishi, expects to launch 1,928,968. That is why the Japs are importing as much iron ore as they can get from South Africa and other countries.

'Japan needs our ore,' Lang said, 'and we can use Japanese capital.'

That capital is on the way. Japan's mighty steel-works have recently signed a contract for 65 million tons of Hamersley ore – a contract worth £400 million. And the Australian branch of the Rio Tinto Zinc Corporation, in collaboration with America's Kaiser Steel, is preparing to spend £32 million on the initial development of the Hamersley iron ore project.

'But if you get Japanese capital won't you have to take Japanese labour?' I asked.

'No,' he said. 'In any case the Japs don't like leaving Japan.'

'What about Hawaii?' I asked. 'They liked that well enough.'

'We have to chance it,' he said. 'Our two great stabilizing forces are America and Japan. We need the goodwill of both. This is an Asian continent occupied by whites.'

I found that rather a chilling reflection. Too close to home! What of the African Continent?

I looked down upon the endless bush, ridged by the wide half-moon of mineral-bearing mountains, and saw it in the years to come when Western Australia's economy would shift its balance from beef and wool to base metals. The towns, camps and steel-mills of the future would people the empty plain with new blood, drawing it together with schools and hospitals, homes and gardens, with young communities eager to build a bright future north of the 26th parallel. I thought too of the heat, the flies, the floods and the pioneering days ahead before Langley Hancock's dream could become reality. They'd need to be brave, those new settlers.

CHAPTER EIGHT

Farewell Western Australia, Welcome Melbourne

The sparkling April days flew by and the trees along the river bank scattered golden leaves. In King's Park the waratahs still put out their stiff pink and yellow blooms but the silver-trees were tarnished as if the shining foliage required a touch of polish. I had once thought that such shrubs grew only on Table Mountain, but Australia's proteas are even more prolific and varied than ours. The yachting season was nearly over, and, in the roof of the house in Peppermint Grove, the possums were peaceful, entering their period of hibernation. The magpies, who are to Perth what the doves are to the Cape Peninsula – only more aggressive – had turned their young ones out of the nests and were preparing for storms to come. Children, riding their bicycles to school, steer clear of trees with 'maggies'' nests, or carry sticks to ward off the infuriated birds who swoop down and peck at their heads.

On a small lake not far from the O.B.H. the cygnets of two black swans were growing rapidly into adolescence, losing the pale downy feathers we had so much admired.

'Like mutation mink,' Elspeth had said, when first we saw the five babies swimming behind their majestic parents.

'Adorable!' I agreed. 'And isn't it extraordinary that black swans have crimpy plumage like an Ethiopian's hair!'

Their long red beaks and white eye-masks lent them a slightly barbaric witch-doctor look. That we saw them at all was thanks to one of Perth's best known naturalists, who, hearing that I was interested in wild life, had kindly telephoned to tell me where the swan family could be found.

On our last night in Perth Piet took us to the Trots at

Gloucester Park. It was dreamlike to me – unreal and spectacular – but exciting too, with a touch of Ben Hur and the ancient Roman chariot races when an overtaking horse and rumble became entangled with the one ahead, bringing down both horses and endangering those coming up behind them.

'That's my horse,' I groaned. 'The one struggling back on to his feet. And he was going so well!'

The night was full of stars, a young moon rose, frosty and cold, a gust of wind whisked my losing ticket into the air and sent it careening away.

Elspeth went to lay her bet and Piet sat beside me on a bench on the steep grassy bank between the Tote and the track. I had been scribbling in my little notebook and he took it from me.

'What do you write about this sort of thing?'

'Nothing really. Only a note or two.'

He glanced at it, half interested, half amused. 'The open sky and stars,' he read. 'The floodlit sand-track skirting the dark oval of turf. Cheap hurdy-gurdy music, lovers hand-in-hand, seedy folk of all sorts. The grass littered with unlucky tickets and cigarette ends. Glamour of the huntsman in his pink coat leading in the field – the fine horses with their elaborate harnesses to keep them from breaking into a canter. (A bit cruel, those straps?) Jockeys sitting in the low two-wheeled rumbles, stick in hand. How they see anything except the horse's rump is beyond me! Perhaps they don't. The thrill of the race! Huge fast strides, mechanical piston movement of strong slender legs trotting faster, faster, faster, gaining fantastic momentum. Manes and tails flying . . .'

He gave back the notebook and smiled at me. 'Yes, that's it.'

We strolled over to the paddock surrounded by open stalls where animals were being groomed. Up-ended rumbles stood against the wall, and out behind was the park from which the big horse-boxes were already beginning to move. We left before the last race, driving home along the lovely river pulsing with its tremulous reflections of light.

Next morning I watched the hardy sunrise surfers for the last time. Glen brought Willie to the beach soon after midday, and later, when his brothers were back from school, we went to the house in Peppermint Grove and had tea in the garden. Two months had slipped away in the blink of an eye. The boys were occupied with gliders now that boats were out of season, and Willie's 'cubby' had been demolished. Tony had shifted his guinea-pig hutches on to a different patch of lawn, leaving a bald square where the little animals had nibbled away all the grass. He informed us with pride that Martha, the trembling bride of a few weeks ago, was about to present Pickles with a new family. Glen's ducks were broody and a new puppy had appeared to keep Bluey company. The frangipani was nearly over, the roses were resting, and the Michaelmas daisies spread early sprays of autumn flowers.

Night fell and we left Willie sound asleep and his brothers doing their homework. Our plane did not leave till midnight, so Piet and Glen drove us to the Airport Grill where we could get a late meal with which we had a bottle of red Australian wine. The loudspeaker called the Melbourne flight and we gathered our belongings together.

'Be seeing you in Sydney,' said Piet.

I nodded, sad that the rest of the family would not be with him for the brief final forty-eight hours we had planned to spend together a fortnight hence.

'You take the window seat,' said Elspeth as we climbed the ladder into the crowded plane.

A few minutes later the lights of Perth and the Swan River fell away beneath us and out at sea Rottnest Island was a tiny jewel which winked and vanished. The little quokkas would be grazing now in the cool of midnight under the huge Moreton Bay figs. As we headed east I looked down upon the great empty waste of Western Australia, dark and anonymous, the infinitely lonely hinterland of the friendly city I had come to love.

The small hours were inky dark with flurries of rain and belts of mist, but we were able to land at Melbourne Airport on time, 4.30 a.m., the last plane to do so before fog closed in fifteen minutes later to put the airfield out of action.

We were met by Mr and Mrs Mervyn Pizzey, who seemed to think nothing of getting up at that shocking hour to welcome a pair of strangers to their beautiful but rain-swept city. I had known

Pam Pizzey's mother in London for many years and was delighted to make the acquaintance of her daughter – even at five on a dismal wet morning.

They drove us to the Windsor Hotel, where we were to spend the next two days, and arranged that I was to dine with them that night while Elspeth kept a long-standing date with her step-nephew and his girl friend. Mervyn and Pam, having thus disrupted their day, left us to bathe and breakfast at our leisure. A porter took our bags to our rooms and a chambermaid came to see that we had all we needed. The atmosphere of the Windsor was discreetly luxurious with pearl-grey bedrooms and deep pile carpets.

Elspeth had decided to •spend the morning resting and exploring while I was to meet Mr Cyril Denny, the General Manager of Cassell's Publishers in Australia, and tie up the loose ends of a plan to enable me to study the Royal Flying Doctor Service and School of the Air in the Outback. In fact, our correspondence on the subject had been considerable and, even before we settled down in the lounge, we felt that we knew each other quite well. Cassell's, at that time, took care of the distribution of Eyre and Spottiswoode's publications and it was to this fact that I owed my introduction to Cyril Denny whose help in so many ways added enormously to the interest and enjoyment of my Australian travels.

'Orm has mapped out an itinerary for you and Mrs Rhodes,' he said. 'We all hope you'll like it.'

Captain Orm Denny, Cyril's brother, a famous and intrepid war pilot, was now the Manager of the Royal Flying Doctor Service of New South Wales. There was nothing Orm did not know at first hand about difficult, dangerous and pioneering aviation. He had piloted all manner of aircraft in treacherous weather conditions over virtually unexplored territory and it was he who had flown the first regular service between the Mainland and the tropical islands of the Great Barrier Reef linking a primitive people with the civilization that was to substitute modern medicine and education for barbarous panaceas and superstitions. Captain Denny had his R.F.D.S. Headquarters in Sydney but he was in constant touch with Broken Hill, the inland part of the service.

I read the itinerary with excitement. We were to fly from Sydney to Broken Hill, where we were to meet Mr and Mrs W. Gall and spend a couple of nights. Mr Gall was that year's President of the New South Wales R.F.D.S. and also of the Graziers' Association. We were to stay the week-end with them at their sheep station, Langawirra, some seventy miles from Broken Hill, and then Elspeth would fly back to Sydney. I would remain to study the School of the Air and, I hoped, accompany the Flying Doctor on a mission or two.

'It's a wonderful programme,' I said. 'I can hardly wait!'

My enthusiasm pleased Cyril, but, in the meantime, he had made sure that we should enjoy the charms of Melbourne and its surroundings.

Melbourne, on Port Phillip Bay, is a dignified city, cultured and prosperous. It is superbly placed on the river Yarra, and it is only from the air that one realizes that it is also a busy port with an alluring coast for holiday-makers. When the mists dispersed we were able to appreciate the full glory of its broad tree-lined boulevards and parks and three hundred acres of Botanical Gardens. The umbrella-shaped elms were shedding their leaves, the fragile golden ash was at the height of its autumnal beauty, and the maples, glowing with the colours of the fall, stood in pools of ruby and amber as light showers of leaves were shaken free by the chilly winds of the dying season. Magnificent old houses bear witness to the golden days of Ballarat and Bendigo, when hostesses entertained in considerable splendour with trained servants to look after all domestic details. Today many of the old colonial houses are once more fashionable town houses or converted into professional chambers and these charming terraces retain a highly individual character with the original wrought-iron balconies and railings that were so much in vogue a century ago.

Pam Pizzey, who drove us round the city, was a knowledgeable and interesting guide. When she showed us the shopping areas she told us, with justifiable pride and no exaggeration, that Melbourne's couturiers were second to none – particularly, of course, in the use of woollen fabrics, most of which are feather-light and in very attractive colours and weaves.

Her own home was above the steep bank of the Yarra which flows through a lush subtropical gorge. From her husband, Mervyn, whose family have exported hides of all sorts for generations, we learned the many possibilities of kangaroo skins that are useful and strong though not quite fine enough for the manufacture of top luxury articles.

Next day my husband's old friend, General Sir Dallas Brooks, G.C.M.G., K.C.B., etc, sent a driver with his Jaguar to fetch us to his home at Frankston. After three terms and fourteen years as Governor of Victoria, Sir Dallas had retired in 1963. This distinguished and democratic ex-commandant General of the Royal Marines had many personal attributes that endeared him to Australians. He had served with the Anzac Forces in the Dardanelles in World War One, he loved and understood Australia and her people and he was a renowned sportsman. So it was little wonder that they took him and his charming wife to their hearts and welcomed their decision to settle among Frankston's green pastures on the fringe of a beautiful seaside golf course within easy reach of Melbourne, where their daughter and her family were already happily established.

Dallas Brooks had also served in South Africa for a time, and it was one of his enduring ambitions to see Australia and South Africa on friendly terms.

'These two great countries have everything in common,' he said, as we went for a stroll after lunch.

'Yes,' I agreed. 'More than Australia admits. A policy of white supremacy.'

His eyes twinkled shrewdly. 'But Australia has no colour bar.'

'So that puts her on the right foot,' I agreed.

He had been genuinely distressed at the South African Republic being forced out of the Commonwealth.

'Tactically – and sentimentally too, if that counts for anything –and for all practical purposes, South Africa should be part of the Commonwealth of Nations.'

'That club has changed its character,' I said. 'The new boys have as much to say as the seniors, and say it louder!'

The sandy path between high hedgerows emerged on to a tee which looked along a tempting fairway. Elspeth admired it with the keen pleasure of a natural golfer and Dallas handed her the Number Three iron he was using as a walking-stick. He watched with approval as she swung it.

'Nice shot!' he said.

'It always is when there's no ball.'

There and then, he insisted on making her a present of that Number Three, a souvenir which fascinated our fellow passengers in various aircraft all the way from Sydney to New York. An elegant lady carrying a single golf club, rather too long for her, presented quite an intriguing mystery.

That evening we dined with Mr and Mrs Cyril Denny. Jim Moad, the sales manager of Cassell's drove us out to their attractive home about twenty minutes from the city. The other member of the party was the Reverend Alf Donnelly, sometime Victorian Secretary of the Bush Church Aid Society which, among other benefits, has given Australia 'flying padres'.

After dinner this very human padre showed us coloured projections of the work done in the Outback by the Bush Church Aid Society. The Church of England in Australia approaches its unique task in an unusually enterprising manner. B.C.A.S. was founded in 1919 to bring spiritual, medical and educational help to isolated outposts. It has established hostels in the larger towns where bush girls and boys can live economically under Christian guidance while attending their nearest State schools. The medical and educational services, developed over the past half century, follow similar lines to those of the Royal Flying Doctor Service and co-operate with it. The first B.C.A.S. hospital was built at Ceduna in the grim hot solitude of the Nullarbor Plain five hundred miles west of Adelaide, and in 1938 the B.C.A.S. inaugurated its own Flying Medical Service with the purchase of a de Havilland Fox Moth. Today it has several Missions, three aircraft that travel about 50,000 miles each year, two doctors, twenty qualified sisters, a dentist, a pharmacist and three pilots! In 1953 the B.C.A.S. built its own short-wave radio Communication Station at Ceduna, its Far West Mission of South Australia, and provided special cheap transceivers for hospitals and homesteads and portable transceivers for the transport used by bush clergy. It also has a Small Boat radio station and special transceiver sets for the fishermen operating in the Great Australian Bight.

To accomplish all this a Church must be well endowed, and if it is to be well endowed it must be loved and trusted. It must prove its genuine usefulness and inspire generosity in the congregations of both the great cities and the thinly populated Inland. When I saw the padre's vividly pictured records of dedication and achievement I was not surprised that this human earthy approach to the problems of the bush people had elicited such a generous response.

Australia's growth and development in recent years makes such services more than ever necessary. There are new water and soil conservation and hydroelectric schemes, the rocket bases of the Nullarbor, extended railroads and miners' camps and the great engineering and agricultural projects that will make use of Australia's rivers instead of allowing them to run dry or turn vast productive areas into seasonal swamps.

Next day we flew to Sydney where we were met by Cyril's brother, Captain Orm Denny, and Herbert Longmuir, the Sydney Manager of Cassell's.

The awe-inspiring magnificence of Sydney's coastline took Elspeth and me unawares. But we would have to wait till later to explore this great sprawling hustling city in its wonderful surroundings.

Within twenty-four hours we were on our way to Broken Hill.

CHAPTER NINE

Charles Rasp and 'Flynn of the Inland'

We boarded the Sydney-to-Broken Hill 'Fokker Friendship' on a sunny April morning, the eve of Anzac Day, when veterans of two world wars and their families travel back to their home towns if it is at all possible. So every seat was taken as we left Mascot and the wide Pacific Ocean behind, and crossed the barrier range of the forested Blue Mountains towards the dusty red plain of the interior.

Broken Hill, seven hundred miles from Sydney and three hundred from Adelaide, is an important mining city which spreads its powerful industrial influence over the three States of New South Wales, Queensland and South Australia. It is also the base of the NSW Royal Flying Doctor Services and School of the Air.

The city was born in the year 1883 when the gold rush of Ballarat and Bendigo was a thing of the past. The inland then was still virtually unknown, except as the graveyard of explorers, but graziers, pressing north from Adelaide in search of pasturage, had discovered that merino sheep could do well on the sparse blue and salt bush that survived the droughts, and prospectors had a strong suspicion that the cruel desert might conceal mineral wealth. That these optimistic fortune-hunters were right was proved by a German-born immigrant called Charles Rasp.

Rasp was employed as a boundary rider on the fourteen hundred square mile sheep station of Mount Gipps belonging to George McCulloch, and one night he chanced to pitch his solitary camp at the base of a queer-shaped hill about twenty miles from the homestead. Like most men of that place and period, he had an eye to the chance of finding some of nature's buried treasure. The broken hill beckoned him. At daybreak he rode out to investigate its possibilities and collect a few samples. He dared hardly credit his good luck. If the 'Prospector's Guide', which he carried with him was right, he had hit upon a rich vein of tin! He staked out a claim, registered it, and galloped back to tell George McCulloch.

'We must stake out the whole bloody hill!' said McCulloch. 'There could be a fortune in it.'

So Rasp and his boss and two dam-sinkers staked out extensive claims, took out miner's licences and impatiently awaited the geologist's report on their samples. It was silver lead, not tin, which was the treasure of the hill. Within a few years the line of lode of Broken Hill was yielding one third of the world's silver and a rich proportion of lead. Zinc followed, and, in less than a decade, 26,000 people were living and working in an area where there had previously been ten! There is a permanency about the 33,000 population of Broken Hill which is unusual in a mining city. The miners work under good conditions and many of them own their homes; the companies are generous and take pride in improving and beautifying the surroundings, and the cultural influence of the eastern coast cities is reflected in the Silver City of the interior.

When Elspeth and I were being met by anyone as yet unknown to us we always left the plane last. We let the other passengers go ahead to their meetings and greetings and then we stepped down into the early afternoon sunshine and keen bright air reminiscent of the Karoo or the highveld.

'Lady Packer and Mrs Rhodes? Welcome to Broken Hill!'

Mrs William Gall was small and slight and her smiling face had a quick birdlike quality. We were travelling light and it didn't take long to stow our bags in her baby Volkswagen.

'We weren't sure what to bring,' I said. 'We thought it would be hot.'

'It can be. It can top the century for days on end, but our autumns are chilly.'

The wind blew cold, puffing up whorls of red dust as she drove down the long avenue towards the Hills surmounted by the skeleton of the rig.

'This is our area of regeneration.'

She pointed out gardens shaded by gums, tamarisks, oleanders, peppers and acacias. New vineyards and citrus groves flanked the Hill, and twin lakes gleamed between the trees. 'In the old days there were plenty of trees round about, but they were all cut down by the early miners to be used as fuel and nobody bothered to replant. As you can see, the desert sand encroached on the houses, and, given a bit longer, it would have buried them.'

On the outskirts of the city a huge WELCOME sign spanned the avenue.

'It's been up nearly ten years,' Mrs Gall said. 'It was put up for the Queen. It was after her visit in 1954 that the Flying Doctor Service was entitled to call itself Royal.'

She parked neatly in the wide street outside the Royal Exchange Hotel.

'Here we are, and the place is packed for tomorrow's Dawn Service.'

On Anzac Day every town and city in Australia, great or small, stages a dawn march to its War Memorial to honour the heroic dead of Gallipoli and the warriors of both wars. After the religious ceremony at the Memorial the day becomes a holiday with horse-racing and parties. The eve of Anzac Day is recognized as an Old Comrades' reunion, a men's get-together, and the wives make their own arrangements. So Mrs Gall swept us off to a Manne-quin Parade, staged for charity, and attended by some four hundred enthusiastic women. The models, rather more substantially built than their English counterparts, showed woollen numbers designed by leading fashion houses, and we admired all manner of garments from top-coats and ski-suits to feather-light evening gowns.

'Ski-suits?' I said. 'Switzerland's a long way off!'

Beth Gall laughed. 'But the Snowy Mountains are on our door-step.'

After the performance we were introduced to Dr A. G. Walker and his wife. Dr Walker was one of the few men present, for the Royal Flying Doctor Service was to get a share of the proceeds, and this strong-featured Glasgow-born New Australian with the deep reassuring voice happened to be the Flying Doctor himself, a general practitioner with a practice spread over half a million square miles – five times the size of the United Kingdom.

George Walker had done his war service in the Royal Air Force as radio operator, air gunner and flying control officer. He had come up smiling after nine crashes, had married a pretty WAAF, taken his medical degrees at Bristol University and had practised in Bristol before settling in New South Wales in a partnership in the industrial town of Wollongong on the Pacific. His daughter was studying music and art at Sydney University when I met him, and his son was in Canberra. Some years earlier Dr and Mrs Walker had visited Broken Hill and, when they had heard that the Flying Doctor was about to retire, George had applied for the post. His experience made him an obvious choice. Now, however, the Walkers had decided to make their final home in Adelaide where George had bought a house and intended putting up his plate. Although they looked forward to the future, both were extremely sad at leaving Broken Hill and the bush people who had become friends as well as patients. They were in the midst of a whirl of farewells and I can hardly imagine a more inconvenient time for them to be asked to occupy themselves with a visitor wishing to learn and write about the R.F.D.S., but neither of them ever allowed me to feel that I was being a nuisance. Both Dr and Mrs Walker were extremely kind and helpful and entertained me in their pleasant official house on several occasions. George's hobby was the growing of rare orchids and he was disappointed at being unable to take his hundreds of plants with him to Adelaide, but the agricultural regulations of South Australia prohibit the import of plants from another State.

'I'll just have to start again,' he said. New starts were a challenge, even orchid growing.

The various States operate the R.F.D.S. slightly differently – according to their own needs – but Broken Hill, the biggest base, has its Flying Doctor on call twenty-four hours a day. Any Outback homestead in trouble can alert the Radio Control Station and arouse the Chief Radio Operator who sleeps on the premises and immediately goes on the air and connects the patient with the doctor's home. His regular morning and afternoon sessions can, if necessary, be conducted from the plane if he is on the way to a case or a clinic. In one typical year (1962) Broken Hill's Flying Doctor made 373 flights, flew 84,415 miles, transported 120 patients to hospital, saw 1,501 patients at field clinics, gave 850 inoculations, and 3,284 consultations by radio.

This remarkable Service owes its existence to the compassion, imagination and devotion of one man whose name is a legend in his own country, 'Flynn of the Inland'. John Flynn, an Australian of Irish and Scottish descent, was born in 1880 in a remote mining town in Victoria where his mother died in giving him birth. When he grew up he became a teacher, a Presbyterian missionary, a journalist and a pioneer. In 1912 he was appointed Superintendent of the Australian Inland Mission. He explored huge tracts of the north-west and the centre on camel-back, and in the course of his patrols for the Inland Mission he saw and wrote about the sufferings and anxieties of those in isolation. A homestead was often over fifty miles from its nearest neighbour and four or five hundred from even the most primitive outpost, let alone a hospital. The wives of bushmen lived in loneliness and fear – fear of accident and illness, fear of bearing babies alone and far from help, fear of seeing their children grow up without education, and fear of the pervasive silence and inertia bred by the unbroken solitude of the bush.

The centre has been called 'the Dead Heart', 'the Dumb Inland' and 'the Great Australian Loneliness'. Flynn knew well the conditions that account for such sinister names. He knew the difficulties of communication and transport over desert that could become a sand-bog in the dry or a swamp in the wet. He saw the graves of little children who could have been saved if there had been some means of getting advice and heard the tragic tales of injured people dying before they could reach medical aid. He understood why women were unable to face the hardship of life in the Outback, and the inevitable disruption of families and the drift back to the towns. Out of his knowledge of these tribulations a dream was born.

Flynn believed that if three vital necessities could be provided the terror of isolation could be overcome. A two-way radio

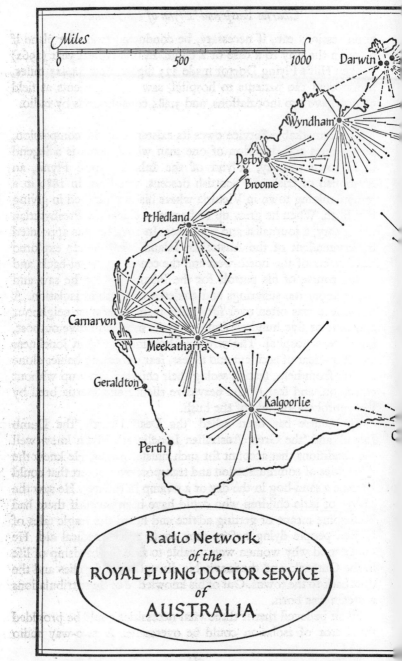

Miles
0   500   1000   Darwin

Wyndham

Derby

Broome

Pt Hedland

Carnarvon

Meekatharra

Geraldton

Kalgoorlie

Perth

Radio Network
of the
ROYAL FLYING DOCTOR SERVICE
of
AUSTRALIA

Thursday I.

Cairns

Townsville

Cloncurry

Charters
Towers

Alice
Springs

Rockhampton

Innamincka

Charleville

Brisbane

Langawirra

tAugusta

Broken
Hill

Menindee

coln

Adelaide

SYDNEY

Melbourne

 Furneaux Group

Hobart

service that would allow station people to consult a doctor in an emergency, air transport to convey a patient to hospital, and a doctor always available to answer the appeal of those in distress. At that time air transport and wireless were still in their infancy and only the boldest and most tenacious visionary could have contemplated using either to bring a degree of safety to the scattered people of the Outback. Flynn was such a man. His unswerving purpose surmounted every obstacle in turn, but it took years of battling to enlist support and translate the dream from theory to reality.

With public meetings, Church talks, articles and publicity the Australian Inland Mission began to interest the nation in an aerial medical service for the Outback.

Among Flynn's earliest and most ardent supporters was Clifford Peel, a medical student in Melbourne, whose greatest desire was to be one of Flynn's Flying Doctors. His ambition was never attained, for World War One broke out, he became a pilot and was killed in action. But before his death he wrote a letter which was published in 'The Inlander' of October 1918 and which went deeply into the technical factors that would enable such a service to operate over the immense distances of the bush. Doctors and pilots who had served in the war threw themselves into the scheme, and Flynn obtained the help of a wireless expert, Alf Traeger, who evolved the pedal-generated transceiver that was so soon to become a feature of Outback homes. The bush people welcomed it and learned the Morse code, but it was far from being the real answer to their problem of communication. It was, however, the forerunner of Traeger's present-day battery sets that have revolutionized life in the wilderness.

In 1928 one of Flynn's young supporters, Dr George Simpson, was sent 4,500 miles by the A.I.M. to see if a medical base could be established at Cloncurry, a hot dusty little town in West Queensland. While he was there a message came through that a miner, two hundred miles away in Mount Isa, was seriously injured with a broken pelvis. The local plane chanced to be in Cloncurry, Dr Simpson boarded it and fetched the injured man to hospital. It was the first mercy flight of the new service and Cloncurry became the first base.

The day after our arrival in Broken Hill Dr Walker took us to the R.F.D.S. Base and introduced us to Mr F. M. Basden, the Chief Radio Operator and his assistant Mr D. Sandercock. The Base building, which incorporates Mr Basden's house, was built as a memorial to the pioneer women of New South Wales.

The Broken Hill Base is more elaborate than Charlie Prideaux's on the hill above Kalgoorlie, but the spirit is the same. The operators, the doctor, the two pilots, Victor Cover and Jack Jenkins, and the callers are all friends. The bush folk can rely on the Base and are confident that no S.O.S. will go unheeded. The pupils of the School of the Air too know everybody, from their invisible classmates and teachers to the operators who connect them.

As I stood in front of the powerful transmitter I thought of John Flynn and Alf Traeger, and of the faith and spirit of those others who had made all this possible – the will to serve, to help, to befriend and never to forget or abandon those who live in the Great Australian Loneliness.

CHAPTER TEN

Langawirra

At noon on Anzac Day we left Broken Hill to her 'get-togethers' and set off for Langawirra. We had copies of the papers, *The Barrier Daily Truth* and *The Barrier Miner*, and I was touched to see that all advertising that day was in the form of a 'memorial box'. Each advertiser had some sort of 'Lest We Forget' theme and no other slogan marred its simple dignity. We also carried bags of supplies and one of Dr Walker's rare orchid plants, a present to Mrs Gall.

Our host's Cessna was parked in the hangar between that of the R.F.D.S. and the Silver City Air Taxi Service. Bill Gall loaded it with the accomplished speed of long habit and we helped push it on to the tarmac runway, marvelling at its lightness. There were other single-engined aircraft in the hangar too, and it all reminded me of the workshed in Peppermint Grove with model planes left lying about rather untidily.

'Don't you get a big kick out of owning an aeroplane?' I asked Beth Gall, but she laughed.

'We did once. Not any more. It's a workhorse, you see. Bill used to fly our boys over to school at the Hill every Monday and back home for the week-ends. They stayed with friends during the school week. I think they'd have preferred to travel in a wheelbarrow at one time!'

Bill Gall had piloted his own plane for over twenty years. His sons, young Bill and John, now aged twenty and eighteen, had said good-bye to their schooldays and were sharing the responsible work of the sheep station with their father. They too had their pilots' licences, and the Cessna was no novelty to them. It was an essential part of station transport.

Elspeth – her misgivings mastered – got into the back of the little four-seater plane with Beth, and I sat with Bill. He was a tall sun-tanned man with a quiet manner and an air of natural authority. His eyes, behind his glasses and in the shadow of his broad-brimmed felt hat, were quick to laughter. He flew us over the Hill to show us the line of lode and then we were over the bush with the Barrier Range jacaranda-blue on the horizon. In the distance were the Menindee Lakes, seventy miles from the Hill, and its favourite playground. But Langawirra had its own two lakes, blue-green in the sun, heavily fringed with trees, and beautifully placed on either side of the homestead. As we came down over them, I said, 'What are those birds on the water?'

'Black swans,' said Bill. 'About a thousand of them.'

So Langawirra, like Perth, had its swans and its blue waters. It had emus too. A flock of them made off into the bush as we banked and landed, running with long swift strides. They lack the glamorous plumage of the ostrich but they have the same ridiculous wiggle and surprising speed when they run. Their faces are streaked with blue and their flat round amber eyes look as if they'd been sewn on to their heads and might easily drop off.

Mr Campbell, the station-hand, was waiting for us with the jeep and, while Bill and he transferred our bags and the household supplies, Beth led us up the slope towards the house. We heard her call 'Noopi, Noopi!' and suddenly a white woolly shape came tearing down to meet us and the air was filled with delighted and reproachful *baaas*. Noopi, the lamb, was on his way, and his raptures were those of a dog welcoming an adored mistress home. Beth laughed as she fondled him.

'He's really John's pet, but very often I feed him – as you can guess from the way he goes on!'

She opened the garden gate on to the lawn (which Noopi helped to keep down) and we stepped into a small oasis. Frangipani and citrus flowers scented air vibrant with the little voices of wild birds and the louder shrilling of the tame parrots and cockatoos in the big aviary that took up one side of the boy's verandah. Young Bill and John had their own bungalow at right angles to the main house. It was curtained with bougainvillaea and golden shower.

Langawirra is run as a 'family partnership', and the only out-side help on that station of 80,000 acres, running some 8,000 sheep, was the station-hand. The house was Beth's job.

The house was over a hundred years old and wings had been added. It had the unusual and attractive features of being faced with log-woodwork and of possessing two front doors at either end of the long verandah. You could take your pick and enter the lounge on the right or the bedroom wing on the left. The big dining-room, kitchen and fly-netted sun-porch were at the back.

There was a bowl of dark red clove-scented carnations in my bedroom.

'From the garden,' said Beth. 'I know carnations mean a lot to you.'

That was how she told me that she had read my books and that I was not a stranger to her. No welcome could have touched me more.

Within minutes of showing us round, she had changed into a washing frock and was busy peeling vegetables for a stew. Cooking for her menfolk meant producing three full meals a day. Breakfast always consisted of cereal, eggs, bacon, chops or steak, coffee, toast and marmalade.

'Then it's not important if they don't do so well for lunch,' said Beth. 'Like John now.'

John had left early that morning to muster sheep and was still away. She turned to her eldest son, Young Bill, who had just appeared and been introduced to us.

'Did your brother take sandwiches with him?'

His teeth flashed and his brown eyes laughed at her, very warm in his sun-tanned face.

'You were away.'

She shook her head with a smile and fetched a loaf while Young Bill began whisking powdered milk for Noopi. He poured the mixture into a quart bottle with a teat on the end and the lamb *baaed* impatiently in the yard outside the fly-wired door.

'Want to feed him?' he asked Elspeth.

'Love to.'

Noopi was a frantically greedy suckling. He practically jerked the teat off the bottle and the bottle out of Elspeth's hand, his little tail wagging feverishly as he gulped his milk. A number of cats lay in the sun outside Mr Campbell's house across the yard. He loved cats.

That afternoon our host took us for a drive. We went in the little Volkswagen, Young Bill in front with his father, to hop out and open gates, and Beth sandwiched between Elspeth and me in the back. At the drafting-yards and woolsheds, a few miles from the homestead, we came up with John in the Land Rover. He and Boots, the black Kelpie, had been mustering and the main yard was already packed with bleating unshorn sheep. Boots was overjoyed to see Young Bill, his master, and John was equally delighted to see his mother, who did not disappoint him.

'You'll find your smoko in the car,' she said.

While the young man tucked into his massive sandwiches, we joined his father and brother who were inspecting the sheep. Beth explained the maze of yards and the three-way gate by means of which the mob could easily be separated into different drafts.

'It's fun to watch,' she said. 'They'll be mustering and drafting tomorrow – separating the ewes and the weaners.'

'On the week-end?'

'Ah, well, next week we'll all be at the Hill for the West Darling. The work has to be done.'

The West Darling Picnic Race Meeting is the family event of the year, one of the highlights of a gay week, which includes the Squatters' Ball, the Flying Doctor Ball, and various other social occasions. The Outback goes to town in a big way, the hotels are crammed, the schools break up, and, when it's all over, the parents take their children home and settle down once more in the loneliness of the bush – haunting, harsh, steeped in the monotony of red earth and pastel scrub that can take so strong a hold on those attuned to its immeasurable vibrations.

It is only when the sheep are on the move or ringing around that they bleat. Once in the pen they settle down, and, after a while, the muffled chuffing of cloven hooves in the thick red dust fades, and a stillness falls upon the scene, a sunset vacuum presently filled by a deep soft sigh stirring the leaves and grasses. It comes from far away, that long sigh, breathing the dry pure air of distant deserts and the chill of an autumn evening.

We left the brothers with the dog and the Land Rover, and Bill drove us home by a considerable detour. He knew every bird and its habits and where it could be found. A flock of blue-bonnets winged out of a fragile, speckly-barked leopard-tree, and Bill showed us an eagle-hawk's huge untidy nest of straw and twigs in a dead nelia; a kestrel-hawk with a wonderful wingspan and a wedge-tail planed and banked above us, seeking his prey. Top-knot pigeons and 'the Twelve Apostles' settled in a mulga tree, and pink-breasted galahs left the branches of a gum with a chorus of shrill cries while a party of drongoes splashed merrily in a clay-pan with loud crackling whistles.

Langawirra land stretched as far as the eye could see – eastward to the purple flat-topped range and west to the herring-bone sky, stained red and gold by the approach of sunset. Kangaroos hopped away to the rim of the world, or sat up to watch us. But they were wary, for the 'roo-shooters had been here and we came, at intervals, on pathetic evidence of their recent presence – a fantastically long foot, or a tiny curled hand with five fingers and no thumb, a skull, some bleached bones and shreds of hide, dried hard and stiff by the sun.

'They skin them on the spot,' Bill said. 'From time to time this is necessary. 'Roos multiply like rabbits.' He looked sorry. Kangaroo shooting is not a sport but a necessity in grazing country.

We came, at sunset, to the lake nearest the homestead, and Elspeth asked Bill to stop.

'There's enough light for a picture. I want to get those swans.'

The swans, though indifferent to a plane or a car, were disturbed at the approach of a human being. As Elspeth walked cautiously to the bank, a few rose with high cries of alarm.

'They need a long runway,' said Bill.

More and more of the swans sped clumsily along the surface of the lake until at last they were airborne with a mighty drumming of powerful pinions lined with dazzling white. The other waterfowl followed them into the air and the beat of hundreds of

wings over the water filled the profound solitude between earth
and sky.

My bedroom formed an angle with the back porch and com-
manded a sunny intimate view of the yard, which was more like
a patio. I was wakened at six next morning by a bird with a sharp
staccato whistle. Although it was only just daybreak, he was very
wide awake. No sleepy chirps from him! A few others joined in
and I lay and watched the golden light brighten outside my
window.

At half past six I could hear Beth moving about in the kitchen.
The cats heard her too, and seven of them sat outside the back
door with their pretty faces glued to the fly-wire. Noopi, still
confined in his pen, lifted up his voice with loud protesting *maaas*
and *baaas*.

At six-forty-five Beth, in her long red woollen wrap, stepped
into the yard and filled a large shallow bowl with milk, and, in
seconds, the cats were crouched all round it, lapping happily.
A few minutes later Mr Campbell let Noopi out of the pen and
strolled across to the kitchen to fetch his morning tea. Noopi
made short work of his bottle, and the birds in the aviary were
given fresh water. Elspeth, who cannot exist without her morning
'cuppa', drifted into the kitchen and I knew that she would bring
me one too, for she is nothing if not kind. I could smell bacon
cooking. The day had begun.

Family breakfast was at eight, and one of the boys turned on
the transceiver in the corner of the dining-room.

'The doctor session,' he said.

I knew what happened at the Base. This was the homestead
side of the picture. At the Base Mr Basden would hear the signals
from the various stations on the network and he would call them
in, each in turn, and make a list for Dr Walker, who would take
his consultations over the air exactly as if his patients were being
shown in by a receptionist. Mr Basden was the radio 'receptionist', connecting him in his own study.

To own a Traeger transceiver set (developed by Alf Traeger
from that early pedal-wireless) and a medical chest you must become a subscriber on the network and promise that you will

respect the privacy of all you hear. You are given a call-sign and it is listed as in a telephone directory. Glancing through the Call Sign Directory intrigued me. Our own call-sign from W. C. Gall, Langawirra Station was 8 AR. And we were only one of many hundreds of outposts, including fascinating stations such as Wompah, Supr. Wild Dog Board; Wanaaring Bush Nursing Assn., and Tibooburra Police Post or Hospital. The information section announces that 'Tibooburra Hospital is available for Medical advice *every* night at 7.45 p.m. on 73 metres; also on Saturdays and Holidays at 3.30 p.m. and Sundays at 11.30 a.m. and 3.30 p.m. (All stations are requested to KEEP THE AIR CLEAR at these times for 15 minutes.)'

This informative Directory also illustrates the signals for use in SEARCH AND RESCUE, a code that can be carried by every vehicle or aircraft with a portable set in it. And it contains a 'Medical Miscellany' of useful hints. Here are a few.

1. KEROSENE OR PETROL INGESTION. The best way to prevent young children from drinking kerosene is to keep it in well-stoppered containers out of reach of little hands. It is a common trap to leave colourless kerosene in lemonade bottles – an open invitation for the children to have what they think will be a party.

If kerosene is ingested, then, contrary to what you think ought to be done, DON'T INDUCE VOMITING . . . Complications of kerosene ingestion are caused by fumes getting into the lungs; if the child vomits he increases the chances of fumes getting into his lungs by two – once on the way down, once on the way up. Give the child milk to drink, inform the doctor, when penicillin will usually be given as a precautionary measure.

2. OTHER CASES OF POISONING IN CHILDREN. This will usually involve various types of tablets (Aspirin, Phenobarb etc.) . . . The first thing is to induce vomiting. It is necessary 'to be cruel to be kind'. This may mean putting a couple of fingers right down his throat or giving him a couple of table-spoons of salt in warm water to drink. He will probably object vigorously to these procedures but gentler methods almost invariably fail.

There are a good many more of these practical 'Mrs Beeton' home nursing hints, and there are notes by the Chief Pilot to the owners of homesteads about the length and maintenance of landing strips.

The School of the Air schedule, which supplements the Correspondence School, is Mondays to Fridays 10 a.m. to 11 a.m. and 2 p.m. to 3.30 p.m., and a note explains that 'these times may be interrupted for Medical emergencies'.

As we listened to Consultation Hour I was struck by the confident and intelligent way in which the patient – or the person speaking for him – came on the air describing the symptoms and general condition of the sick person clearly and without frills. Dr Walker's replies were equally concise. The judgment required to sift the serious case from the simple one comes with experience, but I realized very soon that the bush people are made of stern stuff, neither timorous nor over-imaginative. For instance one man complained of pains across his chest that must have been alarming, and yet there was no hint of panic in his voice. After exhaustive questioning the Doctor said, 'It's definitely not your heart, so be easy on that score, Mr A. The stomach comes right up into the area you describe and those pains could be caused by indigestion or flatulence.' He then prescribed the suitable remedy.

Mrs B. came on to the air, worried about a stockman's hand.

'His hand is swollen – sore right up his arm.'

'Is it discoloured, Mrs B?'

'He's very sunburnt, and his hands are workworn. It's hard to say.'

'What movement has he got? Can he make a fist of it. Has he ever had this before?'

'He's just down at the garage, and the kiddies'll get him. You call me back, Doctor, and I'll have the answers.'

Other consultations intervened, and then Dr Walker called Mrs B. again.

'It looks very shiny, Doctor. No feeling in it. He's never had this before.'

'Well done, Mrs B. Did he lie on it last night?'

'He says not.'

'It's most likely a local oedema. Put it in a sling and tie it so that it slopes *up* towards the shoulder. That'll drain away that fluid. Rest it today. But if pain develops or you feel worried get me on the afternoon session. Cheerio for now, Mrs B.'

One housewife came in from a cattle station about a jackaroo with an acute pain in his back. She was less exact than most of the callers and the Doctor said firmly, 'Now go back, Mrs C, and ask Jim if that pain is worse when he moves about. Make him show you with one finger where it is worst. *With one finger.*'

Young Bill's brown eyes sparkled as we all waited for the answer.

'Doctor's a bit needly this morning,' he said.

When the patient was a young girl of seventeen, the boys opened their eyes wide. There is no privacy. Every symptom, like every telegram, is known to anyone on the network who happens to be listening in. Only once you are in hospital and off the air are you able to keep the course of your malady to yourself.

'It's worse than village gossip,' I said.

But Beth, as usual, put her finger on the spot.

'A village gossip wouldn't stand much chance here. There's nothing she could add or suggest. The facts are in the open and we can all make our own guesses!'

The Sister at Tibooburra Hospital came in to report on a child with tonsillitis.

'Her face was puffy last night, Doctor. Could that be incidental?'

'How is it this morning?'

'A bit better. But Jane usually has such a thin little face, so you notice it.'

'It could be part of the tonsillitis – especially as its dying down. But I know what you have in mind, Sister. So have I. Watch it.'

It was strange, I thought, this world of voices. Every intonation became significant. Already I could tell the difference between someone speaking for a friend or a station-hand and someone calling about a close relation. In the latter case the personal anxiety came through, sharpening the tone, and I realized why a voice on the telephone is so expressive of its owner's mood and health. There's no mask on it, no make-up. It was interesting too that the Doctor never gave an instruction without telling the patient just why it was being given. Doctors without wings are too apt to tell their patients to take this or that without any explanation. The bush people, who have to treat their sick or injured hundreds of miles from the source of advice, like to know the reasons for the treatment.

Soon the men left to attend to the mustering and Elspeth and I gave Beth a hand with the washing up. We could hear the voices still coming from the transceiver in the dining-room – voices of children singing their School Song, and later two women talking to each other across deafening interference when the network was given over to a 'galah session'. They didn't talk about clothes and the cook who gave notice, but of how much rain had fallen on their respective stations some four hundred miles apart, and one of them had a brand new recipe for disguising yesterday's mutton. I'm sure a great many listeners must have been all agog to share that! As city women have music while they work, so the women of the Outback have voices to keep them in touch with the world and their distant neighbours. It was a sort of battlesong, the hymn against the common foe. Isolation.

Elspeth was still intent upon getting a picture of the swans whose curved necks and flat heads made notes of music on the surface of the lake. 'Hundreds of crotchets,' I said, as we wandered down to the water's edge.

'Or periscopes. I wish I had a telescopic lens.'

In the afternoon we watched the mustering which was all done mechanically, with John in the Jeep, Young Bill in the Land Rover and the rest of us in the Volkswagen, collecting the sheep from far paddocks, heading them off this way or that and shepherding them many miles to the drafting yards. The little Volkswagen swerved and turned in the bush as nimbly as a horse. Transport is treated rough in the Outback and traded in after a couple of years.

'Sheep are the most gregarious creatures on earth,' said Bill. 'All you have to do is get one mob moving the way you want it, and the others can't wait to join it.'

Boots, the dog, really came into his own when it was necessary to drive them into the yards, and the speed with which Bill operated the three-way gate to separate them was miraculous. The air was full of dust and *baaing* as they finally clattered up the

ramp and over the grills into the shearing shed, ready for crutch-
ing and wigging next day, a heads and tails 'trimming' operation
performed by the boys with the electric shears. 'To prevent them
being wool-blinded and to give the blow-fly less chance of breeding,' explained Bill.

The last mob was still to come. It was dusk and a huge full
moon was rising beyond the fringe of trees when Elspeth said
suddenly, 'There they are!'

Young Bill, in the Land Rover, was with them. It was a strange
ghostly effect. The darkening bush, the low mulga trees, the quiet
of approaching night, and then what looked like a white ground-
mist rising from the scrub. It came on in a wave, with much
maaing and *baaing* and a soft thuddy pattering as the woolly beasts
materialized out of the gloom. John who had been in the pen,
sprang over the fence and ran along one side of the mob, his dog
on the other, to head it through the open gate. Here and there
sheep jumped like fish leaping in a stream.

At last they were all safely penned and we drove home, carefully, because of the kangaroos who are dazzled by lights. The
night was cold and the air smelt wonderfully dry and clean. We
went into the garden after dinner and stood on the lawn under
the high full moon.

'Listen!' said Bill. 'The swans are trumpeting!'

We were silent and spellbound as the sweet mournful music
came to our ears. Not trumpeting, but a fairy bugling that rose
from the lonely silver lake in an infinitely sad lament.

CHAPTER ELEVEN

The World of Voices

We returned to Broken Hill next day and Elspeth flew back to Sydney on the afternoon 'Fokker Friendship'. I dined with Dr and Mrs Walker that night and George set up his projector and showed some films he had taken in the course of his duties. I was particularly interested by one of Lake Eyre and Donald Campbell's organization for the Bluebird trials. An elaborate camp and a host of vehicles brought the huge salt-covered lake in the 'Dead Heart' to active life. Bluebird herself looked cruel and dangerous.

'In prehistoric times Lake Eyre was an inland sea,' said George, 'then, millenniums ago, it was swampy and forested, inhabited by even stranger things than Bluebird! Giant kangaroos more than ten feet high, emus equally tall, enormous koalas, cave-lions and Tasmanian tigers.'

'Are they really stranger?' I said. 'Our robots today are very frightening.'

About ten thousand years ago, however, the climate began to change, and Lake Eyre, from being well-watered, entered a period of aridity and the great beasts died off. The biggest of the prehistoric marsupials was a diprotodon, a huge slow wombat about twelve feet long. Some years ago a party from the South Australian Museum discovered the remains of hundreds of these diprotodons buried in the mud of the south-east corner of the lake. The poor things had evidently gone there to seek the last water, and had died of thirst.

A lovely shot flashed on his screen of the lake shore after rain, bright with yellow daisies and patches of scarlet and purple bush.

'In the past decade there's been another climate change,' said George, 'and there are hopes that Lake Eyre may once again be watered by rivers like the Cooper, as it used to be. If that happens it'll put paid to its history as a speed track.'

There were pictures too of his clinics for the aborigines, and of his wife helping him to immunize children against diphtheria.

'I don't take a glamorous nurse wherever I go, as flying doctor fiction always suggests, but Bill here has nursing training and she helps me when it's inoculation day at one of the clinics.'

'Bill' Walker, who could achieve glamour when she liked, laughed and sighed. She was torn between the prospect of a settled life in Adelaide and her affection for the people of the Outback.

The next day was a 'schoolday' for me. Mrs K. Hogan, one of the officers of the Parents' and Citizens' Association, took me to the School of the Air, where we were met by the Principal, Mrs Phyllis Gibb, who had recently been awarded an M.B.E. by the Queen. We were to watch her take the Morning Session.

The School of the Air is a highly imaginative conception. Officially it is described as: 'An attempt to give the outback child of school age some of the benefits of school life and at the same time to supplement correspondence education. Using the two-way wireless equipment developed first by the Royal Flying Doctor Service, children hundreds of miles apart participate in the same lesson, and teacher and pupils can talk directly with each other. The first School of the Air was established at Alice Springs in the Northern Territory; it has been followed by similar schools. . . . These nine schools serve children in an area of a million square miles.' (Year Book of the Commonwealth of Australia, 1963.)

Usually Mrs Gibb and her assistants address an empty class-room as they sit at the microphone to give their lessons to pupils scattered over the Outback of three States: New South Wales, Queensland and South Australia. On this particular morning, however, the rows of forms were crowded with girls from a school in Melbourne, and, within a radius of three-quarters of a million square miles, invisible pupils were eagerly awaiting a special treat. They were to hear a talk after the lesson. The visiting speaker was the Curator of the Canberra War Museum, the world's finest monument of its kind. So Mrs Gibb was very busy greeting and seating her guests in the air-conditioned class-room-studio with its wall-map showing the locality of a hundred stations with their total of two hundred pupils. The farthest was in Queensland, 585 miles from Broken Hill.

Mrs Gibb, then on the eve of retirement, made a tremendous impression upon me although she was too occupied to be able to give me more than a few minutes of her attention. This tall slender woman with sparkling brown eyes, a winning smile and grey hair plaited in a coronet round her head, possessed a magnetic spiritual quality. In some curious way one felt that she did not need to 'be seen to be believed'. Her personality transcended the visual and the physical. She was the Queen of the World of Voices.

A little eight-year-old girl from a remote station sat up in front near the teacher's table. She was happy and excited, but tying nervous knots in her small handkerchief which was beginning to look like an ice-cream cone. The visiting lecturer gave the tiny figure a reassuring smile as the Session opened with the School Song. Its words had been written by three young pupils and they were sung with immense gusto by the two hundred to the tune of 'Waltzing Matilda'.

All the little children
Scattered through the outback,
Tune into School of the Air at the start.
And we sing as we listen to many tape recordings,
All joining in tho' we're many miles apart.
Chorus
Parted but united,
Parted but united,
Is our school motto,
And pride of our heart.
And we sing as we listen to many tape recordings,
All joining in tho' we're many miles apart.

Big ones and little ones,
Listen in attentively,
Eager for knowledge our teachers impart,

Then we call in to answer telling them exciting things,
Then back to work with a much lighter heart.
Chorus

The young voices flooded the classroom, but the only singer
present was little Sharon, who joined them with her thin child's
treble. This was followed by the morning hymn, 'The Lord is my
Shepherd'. I could imagine some child alone with his books and
the transceiver in a far station dining-room, like Langawirra's,
singing his head off, feeling himself to be one with his invisible
companions. And suddenly my eyes were full of tears.

Mrs Gibb beckoned Sharon, who went to her at once. She put
her arm round the child as she said into the microphone: 'We
have Sharon with us in the classroom this morning. She would
like to greet you.'

'Good morning, boys and girls,' the child said into the proffered
instrument, and a chorus came back. 'Good morning Sharon –
good morning, all!'

'And now we want to wish Kerry Brown a happy birthday.
Shall we sing the birthday song?'

Sharon stood up and sang 'Happy birthday' in unison with her
distant schoolmates. Mrs Gibb went on to the 'weather report'.

'We have a cloudy picture. I expect you are all hoping for
clouds. Did anyone have any rain?' (One can never forget it? I
thought, this need for water.)

Little voices rushed in, the equivalent of raised hands waving.
Mrs Gibb called them one by one.

'That's splendid,' she commented. 'Five stations have had rain
– with twelve points at 8 EM and nine at 8 MQ. Good! And
now to News and General Knowledge.'

It was a children's news service. Lake Eyre, Donald Campbell was to start his Bluebird trials, a Dutch princess had become
betrothed, the Premier of one of the States had retired – and,
most important, a new teacher had been appointed to the School
of the Air. 'Miss Woodhouse – and, children, be careful how you
pronounce her name. It's a proper trap. *Not* Wood'ouse, but
Wood-*House*.' So the School of the Air concentrated on elocution
and those elusive aspirates!

Some lessons are live, others are recorded; all dovetail well with the Correspondence School of Blackfriars, Sydney. Many of them struck me as being expressly designed to stimulate the imagination and the competitive spirit that is part of the fun of a normal school. Free composition was a good feature, with one child beginning a 'story', another contributing the next sentence, and so on. But this morning the lesson was cut short to allow the guest speaker to address the School.

'And now the Captains. Are the Captains listening?'

Voices chimed in. 'Yes, Mrs Gibb.'

'Well, then, Helen, I want you to introduce our Guest Speaker. And you, Roderick, will thank him.'

As the selected youngsters responded with simple assurance, I understood why they had been chosen as captains (in a secret ballot) by their schoolmates. Those young voices had the quality of leadership. It came over the air like a strong fresh wind from the open spaces. Surely the Australians lead the world in air and radio consciousness! How will they use this special understanding which the circumstances of their lives have imposed upon them? The girls from Melbourne, sitting in the classroom this morning, were quiet and enthralled. The cities are not allowed to forget the Outback, which is such an important part of the nation's prosperity. This wireless educational experiment is of the utmost value. Children, who would otherwise grow up dumb from lack of company, and disinterested in life beyond the bush, are brought into touch with the wide world as well as with each other – and their mothers usually share their lessons with them.

The Australian attitude to education is still that of a people hungry for knowledge and literacy, because their grandfathers – and, in some cases, their own parents, or even they, themselves – have been starved of it. They *know* the handicap of illiteracy. To the bush people the School of the Air and the Correspondence School are lifelines for their children.

'There's nothing we ask that we aren't given by the people of the Outback,' Mrs Hogan told me. 'From donations for scholarships to half a beast for the School Picnic. Our friends in the towns help too.'

After the lecture on the Canberra War Memorial there was a discussion. Question and answer. It was obvious that the invisible audience had been most attentive, and many of the questions had the lecturer scratching his head and promising to get the exact answers and send them to Mrs Gibb.

If a child's voice was faint when Mrs Gibb called it in, because the distant station transmitter was weak, some other child, who had heard the message clearly, would be asked to relay it. This was often done, and most intelligently. I had the eerie sensation that these scattered children knew each other as well, if not better, than normal schoolchildren. They had their uniforms, their school play, and, of course, the all important picnic. Every one of them would be present at that annual event, even if their parents had to bring them over five hundred miles to Broken Hill, for, on that one day of the year, the World of Voices becomes a world of flesh and blood and eager meetings. On that day it is as if the blind look at one another in happy recognition, and say:

'Hullo! It's *you*!'

In the evening Mrs Hogan took me to the 1964 Annual General Meeting of the Parents' and Citizens' Association of the School of the Air, which was held in the same studio-classroom we had visited that morning.

The Meeting was conducted by the President, Mr W. Bolton Smith, with Mrs Gibb on his right and the rest of the committee members on the platform. There was no audience visible, but there was a keen attendance! Forty stations answered the roll-call. Every problem was discussed at length and with great patience, since some of the stations were almost inaudible over the static, which meant relaying opinions – rather like a court case in which the interpreter plays an important part. But one could feel the intense community of interest over the network. It was a tangible presence in that room so strangely devoid of the physical forms of mothers and fathers.

When a call-sign indicated a parent's desire to say something Mr Bolton Smith, at the microphone, invited her to speak. 'Come in Mrs Cody!' He might have been opening the door to her, offering her a chair in the room and giving her his full attention.

The best method of inaugurating a new scholarship was

thrashed out at length, the programme for the next annual picnic was discussed and exciting new innovations suggested, certain hold-ups over the mail-bag courses for some of the least accessible stations were considered and plans made to obviate the difficulties in future. As I listened, I became more and more accustomed to this meeting of voices alone. I came to know those far away parents, to endow them with distinct and special individualities, to prefer some to others, just as if I could see them. It was a strange and illuminating experience. Above all, I was aware of the enthusiasm shared by all 'present'. The education of their children was a matter of vital importance to everyone on the network.

Goodnights were said and the meeting broke up. We, in the studio, shook hands and went to our respective cars. But what of those others – the parents in the distant stations – when the transceiver is off and the deep unbroken silence of the Outback claims the night? Is there a moment of loss and blindness as the last words are spoken, 'Over and out'? Or do they go to bed well satisfied, their minds occupied and stimulated by profitable discussion of Outback education, its problems and its triumphs? They have talked and listened to others; they have contributed and received ideas; they have taken an active part in a national enterprise which affects the future of their children and their country. They and their families matter. A hunger has been appeased. Human beings are, by nature, like the sheep they tend. Without the company of their own kind their very souls disintegrate.

CHAPTER TWELVE

Menindee with the Flying Doctor

The Flying Doctor's Clinic that autumn morning was at Menindee some seventy miles from Broken Hill. It was eight o'clock on a brilliant sunny day with a crisp kick in the air when Dr Walker parked his car near the hangar. He introduced me to the Senior Pilot, Captain Victor Cover, and his Assistant, Captain Jack Jenkins, who was to pilot us.

The plane was a three-engined green and white Drover with red crosses under the wings and the legend ROYAL FLYING DOCTOR SERVICE NSW along the fuselage. When we were settled and airborne I was amazed to see how spacious it was, with several seats and a space for a stretcher.

From where I sat I could see Jack Jenkins at the controls, his narrow-brimmed felt hat resting on his ear-phones and tipped well forward over his nose, the back of his thin neck sunburned and leathery. He was quick and wiry, talked like machine-gun fire and enjoyed a grumble, but he was full of fun too, was much in demand as a singer, and that hat of his was famous throughout the Outback. When it lies about in somebody's living-room it tells its own tale of swift service for the sick.

George Walker had his head-phones on and was taking his morning session. He handed me a pair, I put them on and felt as if I were listening to the continuation of a serial begun at Langawirra. The patients seemed to be on the mend. He had scarcely finished his last, 'Cheerio for now,' when we were circling over the chain of blue lakes said to be eight times the size of Sydney Harbour with four times its volume of water. The lakes are part of an important water conservation and irrigation scheme and those engaged on the work have added considerably to Menindee's tiny community of under a thousand people.

This lovely spot, now a water-skiing and sailing Mecca for week-end campers from Broken Hill, was the natural spring-board for the early Australian explorers. A century ago it was the last outpost of civilization, with a police post, a hotel and a trading store.

It was that aspect which enthralled me, for I was then steeped in Alan Moorehead's book, *Cooper's Creek*, which tells the tragic story of the first crossing of the Australian Continent from the south to the Gulf of Carpentaria in the tropical north a century ago. (Fifteen years before Ernest Giles succeeded in crossing the centre from west to east.)

Alan Moorehead is an Australian himself, who knows the murderous terrain of the centre which lured and destroyed so many who hoped to conquer it. I had met him in 1931, when I was a reporter on the London *Daily Express* and he was a Foreign Correspondent for that paper, and, to my great disappointment, I had just missed him and his wife when they were in Perth. I had devoured his magnificent books about my own African Continent and had been spellbound by *Cooper's Creek*.

But although *Cooper's Creek* describes in full the Victorian Exploration Expedition led by Robert O'Hara Burke, it also gives honourable mention to many who went ahead and were com-pelled to turn back.

There was Edward John Eyre, who braved incredible hard-ships in South and Western Australia, and who, in 1840, set out to discover the inland sea then commonly believed to lie at the heart of the centre. When he reached the dry salt area of Lake Eyre (which had in the distant past been a sort of Australian Caspian) he had abandoned his journey. He wrote of this 'deso-late forbidding region' as 'the Dead Heart of the Centre', and the hill from which he viewed it he mapped as Mount Hopeless.

Eyre's Australian explorations won him fame and the Governor-ship of Jamaica, but, like so many brave colonial pioneers, his career ended ignominiously. That noble Act of Parliament, the abolition of slavery, that had ruined the farmers of the Cape through the method of its application, had an equally disastrous effect upon the planters of Jamaica. Compensation for the West Indian slaves was less than half their value. Great confusion followed emancipation, and, in 1865, a Negro insurrection broke out and thirty innocent people were brutally murdered. The Governor, backed by the planters, put down the rebellion with such severity that a violent outcry ensued in London. Eyre was retired under a cloud despite the fact that a number of prominent individuals, including Carlyle and Tennyson, took his part, believing that his prompt action had saved a massacre of the European population.

Meanwhile, in Australia, many had followed in Eyre's bold tracks, carrying on the bitter and often unrewarding work of discovery. One of these dauntless explorers was Charles Sturt, who, as a young Army Officer, had been sent to Sydney in charge of a convict guard. Lured by the extraordinary magnetism of the centre, he took command of a South Australian Expedition in 1844, and the handful of settlers at Menindee watched it set off with sixteen men, eleven horses, thirty bullocks and a flock of sheep to provide them with meat on the hoof.

Moorehead has this to say of the interior they sought to explore.

Sturt and his men were marching into one of the most appalling summers ever recorded. . . .

The extreme temperatures of the centre are very bearable because of the dryness of the air, but even so the heat this year was unbelievable. It rose to 152 degrees in the shade and 157 in the sun . . . Scurvy broke out in the camp and one man died, but there was nothing to be done; they were alone in the wilderness, even the birds had deserted the inferno, and nothing moved on the cracked earth except the lizards and the ants. . . .

By April it was a little cooler, and thunder clouds began to bank up on the horizon. At last on July 12th a gentle but persistent rain started to fall, and after a few days it developed into a downpour. Now they had floods to contend with, cold nights and even frost, but at least they could move, and as a guarantee that life was returning to the parched earth, swans and ducks and other migrating birds began to reappear.

The explorers crossed terrible wastelands but they made encouraging discoveries. By the end of the frosty winter with its floods and storms, they emerged from Sturt's Stony Desert, and climbed a sandhill to look upon a scene which must have appeared like the Promised Land. A stretch of savannah was intersected by an inviting waterway covered with wild fowl.

> It was a full 200 yards from side to side and the banks rose . . . among groves of flooded gum trees. The blacks had recently been burning off grass, and now the ground was covered with bright young shoots. The water in the stream was vivid green. . . . His (Sturt's) hopes for an inland sea revived, and it was a bitter disappointment when once again they struck the Stony Desert.

Sturt named the creek with its 'splendid sheets of water' after the South Australian Judge, Charles Cooper. He didn't feel justified in charting Cooper's Creek as a river, because 'it had no current'. In the prehistoric past it had flowed into the 'sea' of Lake Eyre.

In the course of his two years in the interior he collected innumerable plants and geological specimens that indicated the great mineral potentialities of the centre. He found many tribes of aborigines to be friendly and helpful, if well treated, and described the wild life that abounded wherever there was water. There were seagulls on Cooper's Creek five hundred miles from the sea! He noted that the black swans 'tended to be on the wing when the moon was shining bright', and observed the sulphur-crested cockatoos and the rose cockatoos commonly called galahs. Moorehead quotes many of Sturt's vivid descriptions, for this explorer had an able and evocative pen. His picture of the little bird, *amadina castanotus*, is deeply touching, for, in a few words, it tells the whole tale of the greatest hardship of those early explorations.

> Never did its note fall on our ears but as the harbinger for good, for never did we hear this little bird but we were sure to find water close at hand, and many a time it has raised my drooping spirits and those of my companions.

Sturt never succeeded in crossing the Continent.

In 1848 Ludwig Leichhardt set out from Melbourne with the intention of making the crossing westwards to Perth and was never heard of again. But the unknown continued to beckon and, in the year 1860, yet another expedition – the most famous of them all – was encamped at Menindee on the shores of Lake Pamamaroo.

The leader was a temperamental Irishman, Robert O'Hara Burke, who had arrived in Australia at the time of the Ballarat and Bendigo gold rush. He joined the Victorian Police Force and distinguished himself in quelling the riots and disturbances of the period. His second in command was a conscientious and loyal young scientist and surveyor, William John Wills. These two, with their comrades, ex-soldier and sailor, John King and Charlie Gray, were the first to cross Australia. Although they never saw the Gulf of Carpentaria, they knew they had arrived when they waded into the salty waters of the northern mangrove swamps, but the return journey destroyed them. All in all, seven men lost their lives in that ill-fated enterprise which had nevertheless succeeded in its purpose. The south-north crossing had been made.

Looking down upon Menindee, I could well understand what that green oasis must have meant to the men destined to leave it for the burning shadeless heart of the centre! Trees waded in calm lakes reflecting the blue of the sky, and both water and branches were alive with birds. Jack flew low over Lake Cawndilla, a wild life sancturary where the pelicans go to breed.

A Combie was at Menindee airstrip to meet us, driven by the Deaconess in charge of the Methodist Inland Mission Nursing Service. George, Jack Jenkins and I climbed in. The fortnightly Flying Doctor Clinics were held in her little house which was set in a small garden where mauve and white cosmos swayed in the breeze. A number of people were waiting on the verandah when we arrived – the families of railway workers, Italian or Greek market gardeners, employees of the Water Conservation Scheme and a few local inhabitants.

Jack Jenkins and I had a cup of coffee with the Assistant Deaconess and then she offered to drive me to Lake Pamamaroo.

'The sights are few,' she said. 'But they might interest you.'

Jack left us to go and see how his allotment was getting on. He had a plot he was cultivating near Menindee and he threatened that one day he would retire to his lakeside retreat.

The young Deaconess had recently arrived from Sydney and was still fairly new to the Outback. She was a teacher as well as a nurse, but I think she often found the loneliness of the bush oppressive after the busy crowded life of her home city.

'Aren't there any aborigines here?' I asked her. 'They seem to be the invisible people of Australia.'

'They have their own reserves,' she said. 'But, yes, there are a few near here.'

She drove me to a leafy grove, where there was a small *pondokkie* settlement such as one might have found in the wattle flats of the Cape. I gathered that these workless people were part of the flock of the Church of England, whose Bush Church Aid Society co-operates with the Methodist Nursing Mission. In the Outback there is this co-operation of the Churches that one meets only too seldom in the world's cities. The abo children received education, and, perhaps in time, the bright ones would be able to integrate with a white community. It seemed to me that most of these were 'twilights', the folk of mixed blood who are so often and so cruelly, rejected by the full-blooded races that have combined to produce them. We left the insoluble problem of the present to glance at traces of the past.

Near the Darling River is Maiden's Hotel among shady trees – an old rambling place built a few years before the Burke and Wills Expedition set out from Menindee. Mr Maiden, a descendant of the first owner, took us to see Room 10, a bare little room such as you might find in any South African hotel in a country *dorp*.

'This is where Burke and Wills stayed before they left with their camel-trains, their horses and their tented wagons.'

We looked round it and I wondered what high hopes had stirred its famous occupants, the volatile Burke, determined to be the first to cross the continent, and his serious companion, Wills, whose devotion never failed his leader.

One of the survivors of the Expedition who had settled in

Menindee was Dost Mahomet, the Pathan camel-driver, whose humble grave lies a short distance from the Main Street. On the tombstone are the words 'DOST MAHOMET. BURKE & WILLS EXPEDITION. 1860–62.'

We drove out to the site of the explorers' camp on the shore of Lake Pamamaroo. It is a lovely glade among tall trees and weeping willows, and even the new dam and weir do nothing to detract from its charm. The pelicans still fish there as they did over a century ago. It is now believed that when Sturt first followed the Darling to Menindee he had come to the legendary 'inland sea' without realizing it. Certainly there had been no other for thousands of years!

As we sat in the shade and watched the birds and listened to the song of the weir I began to appreciate why Wright, the bushman from Kincheca, in charge of the Menindee base, had betrayed his leader's confidence and failed to follow up the party on the Cooper until it was too late. He had eaten of the lotus at Menindee, and there he had loitered too long. Here too, Landells, the camel expert, had fallen from grace by drinking rum which was supposed to be a tonic for his camels! Wisely, but not very bravely he left the Expedition at Menindee and returned to Melbourne, and King, the ex-soldier from India, took over the care of the camels, who, from then on, had to manage without their rum. Most of the stately supercilious beasts perished in the swamps, but to this day occasional wild camels are encountered in the deserts of the Inland, living memorials to that long ago ill-starred expedition. And for many years the children of Menindee played with the camel-shoes they found lying in the dust round Burke's camp.

When I talked to George Walker about my 'sight-seeing tour' he said:

'It's impossible for anyone who doesn't know the centre to imagine what those explorers were up against. They couldn't live off the land alone, as the abos did, because a white man needs a different diet. The abos can subsist through drought on lizards and a sort of native flour called nardoo, but whites need meat and greens. Without them they get scurvy, like the early mariners used to do, poor devils. And in those deserts of the Never-Never it can be so hot in summer that you can hardly crawl from the hangar to the airstrip. You can't see the red cross on the wings for flies. The plane is cold when it comes down and the flies cluster on to it to cool their feet. There've been days when I've got into the plane in my khaki bush-rig, and, within minutes, the whole thing is sticking to me as if I'd been hosed! Once above seven thousand feet, of course, the air-conditioning comes into operation, then it's all right.'

'It's been exciting, seeing the starting point for the first Australian crossing – in the days of no radio and no planes, no Land Rovers or compressed foods or mobile refrigeration,' I said. 'But I wish I could see where it ended – so tragically – at Cooper's Creek.'

CHAPTER THIRTEEN

Mercy Mission to Cooper's Creek

At eight-fifteen next morning the receptionist of the hotel came to my room.

'Dr Walker on the telephone – says it's urgent.'

George Walker's voice was brisk.

'If you want to see Cooper's Creek now's your chance. An old stockman has been thrown from his horse at Innamincka – four hundred and fifty miles from here, on the Cooper. Sounds as if he's broken a few ribs. I'm on my way. Are you coming?'

'Yes. When?' I could hardly believe it.

'Five minutes from now. Could be cold. Wear warm slacks and a jersey.'

Jack Jenkins had the Drover warmed up and soon we were heading north.

'Can you give me a bit of background?' I asked. 'Who's the patient? What's the set-up?'

'The patient is a stockman of about eighty – or so we think. Old Arthur is vague about his age. Mrs Kemp called me from Innamincka cattle station. Her husband is manager. She says old Arthur looks very sick, so you may be sure he is. These people seldom ask me to come unless it's absolutely necessary. They say, "No, we're a long way from the doctor and he's busy. We can manage." I've seen them with ghastly wounds, and they *do* manage!'

'It must be hard to know when you should go.'

'One gets an instinct. They spare their horses too. I knew a boy with a gangrene leg injury take three days getting back to the station in mid-summer rather than ruin his horse by pressing the animal too hard.'

'Is it a big station – this one?'

He smiled. 'Rather more than nine thousand square miles. Not acres. It's owned by the Kidnam Pastoral Company. They used to say of Kidnam that he could drive his cattle from Innamincka to Adelaide without stepping off his own land. But now he might have to cross somebody else's paddock along the route – just once or twice!'

We were flying at about 4,000 feet, a speck between the red desert and the sky, with visibility a hundred miles across and seventy-five ahead. I pictured Sturt with his horses and Burke with his camels plodding along down there under the fierce sun for mile upon endless mile.

'We're flying along the Border Fence,' said George. 'You can see it.'

'And read about it.'

He looked astonished, but smiled when I showed him my source of information. I had brought *Over to You*, the School of the Air Magazine, for light reading on the journey. Two contributions that had caught my attention had come from pupils living along the Fence. They were signed with the station call-sign. One child had written:

I live one hundred and sixty-six miles from Broken Hill on the New South Wales–South Australian Border Fence. This fence is to keep the wild dogs out of New South Wales. There are four children here and we go for walks at the week-end. We roll down the sandhills, pick wild flowers and look for mushrooms after rain. 9CD.

A more senior pupil had been more explicit, if less charmingly carefree, and had included a photograph of a truck descending a dune between the spinifex and the tall wire fence.

The dogproof fence, which separates New South Wales from Queensland and South Australia, is six feet six inches high. Its purpose is to prevent the dingoes or wild dogs from entering the sheep-grazing property of New South Wales. This fence is made of wire netting and steel posts, with railway irons for strainer posts.

Each boundary rider employed by the Wild Dog Destruction Board runs a section of about twenty miles, and is expected to keep his part of the fence in good repair.

The South Australian section is about one hundred and forty miles long, and runs through the country of big red sandhills, where a four-wheel drive is necessary. The Queensland section is two hundred and seventeen miles long and has many river channels running through the fence. These channels cause severe washaways at times. 8NDX.

'What more can *I* tell you?' George laughed, 'except that if a dingo gets into sheep country he'll kill twenty sheep in a night.'

'Like our jackals in South Africa. To say nothing of leopards. We have fences too – aproned to the ground with big stones to stop the jackals digging under the wire to get through.'

The little correspondents of *Over to You* gave a vivid human picture of the Outback to Magazine readers. I was fascinated. 8NEM had a bit to say about Shearing Time.

Shearing is a busy time. Our shed is seven miles from our home. Firstly the shed and shearers' quarters have to be cleaned out. Then the mustering has to be done. I'm always pleased when Daddy musters on Saturday and Sunday so I can go and help him. Daddy uses a jeep and motor-bike to do the mustering.

Ten men come to do the work. There are four shearers, a cook, a woolclasser, presser, and shed hands to sweep up the wool. The wool is put into bales and transported to Broken Hill by truck, and then to Adelaide by rail, where it is sold.

8NCE described her home.

Our home is built of wood and the roof is iron. The walls are painted white and the roof green with yellow trimmings.

The bedrooms open on to a large sleepout where we sleep in summer. The lounge-dining-room has double glass doors opening on to a sun-deck, where Mummy has some pot plants. Around the house is a large garden with many trees, shrubs and pretty flowers.

8NFA loved the family pets.

> We have five pets. There is a little brown and black dog called Sausage, and a black cat with a patch of white under her chin. Her name is Sooty and she is very good at catching mice. Danny is our little white goat. He runs and jumps into the air, he is funny to watch. Bobby is a white lamb who loves his bottle. We have a green budgie called Jack. Jack can whistle. I love them all and feed them every day.

From one little girl who 'got branding-paint all over myself and all down my blouse' I realized that the animals are no longer branded by burning.

'A sandstorm,' said George Walker suddenly. 'Tibooburra's getting it.'

Ahead of us a deep band of red dust about a thousand feet high advanced to meet us, while blessed rain slanted down upon the western horizon. I began to scribble in my soft-cover note-book.

> The dust now blankets the red desert, masking the billabongs and waterless creeks with their lines of vegetation. Even in the aircraft you can smell it, dry and suffocating. We are in it now, bounding about in the turbulence that is causing the storm and Jack Jenkins has signed to us to fasten our seat-belts. It is a sunlit fog, its fine, red, fast-drifting texture visible as we fly through it. We are parallel with the Burke and Wills route and will presently be on the Cooper. On Jack's chart there are names like Mount Hopeless (where Eyre turned back), Mount Dismal and Starvation Lake. Yet the Cooper is a place of fish and birds and mussels. The dust is clearing. East of us, under our right wing, is Queensland, for Innamincka is almost on the border. It's the land of the lizard and the kangaroo, the wild horses that are shot for pet's meat, the dingo and that great builder, the ant. Even the abos are practically extinct.

I was thrilled when George Walker leaned across and said, 'There it is – Cooper's Creek!'

It was a jade green watercourse, dark with trees, snaking across the arid Stony Desert, and it took no stretch of imagination to know how the sight of this large serene creek must have lifted the hearts of the men who had journeyed hundreds of sun-baked miles.

The homestead and outhouses of the Innamincka cattle station looked like toy buildings beneath us on the banks of the Cooper. Jack banked and landed on the airstrip some three miles on.

A big truck was parked there, and, while we waited for Mrs Kemp to fetch us, the two men in charge of it got into conversation with us. They were members of the Geophysical Survey team on the Santos oil rig some thirty miles away in South Australia. This American oil exploration company had bored and found the 'right gases' but the bore had been sealed 'till further notice'.

'Come and see our camp,' said the one young man, a Canadian. 'It's very modern and comfortable – worth a visit.'

His friend, who came from Perth, also urged us to come and see their quarters. I was torn two ways, but the arrival of Mrs Kemp in the station-wagon with two-and-a-half-year-old Christopher settled the matter. We piled in, waved good-bye to the oil men, and Mrs Kemp began to tell the Doctor about old Arthur.

'Well, Dr Walker, he was out on Biscuit yesterday afternoon, and after a while, the horse came back without him. Still saddled. We always feel a bit worried about Arthur on account of his age, so my husband went out right away to look for him. He found the old boy about three miles out, just picking himself up. He seemed a bit stunned. He didn't complain much till later and then he couldn't cough or breathe properly because of the pain. You know how he goes on smoking that tobacco of his—'

'Yes, he smokes too much, but, at his age, who would stop him?'

The Doctor had had Arthur through his hands before, after the old stockman had spent weeks rescuing cattle when the Cooper was flooded. His legs had developed dermatitis from continual immersion in the flood waters.

Mrs Kemp nodded. 'The trouble is that awful tobacco makes him cough. We gave him some veganin and it relieved the pain a bit, but we got you early this morning because he looked very sick.'

'Quite right, Mrs Kemp. Now Biscuit? That's the tame old horse I rode last time I was up here – Arthur's precious horse, nearly as old as he is.'

'Biscuit bucked Arthur off.'

'Bucked? Biscuit!'

'You know how the old man is about that animal. He loves it more than anything else. He's given it no exercise for ages and he's been feeding it oats, so you can guess what Biscuit was like!'

She drew up in front of the homestead which was really lovely – a log house on stilts to avoid the constant danger of flood waters from the Cooper. Her four-year-old daughter ran across a rose garden to meet us, with half a dozen friendly dogs at her heels. Behind them came Mrs Kemp's younger sister.

'My elder daughter's at boarding-school,' said Mrs Kemp. 'So I've only the two little ones to keep me company, and my sister Jennifer, has come from Menindee to stay for a bit.'

Jack Jenkins parked his famous hat on the hall table, and Mrs Kemp showed me round the house, which was very modern with gay colour schemes and comfortable furniture.

'It's all you could want,' she said.

But her tone was less sure than her words and I guessed that she hankered after city lights, restaurants, cinemas, a bit of company and a girls' gossip over a cup of coffee.

By the time the Doctor had examined the patient over at the stockmen's quarters we were ready for the substantial lunch Mrs Kemp had prepared for us, shepherd's pie followed by home-baked bread and scones with honey, and huge cups of tea. Mr Kemp joined us for a hasty meal. He was about to send a mob of six hundred cattle overland to Bourke, some three hundred miles.

'We have to walk them now, but there's a bitumen road being built, so soon we'll be able to truck them right through to Brisbane on the black.'

Four stockmen were to go with the mob.

'How about Arthur?' he asked George Walker.

'We'll take him back to hospital for X-ray. There are several ribs cracked, possibly broken, and he has that shocking smoker's cough. I've strapped him up and he's reasonably comfortable.'

We had to leave right after lunch as it was already near three o'clock. I was sorry, as Mrs Kemp had begun to feel at ease with me. The Outback people, George had explained, were silent and reserved at first. It took time for them to 'warm through'. Certainly, in the immensity of the bush, the 'galah session' would be the only opportunity for chatter! The Flying Doctor gets to know his bush patients well. He is their friend and often their saviour. He eats with them, stays the night, if need be, becomes briefly but intimately a part of the whole family as no general practitioner could be. His voice over the transceiver is part of their daily lives.

Mrs Kemp and I had strolled down to the paddock near the bank of the Creek, where I had been introduced to that aged oat-fed delinquent, Biscuit, and a young horse, 'wild as a brumbie', intended to be tamed and ridden by the children. When we got back the station-wagon was at the gate with old Arthur sitting in the back seat, all strapped up under his jacket and smiling broadly. He was gnarled and bronzed by many summers, with shaggy white eyebrows over laughing blue eyes, snowy hair and one of those hand-knitted faces that is all knots and holes.

'We must show 'er the camp and cairn.' He nodded towards me. 'We got time for that, Jack?'

The pilot grunted and glanced at his watch. Mrs Kemp gallantly took her station-wagon through running water and rough country to the century-old site of the Cooper's Creek depot of the Burke and Wills Expedition. Jack allowed us a few minutes there.

'This is the Dig Tree!' Arthur loved this country and was proud of its history. He pointed out the huge coolibah with a massive trunk and a long branch reaching across the Creek. Carved in the tough wood of the bole was the message.

DIG

5 FT. N.W.

APR. 21 1861

'It's late April now,' I said. 'Those words must have been carved on a day like this – bright and cold.'

George Walker touched the scar on the bark.

'Very likely. But this message spelt death for Burke and Wills.'

Four months before those words had been carved, Burke, Wills, Gray and King bade their comrades at the Cooper good-bye and set out for the long unknown final stage of the journey to the Gulf of Carpentaria. It was a sad parting with Burke ordering the men at the depot to wait for a certain period and then to assume that he and his advance party were lost. The four men had trudged off with their one horse and some camels. It was midsummer, a few days before Christmas.

Unbelievable as it may seem to us, they seldom rode their beasts, except in the last extremity. The animals were strictly for transport of water and supplies. This brave little party of four men marched fifteen hundred miles in four months over the loose stones and pebbles of Sturt's Stony Desert, through sand-dunes and swamps, in sizzling heat and drenching rain. They reached the shores of the Gulf – their objective achieved. They rested and returned to the Cooper under terrible conditions. Camels were bogged and lost; Gray died of dysentery, and the other three, reduced to their last gasp by malnutrition, crawled into the camp on the Creek on that chilly April evening only to find the depot recently deserted, the fires not yet cold, the camel droppings still fresh and the fatal 'Dig' blaze on the coolibah. Their calls were answered by the parrots and the deep silence of the 'Dumb Inland'. They had missed salvation and their comrades by only nine hours!

As I stood in the dappled green light I wondered what sad white ghosts wandered here on April nights.

The three exhausted men dug at the appointed spot and found a camel-box with rations and a letter stating that the depot party had waited longer than the agreed time, that several of their number were desperately ill with scurvy and dysentery, that their camels were dying of scab and they were about to return to the base at Menindee.

Burke, Wills and King, their triumph turned to ashes, the taste of death in their mouths, struggled on hopelessly and finally succumbed not far from the Cooper. Burke and Wills died within a few days of each other while King, cared for by the friendly aborigines, survived in a pitiful condition until Howitt's Relief Expedition found him in September and saved his life, though not his health.

In the course of time the Victorian Government granted the kindly aborigines two hundred acres along the Cooper, but the tribesmen have since then become almost extinct. Missions tried to help them, but the impact of white civilization, slight as it was, brought them few blessings. Australia's black problem, unlike that of South Africa, slowly but surely dwindles.

Mrs Kemp drove us on into the Stony Desert – that harsh gibber country – and there, beside the ruins of the Innamincka Hotel and an open grave containing ten thousand broken beer bottles, powdered by the fierce sun, we found the cairn that commemorates those early explorers who faced their task with so little to sustain them save courage and the determination that never gives in. Two plates are on the rough stone cairn, one above the other. The first is in memory of Sturt.

Charles Sturt discovered Cooper's Creek about 15 miles west of this place on 7th October 1846 in his attempt to reach the centre of Australia. His work prompted further exploration resulting in the pastoral occupation of this locality and Western Queensland. Erected 1956

The second inscription reads:

Burke, Wills, Gray and King, the first to cross the Continent from South to North, passed here 17th December 1860. The sole survivor, King, was cared for by the Natives and was rescued by Howitt 15th September 1861. Erected 1944.

'There's a dust storm coming up,' said Jack Jenkins, pushing his hat a bit lower over his eyes. 'Better step on it.'

Mrs Kemp stepped on it. Soon we were in the air, the green waters of the Cooper behind us and the Stony Desert beneath us. We flew high to avoid the storm and presently old Arthur, in the seat behind mine, tapped me on the shoulder. The old man's face was twisted in acute distress. George Walker was ready with oxygen, but Arthur shook his head and pushed the mask away.

'I'd sooner suffocate,' he managed to mutter.

'We've had this difficulty before,' said George, giving his patient a tablet. 'He refuses oxygen as if it were lethal gas!'

After a while Arthur revived. George put on his ear-phones and prepared to take his four o'clock session. I put on the other ear-phones.

A new voice came in from a sheep station, an anxious mother.

'When Christine coughs she sounds like a chaff-cutter, Doctor.'

'Sorry she sounds like a chaff-cutter, Mrs J. But we'll soon oil that up a bit.'

I heard the smile in his voice, but my attention was diverted by the sight of a leathery hand groping across for the morning paper which was lying on the stretcher Arthur had firmly disdained. I took off my ear-phones and passed him the *Barrier Daily Truth*. I was pleased that he felt well enough to read, but a little surprised that he should be able to do so without spectacles. Arthur nodded his thanks and made a sign that he was now all right. The Doctor, the session over, set aside his earphones and relaxed, his eyes half closed. Arthur, behind us, was very quiet, the open paper concealing his face. Suddenly I sniffed. An unmistakable smell of burning was coming from the seat behind me. The paper was alight and blazing merrily.

George Walker sprang up and put out the miniature conflagration; Arthur's eyebrows, spiky as spinifex, were scorched, so was some of his clothing.

'I told him not to smoke,' groaned George. 'That newspaper was a screen – till he set it alight!'

The cigarette the old man had furtively rolled and packed with his fierce tobacco had gone out in the confusion, and the Doctor relit it for him. Arthur grinned sheepishly as he inhaled and blew the smoke out of his nostrils with infinite satisfaction. George grinned back at him.

'You're incorrigible, Arthur! Indestructible too. I hand it to you.'

An ambulance was waiting at Broken Hill. Arthur eyed it with suspicion.

'I'll get in,' he said. 'But I'm not lying down.'

The Doctor helped him in. 'Of course not. I'll be seeing you at the hospital soon. Cheerio for now.'

Next day I went with Mrs Walker to see Arthur. The indomitable old stockman had broken four ribs, but he looked spruce and perky and he was rolling one of his ferocious cigarettes when we came to his bedside.

It was my last night in Broken Hill. I had dined with the Walkers and we had talked about the strange lethargy that is the true danger of the Outback, and then far into the night I re-read passages from *Cooper's Creek*. Those dogged explorers of the nineteenth century, unaided by modern science, were indeed 'men of positive quality' with an infinite capacity for endurance.

As I thought about them and others, like 'Flynn of the Inland', I saw again the quiet water of the Creek, the birds upon its breast and the gaudy cockatoos in the branches overhanging it. Alan Moorehead knew every mood of that thread of green in the Stony Desert.

> But perhaps the really undermining thing about the Cooper is the inertia that overtakes one there . . . a fatalistic passivity of the mind; one longs to take refuge in a slow, uneventful routine and it is not long before the demands of civilization drop away. One lives upon the bare minimum of effort, one accepts discomforts, and to gaze on and on into the camp fire, *to do nothing, to say nothing, to succumb to solitariness, becomes at last the only bearable existence.*

The italics are mine. I copied out the paragraph into my Writer's Notebook and added a note.

> This is it. This is the true danger. This inertia is what Flynn was fighting. Fear too. And he and his disciples have won the battle.

The moon was high, shining into my bedroom. On the Cooper the kangaroos would be cropping the new young grass and the yellow dingoes would be out hunting. At Langawirra the black swans would be trumpeting – on the Cooper too perhaps. The echo of that silvery lament sang in my ears, swan voices like ghost bugles calling from the vast solitude of the Outback. Tomorrow at sunrise Beth Gall would be up, feeding the cats and the lamb, Noopi.

I shall always remember her thus, in the golden early morning stooping to pour milk into the wide shallow bowl with the cats purring loudly round the hem of her long red gown and the lamb *baaing* impatiently. I shall remember too the vase of carnations that welcomed me to Langawirra and the Outback – flowers from the garden Beth will never see again.

•

CHAPTER FOURTEEN

Sydney, Australia's Melting-pot

What a dramatic place Sydney is! I had never dreamed that it could be so beautiful. In fact, it has the same breath-taking splendour of mighty cliffs and headlands and pounding surf as the Cape Peninsula. After the deserts of the Outback the lush vegetation seemed unbelievably tropical, and the well-behaved Hawkesbury River, banked with meadows, bungalows and boat-houses was a tame and tender affair in comparison with the Cooper, which could run dry or submerge a whole region. Sydney's famous beaches, fringed with Norfolk Island pines, have everything – calm coves for children and huge long breakers for the surf-riders. There are no shark-nets, such as we have in Durban, but the shark patrols keep constant watch from heli-copters and from the life-savers' towers, and, when the alarm bell rings, every bather is out of the water before you can count three.

When the summer humidity becomes too oppressive the Blue Mountains are within easy reach for a picnic or a week-end, and, in winter, the flight to the ski slopes of the Snowy Mountains is a mere 'hop' to the air-minded Australians. Sydney is a teeming higgledy-piggledy city built over innumerable steep hills. Its houses – the decayed elaborate mansions of yesterday overlapped by the angular modernity of today – are jammed together like teeth in an overcrowded jaw.

The Cross, where Elspeth and I stayed at the attractive Belve-dere Hotel, is one of those precipitous hills rising from an en-chanting little yachting harbour to the City Centre. They call The Cross 'Sydney's Chelsea', but to me it felt more like Montmartre. Shaggy bearded artists in weird garments and girls in tights, with fantastic hairdo's and strange ghostly make-ups, mooched around with the aimless tread of those whose working hours are their own, or none at all. The Cross is pitted with little Oriental restaurants and Greek or Italian cafés – mere holes in the wall. There are bright launderettes where odd characters lounge while their grotesque garments go through the mangle. There are shops of all sorts for all tastes, from dress *boutiques* and delicatessens to the lairs of art and antique dealers. You can hear all the languages of Europe in The Cross, and you can see titillating photographs outside curious dives. 'The All Male Revue' was advertised by photographs of men looking like showgirls from the Moulin Rouge. Somehow these 'men' had achieved the feminine form in the almost 'altogether'!

The harbour must be one of the finest in the world and Sydney's fabled bridge was even more powerful and elegant than we had expected, with twin towers at either end of the strong graceful span which carries eight traffic lanes and two sets of railway tracks. At night the harbour is a place of shimmering fantasy. The whole city breathes the most inexhaustible vitality.

While we were there, the University Students held their Rag with an exuberant disregard for life and limb. Their floats were in aid of the Higher Education of Africans in South Africa! I would have liked to suggest that they looked to the education of Australia's aborigines before going quite so far afield. One lad staged a mock suicide from Manly Ferry in the shark infested waters of the harbour, an act which might well have cost him a leg or an arm. And that night his fellow students commandeered another ferry boat and then set about smashing up the contents after the party was over. Yet another group marched on the United States Consulate with hooded figures and a fiery cross – a demonstration which ended in a riot requiring police intervention.

Young white Australia's preoccupation with African higher education and America's Deep South seemed incongruous in view of the fact that her own far north contains countless aborigines who have never heard of higher education or known the franchise.

But in the following year, 1965, a group of Sydney's students travelled thousands of miles on a fact-finding tour of the Aborigine Reserves, encountering some white resentment and a few rotten eggs in the process.

In her aim to populate her vast territory with 'all white' European migrants, Australia has come up against problems similar to those of the United States in the days of Al Capone and the gangsters whose rule of fear made Chicago a name of evil memory for so many sinister years.

While we were in Sydney we witnessed tragic evidence of this. At nine on the evening of May 7th a thirty-three-year-old Croat, Thomislav Lesic, was walking home after visiting a cousin in a suburb of the city. He was carrying a leather attaché case in which a bomb had been planted. The bomb exploded at 9.20, blowing off one of his legs, shattering the other and causing hideous and extensive body wounds and the loss of an eye. Lesic was an ardent anti-Communist and the police soon ascertained that the crime was political. Lesic was alleged to belong to a Croat Group training in Sydney and in Queensland to overthrow Communism in Yugoslavia with the intention of establishing a Fascist type of government in its place. Within the next few days the Sydney papers were full of stories of the Yugoslav 'reign of terror' in New South Wales.

An editorial in *The Sun* on May 11th was headed MIGRANT TERROR:

Federal Security Services and State Police must quickly stamp out the threat of gang warfare among migrants in Sydney streets. In the four days since a Croat was terribly mutilated by a bomb in Petersham, there have been ugly indications that warring factions from overseas have revived their old feuds and jealousies in Australia. . . . Memories of the outbreak of murder and violence among the Italian community in Melbourne early this year are still too fresh to allow any complacency about the latest friction among migrants. The Croats and Yugoslavs living in Australia are a comparative handful of our total population, and the great majority have already demonstrated that they are hard working and law-abiding. . . . The Minister for Immigration, Mr Opperman, said recently that Australia's system of screening migrants had been 'steadily refined over the years'. Even so, it is still possible for trouble makers from other countries to slip through the security net.

There are about 30,000 Yugoslav migrants in Australia with 10,000 in Sydney alone.

There was nothing new or astonishing to me in reports of nationalist organizations training in other countries to bring terror to their own. It is a pattern South Africa knows only too well. There are many 'training schools' in Africa and other parts of the world where extreme African nationalists can study the arts of sabotage and murder. Violence, in the name of Freedom, spreads far and wide, spilling its seeds of hate and death before returning to launch the final blood bath in the land of its origin.

It was quite a relief to read of the purely personal criminal activities of an Italian migrant – a woman who offered a compatriot the handsome sum of £2,000 to murder her husband. The husband had recently inherited a considerable fortune which would be all hers if he were safely out of the way. The would-be assassin failed in the attempt and the husband, after the first shock had passed, forgave his wife and took her back. A cynical little tale – with a happy ending?

But, although Australia has her troubles with a 'handful' of migrants, she has more than a million and a half post-war European settlers who are a credit to the land of their adoption.

'We ought to go to Canberra,' Elspeth said. 'It's not a long flight. I read an article about it while you were flitting round the Outback. Canberra seems to have everything.'

'It's artificially created,' I said grudgingly. 'A federal capital like Ankara, or Brasilia.'

'Or Washington. That doesn't make it less important. On the contrary. An American landscape expert has said that in a few years' time Canberra will be one of the most beautiful, exciting and dramatic cities in the world.' She added, rather wistfully, 'The trees now will be at their loveliest – autumn gold.'

I knew she was right. I too had read about the tree-lined boulevards of Canberra, its parks and lake, its carefully planned satellites that were to be garden towns on a smaller scale, and, of course, there was that wonderful War Memorial which contained the Japanese suicide midget submarine trapped right inside

Sydney Harbour during the war. Canberra also had Sir Robert Menzies, the septuagenarian Prime Minister who was entering his fifteenth year of office, a controversial character whose personality and drive had added so greatly to his country's stature and helped make her an economic and diplomatic bridge between Asia and the Western World. Already Japan is a more profitable market to Australia than Great Britain.

We really did mean to fly to Canberra, yet somehow we failed to do so. It became part of our 'next time' dream – like the Barrier Reef and the Kimberleys, and Tasmania, and New Zealand.

Instead, we spent a glorious day in the Blue Mountains with Herb Longmuir and his wife and small son. We barbecued steak and sausages on the crest of the world, and, on our way home, we visited a park where the koalas live. These greedy, drowsy little fellows are always literally up a gum tree, looking for all the world, like furry teddy-bears with black patent leather noses.

'The eucalyptus leaves are supposed to contain some sort of soporific,' said Herb. 'So it's cumulative. The more they eat, the more they sleep. A glorious life!'

'That from you – the most energetic of men!'

In a delightful article on koalas by Ellis Troughton I subsequently learned that these enchanting beasts were not seen by Captain Cook and his naturalists in 1770 but remained hidden from European eyes till some thirty years later. They were first described in 1803 in the newly established *Sydney Gazette* by the explorer, Francis Barrallier.

An animal whose species was never before found in the Colony is in possession of His Excellency. When taken it had two pups, one of which died a few days since. . . . The surviving pup generally clings to the back of the mother, or is caressed with a serenity that appears peculiarly characteristic; it has a false belly, like the opossum, and its food consists solely of gum leaves, in the choice of which it is excessively nice.

A few weeks later the *Gazette* printed a letter stating that:

5a Temporary sheep yards near Tammin, Western Australia

5b The author with her grandchildren on board *Winnibelle*

6a Mount Tom Price in the Hamersley Range – 'a mountain of iron ore'

6b The Royal Flying Doctor Service NSW in action

Sergeant Packer of Pitt's Row has in his possession a native animal sometimes since described in your paper, and called by the natives a Koolah. It has two young, has been caught more than a month, and feeds chiefly on gum leaves, but also eats bread soaked in milk and water.

I was charmed to know that my namesake over a century and a half ago had been fortunate enough to own such an adorable marsupial family. No one is as lucky as that now. The rare, cuddly-looking koalas, so like Winnie-the-Pooh, are extremely delicate in their diet and health and can only survive in their leafy reserves, protected and contented, nibbling the sleepy hours away among the young foliage of the treetops. Emus share their park and so do wallabies. The wallabies are sleepy people too, who lie about in the sun with juvenile arms and legs sticking out of mothers' pouches in all directions. Then suddenly a leg twitches and vanishes, a face appears, and Master or Miss Wallaby emerges and blinks at the light with long down-curved eyelashes like sun-awnings.

Herb took us for drives along Sydney's spectacular coast. He showed us the green pastures of Botany Bay with its airfield where gulls mewed and screamed on the heights.

'They're a hazard for the planes,' he said. 'They get sucked into the jets and come out plucked and cooked the other end.'

If that bold mariner, Captain Cook, could come back and re-explore his first landing place how stunned he would be!

I have often admired the statue of Captain Cook outside the Admiralty. Apart from his achievements he was a strikingly handsome man. Its inscription reads:

CAPTAIN JAMES COOK
R.N. F.R.S.
BORN 1728   DIED 1779
CIRCUMNAVIGATOR OF THE GLOBE EXPLORER OF THE PACIFIC OCEAN. HE LAID THE FOUNDATIONS OF THE BRITISH EMPIRE IN AUSTRALIA AND NEW ZEALAND, CHARTED THE SHORES OF NEWFOUNDLAND AND TRAVERSED THE OCEAN GATES OF CANADA BOTH EAST AND WEST.

The statue was unveiled by Prince Arthur of Connaught on behalf of the British Empire League on July 7th, 1914, a few weeks before the great Dominions of Australia and New Zealand were mobilising their forces to help the Mother Country in World War One.

I never guessed when I passed it countless times that I would one day follow in the wake of 'the Father of Australia'.

James Cook was born in Yorkshire in 1728, the son of a farm labourer. But the sea was his dream and the wide world his vision. He was blessed with a first-class brain and the restless inquiring scientific mind which drives the born explorer on and on to some lonely, violent or tragic end. Today, with most of the world's geographic riddles solved, our explorers seek the mysteries of space. Planets are the new worlds of our time. In Captain Cook's day whole continents and island groups were still uncharted, especially in the vast Pacific which was to become his hunting ground and ultimately his grave.

Young Cook educated himself and was given employment in the shipping firm of Walkers of Whitby where his ability ashore and afloat was quickly recognized. When he was twenty-seven he was offered command of one of Walkers' colliers, but he decided to join the Navy instead. The Navy was expanding in preparation for the long tussle with France and promotion was swift. Cook gained a reputation as a mathematician and astronomer and was appointed Marine Surveyor of the Newfoundland and Labrador coast and was with the Fleet at the siege of Quebec. There he was entrusted with the unenviable task of charting the St Lawrence River channel under the noses of the French.

In 1769 the Admiralty sent him to Tahiti in command of the 350-ton *Endeavour* to observe the transit of Venus and carry out other sealed orders. He was accompanied by an assortment of distinguished scientists, including the rich and famous naturalist Joseph Banks, and, in lieu of a photographer, there was Sydney Parkinson, a well-known artist to make a pictorial record of the three year voyage.

The transit of Venus was, in fact, no more significant from Tahiti than from anywhere else, and Cook's orders to sail to the Antarctic Circle in search of a 'temperate southern continent' sent him on a wild goose chase. But his surveys of New Zealand and the east coast of Terra Australis Incognita were most rewarding.

On April 28th, 1770 he put into Sting Ray Harbour, thus named for the fearsome barbed flatfish in its waters. But when Banks and his naturalists went ashore they were so impressed by the variety of exotic plants that it was renamed Botany Bay. The terrain reminded the party of South Wales, so Cook wrote in his log: 'Took possession of the whole eastern coast in the name of New South Wales.' Parkinson painted a pleasing picture of the ceremony. As the aborigines appeared threatening no penetrations inland were made. At the same time, Cook was convinced that this country had great possibilities and would be well worth colonizing. Banks was in complete agreement. If only for this reason, it was probably the most important of Cook's voyages. But the three years at sea took a dreadful toll of life. Scurvy decimated those on board *Endeavour*. The losses included three scientists, the surgeon, four ship's officers and twenty-one of the crew, which, out of a ship's company of eighty, was horrifying but not unusual. Cook swore that never again would his men go short of the vegetables and food that would protect them from this scourge of all seamen. His medical knowledge was good and he made a study of his subject. On his next round-the-world tour in the *Resolution* he lost one man out of 118, due, not to scurvy but to accident. Cook had conquered that dreaded disease for the first time in the history of sail.

In 1787, less than a decade after Cook's death, his attempts to interest his country in colonizing the new continent bore fruit, and plans for a penal settlement in New South Wales were launched. Captain Arthur Phillip, R.N., was selected for the desperately difficult task of putting the enterprise into effect. His convoy, carrying 1,100 people, including 750 convicts, with naval escort and supply ships sailed via the Cape where stores were replenished.

Herb Longmuir took us to a spot overlooking Sydney Cove.

'Phillip took a dim view of Botany Bay as a site, so he brought his shiploads of fearsome settlers here. This was the real beginning of Sydney – and Australia.'

I tried to picture this scene as it must have appeared to that dauntless first Governor, Arthur Phillip. It must have pleased him, for he reported that it was 'the finest harbour in the world in which a thousand sail of the line may ride in perfect security'. He named it for Lord Sydney, the Secretary of State responsible for the expedition. It was somewhere here that he landed his Cape sheep and a herd of Afrikander cattle well suited to life in the scrub. But, sad to say, the cattle soon disappeared. When the stock thief, with a few of his stolen beasts, was found, he was instantly and publicly hanged. Phillip knew only too well that his undisciplined and antisocial community must learn to live off this alien land in which edible meat was rare enough. The shadow of starvation hung over the settlement and the theft of food was ranked with murder as a capital offence. But, though his punishments were 'prompt and terrible', his humanity was respected. He rewarded good behaviour with freedom, and his belief that the settlement could be made to prosper survived even those dreadful early years in which Surgeon Bowes wrote, 'The anarchy and confusion which prevails throughout the camp is roused to such a pitch as not to be equalled, I believe . . . in any other spot upon the globe.' So fine was the influence of Arthur Phillip, leader and visionary, that in time his convicts referred to him as 'our good Governor', and when, four years later, he had to be invalided home, they deplored his departure. The settlement by then was – shakily – on its feet and the possibilities of the new land were becoming known.

Phillip's death in Bath in 1814 has been described as 'inconspicuous' – like his life in retirement. It was ever thus. The pioneers of empire sank into anonymity at home, their 'traveller's tales' wearisome, their incredible achievements beyond the comfortable insular comprehension of their fellow countrymen.

Homes, gardens, shopping centres and new industries have engulfed the wilderness Governor Phillip brought to its first reluctant flower. The words of Emerson haunted me. 'The world is a proud place, peopled with men of positive quality, with heroes and demigods standing round us, who will not let us sleep.'

Modern Australia owes much to the 'men of positive quality' who explored her vast territories, settled her cities, developed her Inland, proved their faith in her future and set her on her feet as a proud progressive nation of growing importance in world affairs.

A few days later, when the sun was shining and the autumn air stinging bright, Herb Longmuir drove me to Mascot airport to meet my son.

Piet had a Medical Conference in Sydney and Elspeth and I had planned our departure from Australia to give us the opportunity of seeing him once more, although it could only be for forty-eight hours. How fast it went – the short time we had together! On our last evening he and I dined alone at the Belvedere Grill while Elspeth went with Kitty Denny to see Margot Fonteyn and Nureyev at the Elizabethan Theatre which presents ballet and opera while the new Opera House is in the process of completion. Cyril and Kitty Denny had flown from Melbourne and it was good to see them again.

'By the way, there's this,' said Piet, taking a letter from his pocket. 'Glen forwarded it to me with some other correspondence. It's for you.'

It was a letter from the President of the West Australian Women's Auxiliary of the Royal Flying Doctor Service – a warm interesting letter which touched me deeply. Mrs Edith Miller had written on behalf of the women of Perth who never forget the needs of the Outback families. It was dated April 27th, 1964.

Dear Lady Packer,

This is written on the eve of my departure for a nine weeks holiday to Japan, but I wanted to say how thrilled all the women were, who work for the Royal Flying Doctor Service, when they read of your quick trip to Wittenoom and your expressed interest in the Service.

Our Western Australian Section has a strong Women's Auxiliary of which Hope Hancock – the wife of Lang Hancock who flew you round the Hamersley – was, until her illness last year, the secretary.

When the Service first started in this section my husband was managing Warrawagine Station – a large sheep and cattle

property at the junction of the Oakover and Mulligan Rivers –
80 miles from Marble Bar and 180 from Port Hedland. It covered
over a million acres and it was here that the first pedal set in
this section was installed. After years of having to use my own
common sense in dosing between 60 and 80 natives and an
average of 18 white men I had the thrill of being able to call up
the doctor when accidents happened. This was our only daily
contact with the outside world as there was only a fortnightly
mail service and we were too far away from any telegraph line
to hook on.

And so, because the whole matter was so dear to my heart
and I had personal knowledge of its wonderful help, I accepted
the Presidency of the Women's Auxiliary when we retired and
came to Perth ten years ago. The women would have liked so
much to meet you and hear your reactions to our Outback and
the Service which we regard as the biggest thing in the lives of
the women so far away from city amenities. I never cease to
admire the way the women down here, the greater number of
whom have never seen our north, work so hard to raise funds
to keep the Service functioning.

I hope that your visit to Australia will be very happy and
that perhaps in the not too distant future we will find a mention
of our Royal Flying Doctor Service in one of your books.

With warmest wishes,
Yours sincerely,
Edith Miller.

That morning, too, I had received a letter from 'Bill' Walker,
the wife of the Flying Doctor, written in all the turmoil of
imminent departure. With sharp clarity she had transported me
back to Broken Hill and the bush. Once again I saw the Drover
with its red cross under the wings and the words of comfort
along its body, Royal Flying Doctor Service NSW – so small in
its vast setting of red plain and high blue sky, so significant, the
symbol of safety, the living spirit of 'Flynn of the Inland', the
padre who had translated God's purpose into terms of practical
compassion.

I took the letter from my bag and passed it across the table to

Piet, who read it under the rose-shaded lamp. The rich red Australian burgundy glowed in our long-stemmed glasses, silver gleamed on the polished oak, a waiter brought us tournedos, rare for Piet and medium for me, with succulent beans, grown, no doubt, in the market garden of some Italian migrant.

As I cut into my tender steak I thought of Innamincka and old Arthur, the stockman, who had fed his ancient horse, Biscuit, too many oats, and of Hamersley in the vacuum of the North-West that would one day be the world's greatest source of iron ore.

'Bill's' letter had taken me back to the bush country and its people – the miners, the graziers, the pastoralists and the boundary riders of the Border Fence.

My dear Joy,

Many thanks for your letter – we were very happy to have been of service to you. We have had a hectic farewell week – it ended on Thursday in the Royal Exchange Hotel, at the West Darling Picnic Racing Club's dinner – with George being presented with a nude tailor's dummy laid out before us on our dinner table, by four 'Outbackers' in Beatle wigs, for operation. This was carried out with George's knife and fork! We began our farewell session yesterday morning, at 8 a.m. at the Base. It was dramatically interrupted at 8.30 a.m. by an urgent medical call – a boy of seventeen had been accidentally shot by a 303 rifle. George was giving medical advice, telling Frank to get blood organized from the hospital, getting Don to order a taxi to collect the blood and get it to the aerodrome, getting Jack to get the engines revved up, and all the time we could hear the reports getting more serious. The boy was unconscious, there was no pulse felt – and so on. However George set off, but the lad died when he was about 15 minutes out of Broken Hill, so he just brought the body back. It was a shocking business – but that is life and death out in the bush.

The network came in again this morning with their good wishes – we have recorded it, and it is a magnificent tape, we wish you could hear it.

Arthur is very well – and sends his 'respectful regards', to put it in his own words. He's sweet, and will be going back soon.

          Our love and best wishes,

                    Yours,

                        Bill and George.

Piet gave 'Bill's' letter back to me, his eyes narrow and thoughtful.

'You've seen more of our country than we have.'

'You've all your lives to discover it.'

He grinned. 'It's very big.'

So big that in 1965 New South Wales was expanding her Royal Flying Doctor Service. Today Broken Hill is the base for two Flying Doctors.

Piet's plane left before ours did the next day. We brought presents for Glen and the boys at the airport. There was a koala for Willie with a 'pup' on its back. He would be asleep when his father returned but he'd wake tomorrow morning to find two new furry friends looking at him with shiny black eyes.

The loudspeakers called the Perth flight and Piet and his fellow passengers straggled on to the tarmac. The sun flashed on whirling propellers. Somebody beside me said, 'There she goes!' and I heard the whine of jet turbines overhead.

I watched the plane out of sight. This was the way of my life. I had long since learned to accept it.

PART TWO

American Crucible

*America is God's crucible, the great Melting-Pot where
all the races of Europe are melting and re-forming.*
                                        ISRAEL ZANGWILL

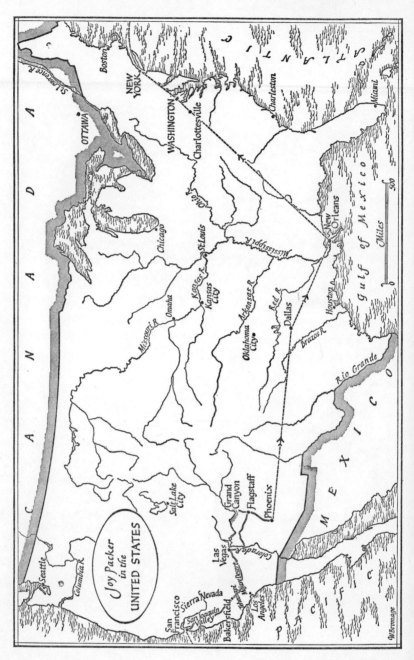

Joy Packer
in the
UNITED STATES

CHAPTER FIFTEEN

Hawaii, Pacific Junction

We fastened our seat belts and I opened my Pan American folder with the excellent relief maps. The red line of our route from Sydney to San Francisco shot across the Pacific for 7,424 miles with a stop at Pago Pago in American Samoa and another at Honolulu, where we were to break our journey for a few days.

As we circled over Sydney that night we looked down upon the jigsaw of the city, spreading in lights from the cliffs to the foothills of the Great Dividing Range, most densely concentrated round the complex land-locked harbour.

'Like grandmother's beaded ball dress,' said Elspeth.

'And the bridge for her tiara.'

Among the yellow diamonds shuttling to and from the city was Herb Longmuir's car. He had brought us to the airport. Our Australian friends had never failed us.

The Captain of the aircraft was saying his piece, welcoming his passengers on board, telling them a tale out of Jules Verne and *Round the World in Eighty Days*.

'It is now 7.45 p.m. Sydney time, May 12th, but, as we will cross the International Date Line between here and Honolulu, we must think of it as 10.45 last night. We will touch down in Pago Pago in about four and a half hours, and we will arrive in Honolulu at 9.00 a.m. yesterday, May 11th.'

Dazed, I looked at my itinerary. But there it was! 'Depart Sydney, Kingsford Smith Airport p.m. May 12th, arrive Honolulu Airport a.m. May 11th (between Sydney and Honolulu cross International Date Line).'

'So last night and today didn't exist,' I said. 'It's the night and day that never was!'

Elspeth laughed. 'Fantasy! Anything could happen in that time. A bright bubble – then nothing!'

But Sydney had been real enough. It was Hawaii that was the bright fantastic bubble, only once reflecting grim reality.

The small first class cabin of our Jet Clipper was for'ard, and from our economy seats we could see the steward pour 'free' champagne into the glasses of those who had paid highly for the privilege. Then he closed the communicating partition and turned off the lights. The tiny blue bulbs glowed in the drumming darkness. Elspeth slept with her head on a little pillow wedged against the window, her long narrow feet resting on her face-case. I tried to follow her example, but I doze uneasily in planes and my mind was full of queer fancies – of twenty-four hours lived in Sydney and lost in limbo, of seagulls plucked and cooked in our searing jets. I thought of nature's birds – so frail compared with man's flying machines – yet so brave, setting off on their great migrations, choosing their mates in one continent, breeding with them in another, stopping to feed here or there in the same way that we stopped to refuel, using air currents and trade winds to cross great oceans, being blown off course by storms and hurricanes, steering by the sun and the stars like the mariners of old, with only a small percentage surviving. The spur for the birds is instinct. For man there are many spurs.

The first human beings to land on the Hawaiian Islands came from the Tahitian Group in the South Pacific eleven centuries ago, driven forth by the age old spur of religious persecution. The fugitives sailed 5,000 miles to the legendary islands in the north. They had only the stars to guide them. In their great canoe with its twin sails they took young women to breed children in the new land, livestock, sugar cane, coconut seeds and other plants, their king, their god and their priest. It was a long and perilous odyssey and the islands to which they came were then uninhabited wilderness aflame with active volcanoes. Yet the settlers survived, others joined them and a happy fruitful life began.

The first white man to sight the Hawaiian Islands was our old friend, Captain Cook. After his two world voyages and many explorations he was unable to settle down at home with his wife and two young sons and a safe shore job at Greenwich. The call of the sea was too strong. By 1776 he was off again in the *Resolution* with the *Discovery* as escort. His orders were to seek the north-west passage between the Pacific and Atlantic Oceans. Incidentally Cook's Sailing Master in the *Resolution* was that tough fellow, William Bligh, whose crew of the *Bounty* mutinied against him in 1789 and set him adrift in the Pacific, and who, in 1805, was appointed Governor of New South Wales, where his soldiers also mutinied and held him prisoner! Cook carried an artist and an astronomer, and also an arkful of live beasts for his South Sea Island friends, including a bull.

He sailed via the Cape, landed most of the livestock at Tahiti, and set off on the same northward tack as the first settlers of Hawaii. The same trade-winds carried him to the same lovely Hawaiian Group which he charted as the Sandwich Islands in honour of his patron, the Earl of Sandwich, who was First Lord of the Admiralty. The friendly handsome natives traded fairly and Cook liked them, but he commented in his log 'they thought they had the right to anything they could lay hands on . . . conduct they soon laid aside'. But not for long! The inquisitive Polynesians were all great 'souvenir hunters' and the possessions of the white men were exciting new toys to them, from compasses to boats.

Cook continued on his northward way towards Alaska. But when the ice of the Bering Strait compelled him to abandon his hopes of finding the north-west passage he returned to Hawaii and the two ships, *Resolution* and *Discovery*, anchored in Kealakekua Bay. The islanders gave the ships an overwhelming welcome due to the fact that the King was under a misapprehension. He believed Cook to be a god. The Captain and his hungry crews feasted on gifts of pork, fowls, fruit and coconuts, and settled down to rest and refit in this delightful winter harbour which provided manna from heaven. But even the gods can outstay their welcome and, after some months, the mood of the islanders changed. On the night of February 13th, 1778 the *Discovery*'s cutter was stolen, and, next day, Cook, who was hot-headed, went ashore with a landing party to take the King hostage till the boat was returned. A fracas developed and Cook was killed by a spear. The white god was only too mortal!

The Hawaiians, when they cooled down, repented. They cremated the gallant Captain with a hero's rites and what little remained of Captain James Cook was taken on board the *Resolution* respectfully wrapped in a cloak of black and white feathers. The relics were buried at sea with a salvo in salute, and the Hawaiian King Terreeoboo mourned 'the loss of a father' with the English crews.

Sixteen years later a Grand Council of Chiefs decided to place themselves and their islands under British protection, but Britain, engaged in her war with France and afraid of over-expansion, did nothing about it, not even when the offer was repeated in a personal letter from King Kamehameha to George IV in 1822. Thus the field was left clear for the American missionaries whose activities shaped the future history of Hawaii.

The narrow rigid Methodist missionaries of New England left Boston in 1821 to convert the happy heathens of Hawaii. Obviously only married men could be selected to work in tropical islands where the women were famed among the whalermen of Massachusetts, and seamen the world over, for their beauty and amiability. The stamina of the zealous missionaries and their wives was almost tested to destruction in the stormy passage through the dangerous Magellan Straits but they reached the Islands and set about their task.

In those days the tall golden girls of Hawaii wore only leaf skirts and *leis* of flowers or shells about their necks, they rode the surf naked, and had the hospitable habit of swimming out to visiting whalers to offer their charms to the eager salts. The missionaries changed all that. The Hawaiians wanted education, and, like many another heathen, they accepted God and garments along with lessons and a certain degree of civilization. The missionary influence was far-reaching and in the course of time the great trading families of Hawaii were founded. Those families, with their roots in New England, were responsible for much of the progress and prosperity of the Islands. As time went by they introduced Chinese, Japanese and Filipino labour for the canefields and pineapple plantations – new human elements that grew and prospered. In 1903, at the request of the Hawaiians, the American flag followed the missionaries and the traders. So did racial intermingling, and today Hawaii is probably the world's best example of a tolerant harmonious multiracial society.

The lights came on in our Clipper, and a few minutes later we were landing at Pago Pago, the capital of American Samoa, our only stop between Sydney and Honolulu.

I had an impression of mountains rising steeply from the sea and the biggest stars I have ever seen. Then we stepped out into the soft air of the tropics. A warm strong wind whispered through the tall palms and the rough thick grass, and, within a very short time, we were back in our places with eighty new passengers to join us. They were wonderfully gay and exotic – the women in printed *muumuus* – shift-type dresses – and the men in short swathed skirts called *lava-lavas*. All of them, men, women and children, wore flower *leis* round their necks and shell necklaces. Every seat was taken and my new companions were a mother and her baby. The baby was sick the moment we took off. The lights were dimmed to blue and we settled down once more to sleep through the second leg of our long flight.

The Samoans were my first experience of the Polynesian type – handsome, intelligent and friendly. The American impact on their lives is dynamic. Education in Samoa has been revolutionized. Television is being used extensively for instruction, and, by means of this new medium, it is reckoned that the backward islanders will catch up in a few years the leeway that would normally take a quarter of a century. Every village has its schoolroom television set and there are teacher training classes by the same method, both in English and in Samoan.

But it was not modern Samoa that permeated my mind as the lights went down and the heavy glistening black eyes of the baby narrowed to slits and finally closed. It was the Samoa of seventy years ago – of Robert Louis Stevenson who ranged the Pacific with the same restless ardour as Captain James Cook had done a century earlier. The teller of tales with a mind unfettered by illness had much in common with the brave seaman who was a humanitarian in a brutal age.

Robert Louis Stevenson was born in Edinburgh in 1805 of well-to-do Scottish parents. All his life he was dogged by tuberculosis and it was during his travels in France in search of health that he met the love of his life, Fanny Osbourne. She was Californian, unhappily married, with two young children, Lloyd and Isobel. Stevenson was frail and not yet famous, earning a precarious living with his writing, but his sparkling intellect, his attractive appearance and a nature, both kind and noble, made him irresistible. Fanny returned to America and obtained a divorce. Stevenson, desperately ill, followed her. She nursed him back to life and they were married in San Francisco on the shores of the great ocean that was to know his name from Tahiti to Hawaii and through the chains of tropical islands so dear to his heart.

When *Treasure Island*, *Kidnapped* and *The Strange Case of Dr Jekyll and Mr Hyde* brought him fame and fortune he chartered a yacht and began the long period of cruising that saved his declining health. Of the many beloved islands Samoa was the dearest. It was home-coming. There, in Vailima among the mountains, he built the mansion he called 'my shining, windy house' and lived happily with his family. Lloyd had become his collaborator and Isobel was his assistant, his widowed mother lived with them, and Fanny was 'at the helm'. In Vailima he enjoyed a measure of health, the love of friends, the devotion of the natives and imperishable success.

In September 1894 he saw his last completed book, *The Ebb Tide*, through the press. A prophetic title. Only three months later he was stricken by a sudden seizure from which he died the same night. Sixty sturdy Samoans, who called him Tusitula – Chief – bore his body up the steep mountain track to his chosen resting place on the summit of Vaea Peak overlooking the ocean he had sailed so often and loved so well. On the headstone was engraved the epitaph he had written himself.

> Under the wide and starry sky,
> Dig the grave and let me lie.
> Glad did I live and gladly die,
>   And I laid me down with a will.

7a 'One-armed bandits' in the Golden Nugget, Las Vegas

7b The chipmunk on the
rim of the Grand Canyon

8a Monticello, the home of Thomas Jefferson in Charlottesville

8b The Kirstenbosch wild garden

Hawaii, Pacific Junction

This be the verse you grave for me:
Here he lies where he longed to be.
Home is the sailor, home from sea,
And the hunter home from the hill.

The mother beside me gently transferred her baby into the carry-cot the stewardess had hooked on to the bulkhead in front of our seats. We could see the waxen brown face of the sleeping child and one little furled hand lying on the light blanket. It was quiet in the plane except for the monotonous drone. I looked out of the window at the burning constellations that winked and trembled as we went our way between the 'wide and starry sky' and the immeasurable Pacific.

Samoa, already far behind us, dreamed in its coral *lei* as we journeyed on into the Northern Hemisphere, across the International Date Line into yesterday.

Honolulu, on the island of Oahu, is the capital of the Hawaiian Group which, in 1959 became the fiftieth State of the United States of America. It is also the great Pacific junction of East and West, playground of the world's millionaires and a vital American military and naval base.

There must be a dark side to such a city, an inevitable hive of dope pedlars and spies, but the face it turns to tourists is brightly angelic, and Elspeth and I were instantly seduced by its sophisticated enchantment.

Our hotel was a rose pink palace on Waikiki Beach within sight of Diamond Head, a headland which is an extinct volcano. In its crater the United States Army has constructed a military arsenal to house both men and munitions.

Nowhere could have been less like the country we had just left than Hawaii. Australia is hard, masculine and challenging, its attitude 'take it or leave it'; Hawaii is feminine, beguiling and frankly out to please. Australia gives you beer out of a can, and Hawaii offers you – at a price – Plantation Punch with a miniature orchid quivering on the sugared rim of the long glass. Waikiki beach is pale gold and palm-fringed, its silky sands washed by courteous waves. The coral reefs, far out, serve as shark barriers and as buffers between the sea and the strand, so that the white-crested rollers surge inshore with ample power to propel cata-marans, outrigger canoes and surf-riders, yet lack the immod-erate violence of Australian and South African breakers. They don't dash their human riders on to the sand in a riot of spray; instead they subside into mild swells at a reasonable distance offshore, as if to allow the swimmers and the children a natural margin of safe, pleasurable bathing unthreatened by collision with surf-boards.

The sunny slopes of the spine of mountains are clothed with tropical vegetation and forests, with cane fields, pineapple planta-tions and groves of banana, pawpaw, ginger, ti trees and, of course, date and coconut palms.

We spent our first morning in lazy relaxation. The bathers' elevator from our floor took us straight to the private walled garden which opened on to the communal beach. Sunbathers lay on the lawn or reclined in garden chairs before wandering down to the sands where the muscular bronze beach-boys taught tourists to surf-ride or how to paddle the outrigger canoes that bring them swooping in on the rollers.

We watched one of the beach-boys teaching a slim girl in a bikini how to stand on her board and keep her balance. She was graceful and quick to learn and even found time to adjust her costume as she rose from her knee to her feet. The tall man with her was having more difficulty, or perhaps his instructor was less interested! Long-sighted Elspeth spotted the identity of the surfers before I did.

'Why, yes, it must be them!' I agreed. 'But she looks so young – like a very pretty little girl.'

We had been reading the *Honolulu Advertiser* in the garden, and the gossip column, called 'Party Line', had informed us of the presence of Lord and Lady Blandford at the Royal Hawaiian Hotel.

Lord Blandford's full name is George Vanderbilt Henry Spencer Churchill. His wife, Tina, is the daughter of shipping magnate Anthony Lovinos and the former wife of Aristotle Onassis whose shipping lines circle the world. They're en route to Japan where she will christen one of her father's ships, a 78,000 ton tanker, which will be named 'Atlantic Princess'.

'One of the Japanese shipyards that'll soon be buying Hamersley ore,' Elspeth suggested.

'And is probably using South African iron right now.' I added.

The same paper told us that Frank Sinatra was making a film on the neighbouring island of Kauai – a war film, 'None But the Brave'.

You sit on the sand near the twisted fuselage of a C-47 transport and watch U.S. 'Marines' and Japanese 'soldiers' playing touch football. They laugh and joke among themselves . . . You are struck by the tremendous irony that twenty years ago the older brothers and uncles and maybe the fathers of these young men were shooting at each other. . . .

'War in Hawaii!' I said. 'It could only be make-believe.'

'That catamaran out there – it takes parties to Pearl Harbour,' said Elspeth. 'That was real enough!'

We waded into the clear sparkling water, gloriously refreshing and not too cold, and swam out over the gentle waves lightly feathered with spray. The outrigger canoe swept past us with its laughing American complement, the young women glossy with oil, glowing with carefully acquired suntan, wearing itsy-bitsy bikinis that were a gay affront to the memory of the first Americans in Hawaii – the straight-laced missionaries who'd striven to persuade the pagan Polynesians that nudity is shameful. How shocked and bewildered they would be if they could come back now, after a century and a half, to find their own people 'going native' with such joyous abandon!

'We must buy muumuus,' said Elspeth, floating on the softly rocking swell. 'Everybody wears muumuus here. I've noticed.'

There are things Elspeth notices much better than I do, so, when it comes to matters like *muumuus*, I follow like a sheep.

'Of course. Where?'

'Anywhere – everywhere. I shall get an A-line. Severe. You can have a frill.'

'No frill. When shall we buy them?'

'This afternoon. I'm going in now. I'm ravenous.'

We had lunch on the terrace. The waitresses were all in long flowered *muumuus* and the guests in short ones. The waitresses looked better because they had the right faces to go with them and wore white cotton Japanese socks with cleft feet to allow the strap of their sandals to pass between the big toe and the next one. They were pretty and heavily made up, and most of them appeared to be a mixture of Polynesian and Asian with a dash of white – a cocktail as intoxicating as any they serve.

'I suppose these muumuus are the Island's version of the original missionary Mother Hubbards,' I suggested.

'Nothing could stay austere and ugly in Hawaii,' said Elspeth. 'Everything develops a different character – a touch of orchid, a taste of nectar.'

She took the little pink orchid from the edge of her glass and sipped her *maitai* with its fragrance of fruit and rum. The orchid rested like a butterfly upon the table. The waitress smiled as she brought us sea food fit for Neptune himself, and when we got up to go she patted Elspeth's arm with a small smooth hand.

'Enjoy yourselves, my dears! Have fun!'

We enjoyed ourselves in the Hilton Hawaiian Village, where you could choose *muumuus* by the score and where Elspeth found the A-line she wanted, and I bought a gaudy cotton sun-dress with a stole to match and a huge hat.

'It'll be a nuisance in the plane,' said Elspeth, with a glance at the hat.

'I'll wear it. That's more than can be said for your Number Three iron!'

That evening the manager of the hotel gave a cocktail party. When we told him how pleasant we found the waitresses with their smiles and charming manners, he said:

'It's genuine, you know. These little things love to please you.'

One of the 'little things' brought us each a Princess Kaiulani punch and presently we found ourselves in conversation with a dark masterful-looking man wearing a light-weight white and red pin-striped dinner jacket, and his elegant tall blonde wife. The Social Hostess had introduced us, and, being American, she

164

had made sure that we knew each others' names. There was the usual cautious foraging that goes on when strangers meet each other without a clue, and, in our case, we could not even claim acquaintance with our host. There is, of course, the usual guide – accent. Professor Higgins would, no doubt, have pin-pointed us, but Robert Murray did better than usual in assessing us as British and, since his ancestors hailed from Scotland and he had served with the R.A.F. in World War Two before his own country had opened hostilities, we were soon on common ground.

The Murrays were well acquainted with Hawaii, and before long we discovered that their home was in San Francisco and that Robert Murray was Head of the Pacific Section of Pan American Airways.

Waikiki at night is something to dream about for ever more. Fairy lights festoon the monster baobab trees, and the paths are lit by torches on crossed stanchions. These are so cleverly hooded that the soft breeze does not blow them out but tosses the living flame hither and thither like the fluttering tail of a golden kite showing the way of the wind. The tall palms reach for the stars, guitars thrum and romantic Hawaiian songs float up from shadowy sea gardens. Somewhere a clock chimes the hour in notes of music.

We dined in the Monarch Room and saw the Polynesian cabaret, polished and brilliantly glamourized. The dancers wore Hawaiian costumes adapted by Hollywood, a throaty-voiced *diseuse* crooned the love songs of the Islands with such temperament that tears stung the eyes of the listeners, and the Polynesian dancers provided exciting contrast with their incredible performance of the *hula hula*. Every muscle of a *hula* girl's body is separately controlled. It dances its own frenetic dance in its turn. Bare stomach and buttocks jerk and gyrate like the body of a snake in the writhing hours of its death, while shoulders, breasts and diaphragm remain immobile. A leg, from knee to thigh ripples in frenzied activity while its flexible brown partner stands quite still as if politely disinterested. Finally the entire body joins in the dance and every muscle is in simultaneous co-ordinated play. Elspeth, who has studied and taught deportment and muscular control, was awestruck.

My bedroom opened on to a little balcony overlooking a far quiet corner of the beach. A very tall date palm was silhouetted against the moon. Doors were all slatted to allow the draught to pass through, there was no mosquito net and no need for one. I lay in bed and listened to the night. Slap of the waves, songs that grew ever sadder as the night advanced, throb of planes coming and going, sleep. Dawn and birds – whistlers, warblers, trillers, chirpers and hooters, the sea heavy in the hour of daybreak and the needly treble of the breeze in the palm fronds. I went to my window and marvelled at the colours of the sea, separate as the muscles of the *hula* girls – jade, coral, violet and cobalt, each with its own current of life and movement. I returned to bed, and presently an amiable waiter brought me breakfast with a luscious pineapple grown in the Garden of Eden. There was a rose beside my coffee cup. The beach and the sea called.

We strolled through the International Market. It would be easy to spend all day and all night there, watching the lazy holiday world go by, sauntering into the various bazaars and watching the side shows. There were *muumuus* galore, *aloha* shirts, many versions of the *kipeka*, a sort of *sarong* in brilliantly figured cotton, and gay little skirts made of *tapa* cloth refined from the beaten bark of the mulberry tree. There are no grass skirts in Hawaii. In the South Seas, maybe, I was told, but in Hawaii, certainly not! The leaf and the bark skirt were the traditional garb till the missionaries introduced the shapeless cambric 'Mother Hubbard' that has finally evolved as the cool, practical and pretty *muumuu*.

You can choose an informal meal according to your fancy in the International Market – Mexican, Italian, Japanese, Chinese, or you can just take a Hot Dog or a Hamburger and sit in the shade and watch the lovely Hawaiian girls and boys engaged in their native crafts, the boys thatching huts with *pili* grass and the girls kneeling on the soft turf plaiting big elliptical ti-leaves for sun hats, or stringing floral *leis*. Every *lei* has its meaning and every island its particular flowers. When night falls you can go to King Kamehameha's Cabaret with the long royal canoe outside it, or watch the Polynesian dancers in the 'Village Hall'.

Next morning we took a motor launch tour round Pearl

Harbour, pitching across the rough open waters of Honolulu bay into the sprawling mushroom-shaped inlet that is now once again a busy naval dockyard. We were shocked by the evidence of treachery and unpreparedness still only too visible in the harbour creeks under the lovely Waianae Range clothed with emerald cane-fields.

All cameras were temporarily confiscated as we entered the harbour, and a guide with a megaphone pointed out hulk after rusty hulk as he told the sad story of the fleet and shore installations destroyed in 1941 by waves of Japanese bombers while the Japanese Envoy in Washington was still engaged in peace parleys between his country and the United States. It was not the first time Japan had jumped the gun. It was thus that Vice Admiral Togo had surprised and paralysed the Russian squadron in Port Arthur on February 8th, 1903 two days before any formal declarations of war.

The Japanese shock plan of December 7th, 1941 had been well thought out and met with no resistance. A task force of thirty-three ships, including six aircraft carriers, took up position two hundred miles north of Oahu and at dawn the first wave of three hundred and fifty-three carrier-based aircraft launched the attack on the unsuspecting U.S. Pacific Fleet in Pearl Harbour. Aerial torpedoes and bombs tore into the helpless warships of a nation still at peace; dockyards, shore installations and airfields were soon ablaze and within hours eighteen ships had been sunk and 3,067 American servicemen had lost their lives. Most tragic of all was the end of the 32,000-ton battleship *Arizona* hit amidships by bombs and an aerial torpedo which plunged down her smoke stack and exploded. A memorial bridge spans the twisted iron casket which still entombs the 1,102 navy men who went down with their ship. (Yet the *Arizona* remains 'in commission', the ghost ship of the Pacific Fleet!) Thirteen of the sunken ships were salvaged in time to take station with the greatest fleet ever assembled in revenge. Retribution was to be complete and final.

I was deeply interested to see the camouflaged United States submarines lying in their berths. It was from this same harbour that the world's first atomic-powered ship, the famous United States nuclear submarine, *Nautilus*, set out on the record-breaking cruise that transformed the north-west passage from an impossible dream into a fantastic reality.

Commander William R. Anderson took the submarine which was his pride and joy out of Pearl Harbour on July 23rd, 1958. Like Captain Cook, two centuries earlier, he sailed under secret orders, with the same objective, and on the same course. But, unlike the *Resolution*, the *Nautilus* had everything. There was no comfort lacking for the crew, no scientific device missing. She could dispense with the guidance of the stars, and, when the seas were rough, she could submerge and travel in her own calm subway with her juke boxes, cinemas, television and many other home comforts, exemplifying the capsule explorations of the mid-twentieth century. Today's explorers can exist in a caul and a climate of their own. Captain Anderson writes of the nuclear heart of his ship with almost mystic respect.

> Our reactor, the powerful source of energy that drove us, gave us light, cooked for us, and shaved us, performed silently and majestically. . . . Ours was a world of supreme faith – faith in instruments, faith in the laws of physics, faith in each other and in Him who guided our destiny in the unknown seas ahead.

Like the *Resolution* she followed the coast of Alaska and entered the narrow Bering Strait which separates North America and Asia, but where Cook had found his way barred by 'a continent of ice rising twelve feet from the water and stretching as far as the eye could see', the *Nautilus* plunged beneath the Polar pack and explored and accurately surveyed the peaks and valleys of the uncharted ocean bed, 'undersea ranges as grotesque as the craters of the moon'.

It is history that the *Nautilus* succeeded in her mission and sailed from the Pacific to the Atlantic across 'the top of the world', thereby earning a Presidential Unit Citation which described her exploit thus:

> . . . During the period, 22 July 1958 to 5 August 1958, U.S.S. Nautilus, the world's first atomic powered ship, added to the list of her achievements by crossing the Arctic Ocean from the

Bering Sea to the Greenland Sea, passing submerged beneath
the geographic North Pole. This voyage opens the possibility
of a new commercial seaway, a Northwest Passage, between
the major oceans of the world. Nuclear powered cargo submarines may, in future, use this route to the advantage of world
trade. . . .

We returned from Pearl Harbour, that cemetery of the sea, in
a thoughtful frame of mind, but Honolulu was in gala mood,
smiling its sweetest *aloha* for the Crown Prince of Japan and his
Princess. Nothing retains its character of cruelty in Hawaii. The
enemy of yesterday is the dear friend of today!

The *Honolulu Star-Bulletin* told us all about the glamorous
young couple who were met that afternoon at the International
Airport by Governor John A. Burns and Mrs Burns, heading a
group of 'dignitaries'. The paper carried a picture of Crown
Prince Akihito, in a Palm Beach suit, and Princess Michiko,
wearing a Japanese kimono as they walked in the garden of the
Royal Hawaiian Hotel. It was accompanied by a glowing article.

Crown Prince Akihito and Princess Michiko, popular symbols
of a 'new Japan' born out of the ashes of defeat, have been
instrumental in winning friends and restoring their nation's
shattered prestige. . . . They've been a tremendous hit wherever
they've visited – even in the Philippines which still harbours
bitter wartime memories of the Japanese Occupation. . . .

Prince Akihito and his wife speak several languages. Their childhood coincided with the American Occupation of their country
and both had a democratic education and are keen on sport.
Akihito travelled extensively and married the girl of his choice,
a commoner, the daughter of a wealthy Tokyo flour miller, a
gesture both romantic and democratic. He is a naturalist with a
special interest in fish and birds, and a keen tennis player – though
his wife is a better one – and he loves poetry. Their four-year-old
son, Hiro, attends a kindergarten. In fact, the claustrophobic
seclusion of the centuries old 'Chrysanthemum screen', which
imprisoned the Sun God Emperors of Japan, has been pierced

169

for ever by the Western influence that followed Japan's defeat.

So, with the tragedy of Pearl Harbour still fresh and vivid in our minds, we watched the people of Hawaii, the fiftieth State of the United States of America, smile and bow before the heir to the Japanese throne and his young wife.

'See how all is forgiven!' said Elspeth. 'Makes one think.'

Next day, as we waited for our car, we had a few minutes in which to watch a lady with an American accent and a Hawaiian assistant giving a lesson in flower decoration on the *lanai* (verandah) of the hotel.

'This little flower lasts very well,' she was saying. 'It fills in nicely when you have a gap needing something white. We call it Star of Bethlehem.'

I looked at the Star of Bethlehem and recognized it. I whispered to Elspeth:

'In South Africa we call it a chincherinchee.'

'Star of Bethlehem is a better name.'

As we prepared to step into the limousine that was to take us to the airport, the hotel porter detained us for a moment so that he might put a *lei* of pink plumeria round our necks.

'Aloha, enjoy yourselves! Happy journey! Come back!'

CHAPTER SIXTEEN

San Francisco, Golden Gate

Although, strictly speaking, we were already in the United States, our luggage was opened and examined before we could leave Honolulu Airport.

'Any shells? Any plants or roots?'

Nothing must be taken out of the Islands that might inadvertently introduce some harmful element into the agricultural mainland. We were travelling on the same plane as the Head of Pan-American, Robert Murray, and his wife, Eleanor, and we were astonished when the contents of her dressing-case came in for a cursory glance. She shrugged her shoulders.

'A necessary precaution, I suppose, though goodness knows we do this flight often enough! California's agriculture is very important.'

We lost two hours the moment we entered the Boeing, so it was 5.30 p.m. San Francisco time as we took off. The Islands lay within the perimeter of their coral reefs, like blossoms cast upon the ocean. Oahu was velvet soft in the afternoon light and the crater of Diamond Head yawned up at us, innocently grass-lined. Yet that extinct volcano could, if need be, disgorge flame and fury once again, only now the fire and thunder it held in its throat was that of man and not of the gods. Diamond Head was an arsenal. The arms of Pearl Harbour, cradling their tragic dead and their virile living, gleamed as they reached into the richly cultivated foothills, and in my heart I said 'aloha', the word that can mean farewell or welcome.

I took off my *lei* and put it on the rack, but the sweet lingering scent of plumeria was with me far into the night when Hawaii was already a memory thousands of miles away. It was nearly midnight when Bob Murray leaned across to tell us that San Francisco was in sight.

San Francisco is on a peninsula and its glamour is reflected and doubled, especially at night. The long bridges flung their arcs of rainbow light across San Francisco Bay where ships, great and small, blinked at the stars and at their own mirrored reflections. The great freeways and railroads raying out into the hills, along the coast and away across the deserts, were glittering threads knotted with incandescent clusters of towns and villages.

We disembarked straight from the Boeing across a covered way into the airport. Bob Murray gave our keys and our baggage checks to an official.

'Your car has been ordered,' he told us. 'We've just time for a nightcap in The Clipper Club.'

We were whisked up to a very attractive Club where the Jet Clippers of today pay homage to the ocean-going Clippers and Cape Horn Windjammers of yesterday when man's only wings were canvas flying before the trade winds to the faraway lands that air traffic has brought so near.

The Murrays very kindly invited us to visit them at their country home.

'A car will be waiting for you at the Mark Hopkins at eleven o'clock the day after tomorrow,' said Bob. 'In the meantime enjoy yourselves!' Delightful advice, easy to follow.

San Francisco, premier port of the Golden State of California, must be the world's most exciting city. Her essence is profoundly feminine. She has the magnetism of a great courtesan with incomparable beauty bestowed by nature and adorned by many lovers. Although she matured in the Gold Rush of the naughty nineties when the Railroad millionaires and Nevada Silver Kings crowned her heights with their palaces, her history really dates back to the sixteenth century.

After the Genoese navigator, Christopher Columbus, under the patronage of Spain, discovered America in 1492, the Pope issued an edict dividing the 'New World' between those two great Catholic maritime powers, Spain and Portugal – the eastern half for Portugal and the west for Spain. By the end of the sixteenth century both participants in the new source of wealth were doing very nicely. Portugal had a string of trading bases on the eastern sea route to China and Japan via the Cape and the Indies, and Spain had established her profitable military empire from the West Indies, across America, throughout Peru and Mexico to the Philippines and beyond. Her great galleons, manned by slave oarsmen, sighted the Californian coast regularly as they plied between Mexico and Manila, but for two centuries they did little about charting it.

Then, in 1577, that dashing Elizabethan Protestant privateer, Sir Francis Drake – who thought nothing of Papal Edicts – went his meteoric way into the Pacific through the Magellan Straits. After a series of highly successful raids along the western seaboard of the Americas he decided to 'go forward to the Islands of the Moluccas and there-hence to sail the course of the Portugales by the Cape of Good Hope . . .' but, finding himself becalmed, he was forced to sail north 'to get a wind'. This wind bore him on towards San Francisco. A vivid description of the coast and its natives is given by one of the ship's company of the *Golden Hind*.

The fifth day of June . . . we found the air so cold, that our men being pinched with the same, complained of the extremity thereof . . . whereupon we thought it best to seek land, and did . . . till we came within thirty-eight degrees towards the line. In which height it pleased God to send us into a fair and good Bay (still called Drake's Bay, near San Francisco) with a good wind to enter the same. In this Bay we anchored the seventeenth of June, and the people of the Country, having their houses close by the water's side, showed themselves unto us, and sent a present to our General (Drake). When they came unto us they greatly wondered at the things which we brought; but our General, according to his natural and accustomed humanity, liberally bestowed on them necessary things to cover their nakedness, whereupon they supposed us to be gods, and would not be persuaded to the contrary. . . .

The Indians, in spite of the cold weather, went naked and their women – 'very obedient and serviceable to their husbands' –

wore loose garments with deer-skin cloaks. So favourably did Drake and his men, and no doubt his gifts, impress the natives that the King implored him to take possession of the country and, says our narrator, sang a joyful song and set a crown upon his head.

> Wherefore in the name, and to the use of her Majesty, he took the sceptre, crown and dignity of the said Country in his hands; wishing that the riches and treasures thereof might so conveniently be transported to the enriching of her kingdom at home.

After these highly satisfactory ceremonies Drake and his followers went inland to the villages in a sort of royal progress, saw huge herds of deer and various strange animals and observed that 'There is no part of earth here to be taken up wherein there is not some special likelihood of gold or silver.' The scribe remarks furthermore that 'It seemeth that the Spaniards hitherto had never been in this part of the country, neither did ever discover the land by many degrees to the Southwards of this place.'

Two centuries later, when Drake and his 'white gods' and their treasure ship had become no more than a legend passed from father to son down the years, the Spaniards decided to occupy California lest the British, the French or the Russians from Alaska get in first and threaten their Mexican border. So one fine day Don Manuel Ayala sailed through the Golden Gate in a Spanish man-of-war and very soon a military and clerical base was established – the Presidio and the Mission Dolores – for that was the pattern of Spanish colonization. The Cross and the Sword went hand in hand and, only too often, the tribunals of the Inquisition followed, though these had no jurisdiction over the Indians.

In exchange for gold, silver, spices, precious stones, tea, tobacco, sugar, cotton, or whatever other commodity it might be, the natives of Spain's dependencies were forcibly fed with Christianity. Thus a chain of Franciscan Missions was presently established in California, where the Indians were taught husbandry, crafts and the proper care of flocks and herds.

But the voices of the French Revolution reverberated throughout the New World, and soon the Indians and Creoles and the Negro slaves of Mexico combined to stage a series of revolts that threw off the yoke of centuries and culminated in Mexico gaining her independence – and California, into the bargain.

Then, in 1846, America and Mexico went to war and two years later Captain John Montgomery of the United States Navy arrived in the warship, *Portsmouth*, and ran up the American flag on the Plaza at San Francisco. It was the year gold was discovered – the year all California went mad.

By the time the 'forty-niners' had surged into San Francisco the Wild West was a law unto itself, for the law of the land – when most it was needed – had ceased to exist. With the coming of peace between the United States and Mexico, Military Law had disappeared, Mexican Law was no longer valid and American Law was not yet enforced. Congress had not decided what to do about the new territory while the world flocked, regardless, into this golden no-man's-land.

It is estimated that in 1849 80,000 men arrived at the coast, half by ship, half overland, and three out of four were Americans. Soldiers deserted wholesale from the Army, sailors left the sea; the lawcourts and churches were empty, merchants abandoned their shops and every man in the country flocked to the foothills in search of a fortune. The only effective law was that imposed by the Vigilantes – the lynch-law of the Wild West.

The Central Pacific Railroad (known today as the Southern Pacific) was built at this period of riotous growth, and a vast Chinese labour force was imported. When the task was completed and the Chinese disbanded they flocked into San Francisco by the thousand and the city, unable to absorb this workless Asiatic invasion, was torn by bitter anti-Yellow agitations. So, one way and another, San Francisco grew up in a constant state of hectic excitement which reached its tragic climax in 1906 when, in a terrifying Act of God, the sea rose, the earth split asunder, palaces tottered into crevasses, and fire raged up and down the hills, reducing the homes of rich and poor to ashes, and leaving a trail of desolation and disease in a city bereft of hospitals and all the amenities of civilization.

In the next half century the new State and the Gold Rush City, chastened by earthquake and fire, settled down. In time San Francisco, fairer than ever, enhanced by new stateliness and dignity, rose again from the holocaust. Her Opera House was the birthplace of the United Nations, and now, mellowed and cultured, she serenely stirs the mixed human elements in her melting-pot. Nowhere, not even New York, has a more exotic brew to pour into the great American crucible!

Take just a few of the newspapers you can buy – Chinese, Japanese, Spanish, French, Greek, German, Italian, Hungarian, Yugoslav and Swedish. And there is an even greater variety of restaurants. You can pray in the churches and temples of West or East, and, from their positions, you will know the second language of the district. The new generations speak American, but the language of the speaker's origin is still part of the voice of San Francisco, whether it emanates from Europe, the Orient or Africa.

The city rises from the Bay in a series of almost perpendicular hills, turreted with skyscrapers and veined with funny little cable-cars that rattle up and down with a cheerful ding-a-ling, ding-a-ling. We stayed at the Mark Hopkins Hotel. The original Mark Hopkins, for whom it was named, was one of the transcontinental railroad Titans, who built his palatial home on the summit of what was called 'Nabobs'' or 'Nob's' Hill.

It was Mrs William Bayless who introduced us to the charms of Chinatown and the Downtown shopping centre. This kind San Franciscan knew South Africa well and loved my country and I believe she enjoyed sharing our appreciation of her city.

Chinatown goes from Grant Avenue, just off Nob's Hill, right down to Fisherman's Wharf.

The little Chinese stores and restaurants cater both for tourists and for the Chinese community and we heard there the jingle of windbells, the whisper of bead curtains and the whine of Oriental music combined with the Occidental juke box. A century ago San Francisco's Chinatown was a place where hunger, unemployment and the hostility of the White citizens drove its denizens into crime. Opium dens, brothels and gambling houses flourished and many evil 'protection' rackets endangered the lives and properties of peaceful people. Now it grows more and more westernized as the American-educated youngsters turn away from the traditional customs of China towards those of the United States.

'But you'll want to see our big stores,' said Mrs Bayless, who knew that every woman loves to go shopping in somebody else's city. 'And the White House has window displays showing the history of San Francisco. You might be interested.'

We certainly were. Elspeth couldn't be dragged away from the Pony Express and the Wells Fargo stage-coach exhibited in one of these informative windows.

'There it is – a real Wells Fargo coach! I always doted on the TV series of Wells Fargo, but somehow I never quite believed in it till now!'

In the History Room of the Modern Wells Fargo Bank you can see the old maps and letters of the Gold Rush days, posters of Wanted Highwaymen, gold nuggets, strong-boxes and the heavy firearms used by the guards of that stage-coach so familiar to television viewers.

San Francisco is a city of temperate climate and morning mists, 'air-conditioned by nature', as Mrs Bayless put it. I'd wake to hear the *moo* of the fog horn from down in the Bay where the water-front clings to her mantle of mist like a lazy woman unwilling to rise and throw off the blanket of the night. But the sun's warm fingers wake her and strip her, and I'd watch the lovely scene emerge from the grey veils of fog into the strong light reflected by the blue of the Bay. At night, when she is clothed in jewelled darkness, San Francisco can be dangerous. I'd hear the sirens of police cars down in the concrete canyons where crime, the night prowler, pounces on its prey. In my many travels I have never heard this sinister banshee voice raised more often than in the small night hours of America's great cities.

I was having breakfast in the big bay window of my bedroom on the nineteenth floor when Elspeth came in. She sat down and helped herself to an orange and began to peel it delicately.

'The Manager sent a basket of fruit to my room too. Enchanting of him.'

'Everybody says "you've come from so far away!" and then they set out to make it worth our while.'

'This morning, while you're scribbling in your note-book, I'm going to fix our car,' Elspeth said. 'There's a Hertz Motor Agency just down the hill. I have all the papers.'

Both Britain and South Africa had a restricted currency for travellers in dollar areas, so Elspeth had arranged that the hire of a car for part of our American journey should be paid for in England, including petrol – which we now learnt to call gas. When she came back an hour later, she looked pleased.

'It's a commodious Chev with an automatic gear shift. Everybody has the automatic here. And if we get a puncture and put the tyre in the boot, we say, when we take it to the garage, "Hi, there's a flat in the trunk!" We must learn this language. Its expressive. Now look!'

She spread a large coloured relief map on the table. If it had been a chart of buried treasure I could not have felt a greater thrill.

'Here's where we are and here's where we go.' Her long index finger with the scarlet filbert nail traced our course. 'San Francisco – and across Bay Bridge which you can see from your window when the mist lifts – the one to Oakland – you driving—'

'You know very well it'll be you driving! a new city, a new car, the automatic neither of us really understands, and right side of the road! That's not for me. Not yet. That's for you.'

'Me driving,' she corrected. 'You taking your turn later on. Then down the San Joaquin Valley to a place called Bakersfield, and somewhere here we cross the Sierra Nevada.'

'What about the Yosemite Valley?'

'I thought that would come up. Your mother went that way when she was nineteen and said it was beautiful. But you've no head for heights. You'd never dare look into the Gorge. Anyway, its north and we're going south.'

'And Death Valley. We could cross here and go into Death Valley—'

'And be baked to a frazzle! Do you know the temperature in Death Valley? No? Well just think of Burke and Wills in Central Australia in mid-summer.'

'So where do we stay our first night?'

'In a motel. Anywhere. Pam and Peter say the whole of America bristles with splendid motels. You take your hooch and they give you ice and a TV for free and you just stop where the spirit moves you.'

Pam and Peter, Elspeth's step-daughter and her husband, who had travelled extensively in America, which they loved, had briefed her thoroughly, and, from now on, these two travelled with us like friendly helpful ghosts. Between them, Pam and Peter had mapped a route for us to follow which included the places we were determined to see, and Elspeth was not to be diverted from their plan.

'Then we cross this Mojave desert to Las Vegas, where we get together with those sweet Folwells we met in Hawaii and they tell us where to lose our dollars at the tables. Then it's quite a short day's run to the Grand Canyon.'

'We haven't booked rooms at the Grand Canyon.'

'You may be sure there'll be a motel. And from there we drive due south to Phoenix, stopping at Flagstaff for a night. Peter says there's a gorgeous little trout fishing valley between Flagstaff and Phoenix. It's a canyon really. At Phoenix we ditch the car – just toss it to the Hertz agent at the airport.'

'Then fly to New Orleans via Dallas, Texas. My goodness, New Orleans is Deep South all right! And the Mississippi – dat Ole Man River! Elspeth, it's terrific, isn't it? The whole thing, I mean.'

'Stupendous. And, after that, we fly to Virginia to see Frances and to New York via Washington.'

'We ought to go to Mexico – Acapulco, and Florida – Miami Beach—'

She folded the map firmly. 'And launch out over the Caribbean, I suppose, by-passing Cuba to say hello to Noel Coward in Jamaica. There's an awful lot of world, my friend. You can't have it all in one bite.'

'Talking of bites, where are we going for lunch today?'

'Peter said Alioto's on Fisherman's Wharf. We take the cable-car.'

179

The cable-car rattled along like a miniature tram and its occupants were of many different complexions and walks of life. They smiled at us because we were obviously foreign and they wanted to make us feel at home. The fat dame squeezed up against me had a swarthy slavonic face and probably originated in Macedonia.

'Your first time in San Francisco? You must wait and watch the grip-man turn our car around at the terminus. Sure is a very neat trick. You from Australia?'

'Yes.'

'Ah, I guessed so the moment I heard you and your friend talking. You can always recognize that accent.'

We were astonished, but we soon got used to being taken for Australians. When we'd explain that we came from England and South Africa respectively the information invariably elicited the same response, 'My, but you're far from home!'

Our track was lined with tall narrow rococo houses so close together that they form light decorative walls on either side of the street. Windows are bay-fronted and every façade is richly embellished. San Francisco loves ornamentation. Even her houses are frilled and lacy for she cannot let one forget that she is, at heart, completely feminine.

On the water-front we duly watched our cable-car whirl round on its turntable and then we strolled along the wharf to the Fish Market outside Alioto's. The catches are sold straight from the sea with huge cauldrons kept at the boil for lobsters and other crustaceans. The vendors are Greek, Italian, Chinese and Portuguese, and there are many Negroes who work on the water-front. It is noisy, picturesque and intensely alive – even unto the freshly caught fish flopping on the marble slabs and the lobsters wandering about till they are rudely popped in the pot.

Alioto's has a wonderful view of the Golden Gate bridge, and, while we ate our seafood lunch, we gazed across the water to that thin span, or down into the crowded lock where yachts and powered fishing boats come and go. Our waiter was German and his colleague hailed from Yugoslavia. But they might equally well have been French, Italian or Hungarian. The clientele was varied and affluent. There were tourists, like ourselves, and San

Franciscans too – the sort who would go to the ski slopes of
Squaw Valley in winter and to the Lakes for summer week-ends.
San Francisco is no oasis. Her surroundings are as lovely as she
is herself.

CHAPTER SEVENTEEN

American Freeway

The fog horn had given way to chiming church bells and the Sunday morning sun was primrose soft as we bowled along the freeway in the limousine Bob Murray had sent for us. The countryside where our hosts lived was a residential area centred upon a golf course and a country club which had once been the mansion of one of California's famous millionaires.

Although California is a young State she has grown up with a legend of splendour which is all-pervasive. We found it in Robert and Eleanor Murray's lovely home set in spacious grounds shaded by exotic shrubs and tall trees. As we sauntered across the lawn to the swimming-bath with its own summer-house, changing rooms and little cocktail bar, Eleanor told us that she ran the place with a Swiss couple. Chinese and Japanese are no longer permitted to flock into California from their own countries in search of work and, in any case, the younger generation either follow their fathers by owning laundries and shops or aspire to some more ambitious place in the community.

I have always wondered what 'the height of luxury' really means. Gold-plated bathroom fittings? A cocktail cabinet masquerading as a library of specially bound classics? A remote control record-player that makes all its own arrangements at the touch of a button? A hearth-rug of golden seal? No, none of these, I decided. In the Murray's garden I came to the conclusion that 'the height of luxury' meant a full-sized outdoor swimming-bath warmed to any temperature you might require.

'It can be cold in California,' smiled Eleanor. 'And it's good to swim in any weather.'

I thought of those tough Australians who bounded into the waves at Cottesloe, summer and winter, and agreed with her.

Friends of our hosts joined us and later we all went to the Country Club and had drinks on the sunny terrace and afterwards lunched superbly in a lofty perfectly-proportioned dining-room. Our new acquaintances showed us the kindest hospitality and insisted that Bob and Eleanor bring us to their home after lunch. No one would hear of our going back to San Francisco, and, by sundowner time, quite a number of people were re-organizing our schedule for us.

'Oh, not the dreary desert! The Californian coast is indescribably beautiful! You *must* go that way.'

Someone found a road map. 'Look, it's not much out of your way – a mere couple of hundred miles, perhaps a little more. You really *ought* to stay a night at Santa Barbara. There's a divine hotel there overlooking the sea.'

'There's Pebble Beach and—'

'We'd have to make a reservation—'

'That's no problem.' Bob Murray reached for the telephone. 'And then, when you get to New Orleans, you must meet our friends, the Wisdoms; you'll love the Wisdoms.'

Everything happened in minutes. We heard him booking a suite overlooking the sea and then he was calling New Orleans two thousand miles away!

'Long distance calls no trouble, no fuss,' I said to Elspeth when we were back in our hotel that night. 'You're connected with any place right away. Instantly. That's how telephones *should* work. No wonder Americans think nothing of calling the ends of the earth!'

She nodded, but something was on her mind.

'Look,' she said. 'We've got to undo all that stuff about Santa Barbara and Pebble Beach. We allowed ourselves to be rushed.'

'But don't you think it's a good idea.'

'Not in the time at our disposal. We don't want to pitch up at Las Vegas like dead dogs about two in the morning, and that's what'll happen if we do this coast run. Nor do we want another smart hotel where we've got to dress up tomorrow night. We want to do as Peter and Pam suggested – cross this desert and stop at a simple motel on the way to Las Vegas.'

'What about Hollywood and Sunset Boulevard and all that?'

'We considered that in Hawaii and decided against it. We can't do everything.'

'There's a bank designed like a gigantic birdcage, and a magnificent university—'

'And film stars' homes by the score. I'm sorry. It isn't on.'

I realized that the spirit of Peter was breathing down Elspeth's neck. She'd made up her mind not to be deflected and the momentary lapse must be put right.

'Suits me.' I was relieved to stop vacillating. 'But we're booked—'

She flashed her eyes and lifted the receiver.

'As Bob says, that's no problem.'

She asked for Santa Barbara.

'But it's the middle of the night!' I protested.

'This is America,' she said with great satisfaction. She had an affinity with America. From the moment she had stepped from the Boeing on to the Mainland she had felt herself at home.

Elspeth and I are both punctual, which, from now on, was a mercy. The tempo of our Australian visit had, on the whole, been leisurely, whereas our journey across America was governed by a time table and certain key reservations that had already been made in London. By nine next morning our commodious Chev had arrived and was ready to take the road. Our luggage had been stowed, Elspeth had been once round the block with the Hertz driver 'to get the feel of the automatic', we had heard again those pleasant words 'Enjoy your journey! Come back!' and we were on our way. I was navigator.

America's great highways and freeways are exemplary – if you know your way. If not, an ambiguous signpost can side-track you, and, once in the city you've intended to by-pass, the way back on to the freeway is fraught with tribulation for the stranger.

Somewhere on or after the long Bay Bridge we took the wrong turning and found ourselves in the heart of Oakland.

'This is a city we'll remember,' said Elspeth, when I'd brought her back to the same point three times. 'We can forget about Las Vegas and the Grand Canyon and just stooge around here and

184

keep coming back to the Town Hall. It's a splendid Town Hall.'

But at last we wormed our way out of the maze and Elspeth, now fully conversant with our car and safely back on the freeway, put her foot down and made up for lost time. I let the map rest on my lap and relaxed. We had been going for some time when a particularly large signpost informed us that we were only a few miles from Sacramento. As navigator, I felt rather winded.

'Hold it, Elspeth! We're going north instead of south.'

'Since when?'

'Since the start. Since Oakland.' She stopped the car and lit a cigarette. Her gloved hands gently took the map from me.

'Sacramento! A lovely name. True enough, we're going the wrong way.'

She turned the Chev without reproach and drew in at the next coffee stall.

'I've always longed for a real American Hamburger. After this you take on.'

I found the Hamburger greasy, and the automatic drive surprisingly abrupt. When I put my foot on the brake Elspeth shot into the windscreen like a cannon ball.

'You're awfully good,' I said. 'You haven't complained once.'

'It builds up inside.' But she was laughing, her eyes moist. 'You had us on the right road, when all's said and done.'

'Like catching the right bus going the wrong way.'

'Do you realize where you were heading?' She tapped the map. 'Sacramento.'

'*And* the Yosemite Valley. Your old Mum's ghost was prodding you.'

My old Mum's ghost hadn't a chance against the potent spirit of our absent friends, Peter and Pam.

'Here we are at Modesto,' said Elspeth. 'Practically where we started from. This time we really are on our way.'

After that I braked with respect for my passenger and we settled down to enjoy the run through the San Joaquin Valley. The rolling green hills gave way to an agricultural plain with vineyards, olive and orange groves, fruit orchards and acres of cotton. Near Bakersfield we found ourselves in an industrial area. Then oil rigs and refineries etched their gaunt silhouettes against the evening sky.

'It's time we found a motel,' said Elspeth. 'But not here. We want somewhere beautiful.'

So we began the ascent of the Sierra Nevada which grew more beautiful with every winding curve. Blossom clothed the slopes, cattle grazed in rich pasturage, and the roseate glow of sunset touched the peaks and flooded the valleys. Two centuries ago the Franciscan monk, Padre Francisco Garcés, had blazed this trail in his 2,000 mile trek from San Xavier Mission in Sonora, Mexico, to the San Joaquin Valley. Those zealous missionaries of old were brave, resourceful and practical explorers. They never lacked secular support and their missions prospered. Nowadays the Southern Pacific and Sante Fe Railroads follow his path over the Tehachapi Pass on their transcontinental journeys to the Californian coast. During the building of the railroad, gold had been discovered near Tehachapi and many of the Chinese labourers had found subsequent work in the diggings.

'Tehachapi – this is it,' I said. 'This is the night stop we've been looking for!'

'The Ranch House Motel. Looks fun. Shall we give it a go?'

'Let's!'

We were 4,000 feet above sea level and the mountain air was icy cold. A week ago Tehachapi had been under snow. Now the plumes of peach, pear, almond and cherry blossom glimmered among oaks and firs. In the gardens of holiday chalets English may and lilac nodded and blossom was feathery above clumps of crocuses, cyclamens, daffodils and narcissi.

'You know something,' said Elspeth. 'It's Spring!'

'And in Perth it's Autumn – the Fall.'

'As they always tell us, we've come a long way.'

The Ranch House Motel offered its patrons clean comfortable rooms each with a bath, television, an electric jug for making tea or coffee and an ice bucket. There was a slot machine outside for cool drinks. It was, like most motels, unlicensed and situated on the highway – in this case, right opposite the Railway Station. We gazed in awe and delight as breath-taking trains rested or shunted – the Pacific Fruit Express with its colossal locomotive and refrigerated trucks, the all silver Santa Fe transcontinental with a silver crest, and a blue and gold Southern Pacific passenger train.

'They're riveting,' said Elspeth. 'But I'm not sure if we want them on our doorstep.'

'I doubt if anything could keep me awake!' But I did the night traffic an injustice.

Tehachapi, with its invigorating mountain air, offers its visitors fishing, ski-ing, riding and deer-stalking. Its name derives from the Indian for 'plenty of acorns and good water'. The acorns, we found, were concentrated mainly in a charming oak park and in avenues just coming into young leaf. A lovely little green building bore the crest of the Sheriff of Kern County and a young policeman emerged looking like a character from a Wild West film and gave us a friendly greeting.

We dined in a small restaurant recommended by the Motel Manager and all the types there were in fancy costume too, with tight denims, wide-brimmed cowboy hats and short plaid jackets in loud colours. We tucked into juicy steaks and Elspeth looked round with approval.

'What price that hotel over the sea at Santa Barbara?'

'This is right up my street.'

We soon found that there was a great deal else right up our street. American heavy traffic moves at night, and enormous Diesel trucks with funnels thundered up the mountain road unceasingly.

'Their lights are glorious,' I said, as we strolled back to the Ranch House Motel. 'Four in front and six each side! I've never seen anything to beat it!'

Elspeth, who is not a very good sleeper, was silent.

The trains said 'tring tring' all night, the trucks blew their horns as they rumbled round the bend, the motel trembled, and in the dawn a hundred birds sang madrigals to the Spring and to each other. We breakfasted at a Snack Bar and, while Elspeth smoked her first cigarette of the day, I drove. She was firm with me when a crossroads offered us Los Angeles on our right and Death Valley on our left.

'Forget Hollywood and the death wish,' she said. 'We're going to Barstow.'

'It's an ugly name.'

'It's probably an ugly place, but it's on the way to Las Vegas.'

We passed a lilac grove and a white cement-producing mountain and found ourselves in a strange golden landscape. The pale mountains were devoid of vegetation save for cacti, and large notices told us to 'Watch out for rocks'.

Elspeth was sorry to leave agricultural California, as her stepdaughter and son-in-law had been very much with us there. Peter is a manufacturer of high grade British agricultural machinery and Elspeth scanned every field and orchard for evidence of his products. When she discovered one of his tractors she was jubilant and when she saw a plough rusting in a dump she mourned.

'That's Peter's! They *never* wear out. What can have happened to it?'

She had missed her vocation. She ought to have been in charge of the Sales Department. She is the only truly elegant woman I know who can wax lyrical over a muck-spreader. She had practically sold one to Herb Longmuir in Australia when we were halfway up the Blue Mountains before Herb came to earth and realized that Peter's muck-spreader was not what he needed in his quarter acre plot.

When we reached the borax deposits of the Mojave Desert Elspeth perked up.

'I've shares in those,' she said.

'What's borax for?'

'But everything! It's extremely fundamental!'

'Ah, yes, infants—'

'That's the least of it. It is used in glass making, welding, all sorts of things.'

I could never have believed that any desert could be as busy as the Mojave. After the vast empty spaces of the Outback this desert seemed packed with people and things. We were interested to find notices imposing speed limits. '60 m.p.h. by day. 55 by night.' There were truck weigh-in-bays at regular intervals and drive-ins with notices outside them 'Ten-inch dogs. Broiled burgers.' Entire houses on wheels – not caravans, but complete prefabs – travelled along the highway bound for some destination where humans would instantly convert them into homes; United States military vehicles of every variety roared across the parchment scene straddled by columns of giant pylons. The blanched sky above us was criss-crossed with the white vapour trails of military jets and the light was pitiless. Never, not even in Australia – that land of high skies and baking sun – have I been so acutely aware of light pouring down from infinity with nothing to break its blinding impact.

We passed a U.S. Air Force camp and the turn off to the Rocket Base.

'Quite a thing to have a desert to play with,' I said.

'Like the Nullarbor – with Woomera. But poor old Europe has to go to other continents for her nuclear experiments.'

'Not all of Europe. Not Russia.'

'No, Russia has her Steppes and she has a foot in Asia. She is one up on Britain and France.'

'And, in some ways, on America? Or not?'

'Wait for the show-down,' said Elspeth.

We shivered although it was growing hotter by the minute as we descended into the burning plain.

CHAPTER EIGHTEEN

Sagebrush and Touch of Satan

The moment you cross the Californian border into Nevada you get the form. The Border Road House blazons it forth with a dashing sign. '*Hot Dogs. Gambling. Never Shut.*' The heart of it all is, of course, Las Vegas.

Nevada, the Sagebrush State, is a territory of deserts and high snow-capped mountains and of horses, cattle, sheep and pigs. Since the sky is blue all the year round and the rainfall scanty, agriculture depends upon artificial irrigation, but hay and grain do well.

Until 1859 Nevada was really only the highway for the American overlanders – many of them leaving dust-bowl areas to chase California's newly discovered gold. Then, suddenly Nevada had her own silver and gold bonanza. Apart from silver, gold, lead-zinc, turquoise, manganese, tungsten and other minerals she produces quicksilver and arsenic. A more artificial source of revenue is gambling. Reno and Las Vegas are fashionable divorce and remarriage cities as well as gambling holiday resorts. Six weeks' residence suffices for a Nevada divorce. Reno and Las Vegas are wonderfully gay. The end of a marriage is sad. Make it fun! Executions too are said to be painless in this cynical little State. An odourless lethal gas takes care of criminals.

The first white man ever recorded in the sagebrush plain, so good for grazing, was that same indefatigable monk, Francisco Garcés, who, in 1776 had crossed the southern corner of Nevada in the course of his long trek from Mexico to north California by way of Tehachapi. The first settlers were Mormons from Utah.

Here, nearer the Mexican border, the Spanish influence of Latin America seemed more potent. It was no longer the Ranch Motel but El Rancho we saw at the roadside. Notices were often bi-lingual – English and Spanish – and Mexican food was the speciality of restaurant drive-ins.

How powerful the influence of Europe has been! Down the centuries and throughout the world, she imposed her will upon the indigenous peoples of other continents, conquering, converting, exploiting and, if necessary, destroying them. The long greedy arms of the Old World reached across sea and land, sowing the seed of Christian civilization from a cornucopia filled with good and evil. It is strange and wonderful today to contemplate the plants that have sprung from that seed – whole nations, transformed and conditioned by the continents of their growth. Americans, Canadians, Australians, New Zealanders and South Africans are a few of the different families of the same parent – Europe.

Among those who suffered most from Europe's invasion of the New World were the Red Indians. Those early Spaniards, so eager to give the natives God in exchange for gold, introduced a terrible invisible killer into the lands they conquered. The villain was venereal disease which proved deadly to people who had hitherto never known it. Gunpowder only carried on the work of decimation.

Today the survivors of the Red Indian tribes are protected, existing in their own reserves. In Nevada we saw their arid territories fenced for long miles.

The United States Indian Reserves are administered by the Bureau of Indian Affairs and whites cannot buy land there without official sanction. This measure prevents exploitation of the Indians. They receive free education and have the franchise – if they care to exercise it. Individuals who feel that they have outgrown tribal existence can live and work wherever they please and marry as they wish. They are free. But those who wish to compete successfully in the white jungle require an aggressive temperament and an intellectual capacity not characteristic of their people. Out of three hundred original tribes only one ever evolved a written language. Once they were a threat, now they are a responsibility. The covered wagons of America's pioneers represented the last phase of Europe's long drawn out occupation of their land. The Indians, by then, knew better than to mistake the pale-faced invaders for gods; they sang no 'joyful songs' to welcome them; they preferred to scalp them. America's early history is an epic of warfare, and the westerns that thrill men, women and children on the world's screens are only tiny slivers of the long turbulent history of a nation that has fought continuously for the possession and expansion of its chosen territory, for the independence of its people and for the principles of freedom.

We stopped for a snack at a drive-in and Elspeth read the list with hungry anticipation.

'What splendid sandwiches! Ham, turkey and cheese, one dollar; turkey on rye, cole slaw, Russian dressing, ninety cents – I'm mad on cole slaw! De luxe cheeseburger and sesame roll, seventy five; tuna salad or liver wurst, sixty five; melted American cheese, fifty. With onion ten cents extra.'

We went on soon after midday. The desert heat and merciless light attacked us with dizzy ferocity. I groaned.

'Mad dogs and Englishmen! Pity Noel Coward isn't at Las Vegas. Really, Elspeth, I think we ought to swop this car for one that's air-conditioned.'

'It won't be so bad tomorrow,' she said tautly. 'We climb again tomorrow.'

I knew she hated the heat. When she plays golf in summer she walks round with a little sunshade and puts it up between shots, yet in this oven she didn't grouse, just went rather quiet. I stole a glance at her profile and thought she'd make a good model for Lot's wife – pale and carved out of salt – or cement or borax. I wondered if she felt the heat more or less than I did? This infinitude of light should surely reveal one person to another. Or did it simply pass through the outer casing of a human being like X-rays, significant only to the initiated who can read the signs? One could become very fanciful in the desert. A bit light-headed. The black highway turned to water and distant ranges stood with their feet in lakes of mirage, withdrawn and remote, behind curtains of shimmering lavender gauze.

'We're getting near,' said Elspeth. 'Look at that!' A huge hoarding announced that the fashionable place for wedding receptions was 'The Little Chapel of the Flowers'.

9 Sydney Harbour from the north

10a The black sands of Honaunau on the Big Island of Hawaii are made by the surf pulverizing lava into minute particles

10b Cablecars in San Francisco

'That's what Las Vegas is in aid of,' she added. 'The quick change-over.'

It was then, I think, that the evil of Las Vegas leaned out and touched me lightly. From now on monster hoardings bordered the highway and broke the golden monotony, yet were in themselves monotonous. 'Tropicana. Folies Bergere Casino.' 'Riviera Hotel. Casino. Tony Martin – Cyd Charisse 8.15 and midnite.' 'Casino. Danny Kaye 8.15 and midnite.' Familiar faces of show people leapt from tawdry posters into the pale glare side by side with the names of the glittering hotels along the famous Strip. Downtown Casinos and gambling houses beckoned their eager victims.

There it was at last! A tinsel gauntlet flung onto the sand at the feet of fate. The lifeline down the palm of this grasping gauntlet is the Strip, where every building is an ultra-modern hotel or motel with its own pool, Casino and floor show. The Casinos are never closed.

Why should anyone come to Las Vegas? There are a number of reasons. It's on the way to other places, a desert junction, a night stop with a difference. Las Vegas welcomes the visitor with open arms and caters for human frailty. It is coldly calculating. It'll give you a good time and take your money, it'll sever your marriage, break your heart, tie a new knot and wait mockingly for your return. All hotel rooms are doubles, one person signs, no questions asked. Everything goes. Wear what you like, do what you like, nobody worries.

Mr and Mrs Paul Folwell, whom we'd met in Hawaii, had booked us in at the Sands Hotel on that famous Strip. We arrived in the afternoon and Elspeth was driving, so I went in to check our accommodation. I shall never forget the curious cold shock of that entrance. Yet it was commonplace enough in Las Vegas.

I walked straight from the fiery desert air and the purity of immeasurable light into the cool air-conditioned gloom of a lobby that was like no other hotel lobby I had ever seen. It was not a place where people met and chatted and wandered through to other reception rooms. It was a Casino. On the right was the reception bureau; on the left a regiment of fruit machines – the 'one-armed bandits' – glowed in the semi-darkness. The bar backed the gaming tables, roulette, chemin de fer, vingt-et-un. Over each a single harsh light concentrated its beam on the spin of the wheel or the turn of a card. There was no glamour of Monte Carlo here, no chant of the deep-voiced croupiers 'Onze, noir, impair et manque . . . messieurs, faites vos jeux, rien ne vas plus.' These croupiers wore eye-shades, their faces were blank and bloodless, they did not speak. Why should they? You could see the winning number, no need to call it. Get on with the game! They moved with mechanical rhythm – flick of the wheel, sweep of the rake, flick of the wheel. Dull-eyed men and women loitered round the tables.

A glass door near the reception desk swung open and a young woman entered and walked straight to the roulette table. Outside was the swimming-pool. No need to warm the water in Las Vegas! The young woman wore a bikini. She leaned forward to put a counter on zero. The croupier's pallid face was expressionless. I wondered if he'd have blinked under that eye-shade if she'd forgotten to put on the bikini. A bald man in bathing trunks with a grey fur rug on his chest was playing the slot-machines. Crack, rattle! One vomited into its tray. He gathered his coins and padded, bare-foot, back to the garden and the pool.

I went out to the car with the bellhop and the key to our rooms.

'We're in the garden block,' I said to Elspeth.

'You took your time to find that out.'

'Wait till you go into that lobby! It holds you.'

The bellhop told us which way to drive to our annexe in the garden near the lido-blue pool. He trundled round to meet us in one of the little motor-trolleys that serve the various blocks and took our bags to our rooms, which were large and air-conditioned. Mine had mulberry walls, a plushy carpet and heavy woven curtains in an abstract design. There was a large abstract picture on the wall over the huge double divan. It seemed to say, with derision, 'Make what you like of me! I couldn't care less!'

There were face tissues and a jug of iced water in the bathroom. There always are in American hotels. I flung myself on to the enormous bed and slept for two hours. We met our friends, Paul and Aileen Folwell, in that crepuscular bar and then dined at the

Tropicana where we saw a lavish spectacle – scores of gorgeous girls, clad only in fig leaves, and a charming man whose perform-ing dog – a real shaggy dog – refused steadily to do anything he was told. The usual act in reverse. The moment the show was over the diners were expected to disperse like an audience after the first showing of a film, and the tables were rapidly cleared in readiness for the next session. There was no intimate night club act about this. It was theatre while you eat in the stalls. No time was lost between courses either. Get on with the act! Get on with the meal! Time is money in Las Vegas. If possible, do two things at once. Afterwards we went Downtown with the Folwells. The streets blazed with neon signs. 'A Jackpot every 27 seconds!' Everything was open all night. The Casinos, the shops, the bars, the cafés and the chemists. Strike it lucky at the Golden Nugget or some other joint and spend your winnings fast! The 'bandits' are so densely massed in the gambling houses that there is only room for the victim to confront his chosen robot and pull that one iron arm.

'I'm going to the vingty table,' said Aileen, as we went in to the Golden Nugget. Paul, who had a new toy – an extra special camera – wanted to take photographs of the Downtown scene. Elspeth went with him and I foolishly settled down to a session at roulette. Hours later, when Elspeth appeared at my elbow to 'drag me away', she had no difficulty. I was cleaned right out.

'But you had a pile of chips when last I looked in on you! Did you cash some in?'

'Just as I was going to do that thing a man came round with drinks on the house. I went on playing.'

Outside, the desert night was gloriously fresh and dry. The fading stars were small, innocent and comfortably stationary above the gold, green and blood-red lights whirling and blazing along the Strip and in the crowded Downtown alleys.

'It'll be dawn soon,' I sighed. 'What time do you think we ought to leave tomorrow?'

'Around ten thirty.'

'Are we going right through to the Grand Canyon?'

'Let's see how we go.'

We said good night to the Folwells and made a plan to meet

again in New York. Aileen Folwell was going to fly to Salt Lake City next day to see her sister and Paul was returning direct to New York. We should have included Utah, I thought, as I turned out my bedside light. Pity to miss the Mormon State. How greedy could one become? The spirit of Las Vegas was infectious. Miss nothing! It's later than you know.

CHAPTER NINETEEN

Grand Canyon

We left the tawdry Strip of one-armed bandits, triple zeroes and silent croupiers and drove north-east in the clean morning desert sun.

After Boulder City and the Hoover Dam, where the peacock-blue Colorado River is harnessed between its black volcanic cliffs and man-made locks, we passed into the State of Arizona, a scene as desolate as Sturt's Stony Desert in Central Australia. It was indeed the arid zone, with heat striking off the polished rocks and pebbles as if from a mighty anvil. But after a while we came to open plains with sparse grazing – the land of Indian Reservations and great ranches, of far horizons and distant tumbled snow-crowned peaks.

As we headed due north towards the upland plateau of Grand Canyon National Park the air cooled and sweetened until in the late afternoon we entered the forested Park on the South Rim.

I had been tired and cross all day, unreasonably irritated with Las Vegas, which was, after all, exactly what it purported to be – one great gamble with cinema stars as entertainers and quick divorce as a source of revenue – and I was furious with myself for joining the multitude of suckers on whom it feeds and fattens.

'I don't see a trace of this Canyon,' I said, 'and we must be right on top of it. I wonder if it's going to disappoint us.'

Elspeth took off her dark glasses and I put them into her bag for her. She had relaxed the moment she drove our car into the fragrant pine and juniper woods. Dappled shade is her element, like the deer who live in the Canyon forests.

'Pam says nobody can be disappointed in the Canyon and nobody can describe it.'

A signpost indicated the way to our destination, Grand

Canyon Village, and a viewpoint turn-off. She took the way to the viewpoint.

'We're nearly there. The Village can wait.'

One of the strange things about the Grand Canyon is the shock of seeing it for the first time. It doesn't show itself gradually. It appears suddenly and impressively with the awe-inspiring impact of a revelation. Wherever it meets you it finds you unprepared. Only when you have walked to its brink do you see it.

We emerged from the sheltered woodland glade into the full radiance of a scene of breath-taking splendour. We left the car and stood by a rough stone parapet right on the lip of the mighty crevasse a mile deep and ten miles wide and gazed across to the North Rim and mountain ranges bathed in jewelled colour. Rose, topaz, amethyst, aquamarine and coral glowed in remote majesty.

I drank in the unspoilt beauty of the great distant vista, knowing that when my eyes and being were saturated there was still the Canyon, the true heart of this unearthly revelation. I am afraid of heights but at last I dared to look down, down, down, thousands of feet into the remote past, to the desert floor that was a sea bed before the first life stirred; and, as I looked, there was no more fear or vertigo, there was only wonder.

The golden evening poured its rays into the Canyon, gleaming on the fast flowing Colorado River, a thin green snake winding its tortuous way between peaks and buttes soaring from the depths, every plane and facet bathed in pastel hues, ethereal and sublime. Those eagle-haunted minarets and towering temples, wrought by nature's violent hand and the waves of seas before the memory of man, have been Sacred Places from time immemorial. Here in the Canyon prehistoric man was aware of God. He turned his face to the life-giving sun and worshipped earth's great ancestor.

The silence and solitude were absolute. Even the torrent of the raging turbulent river was mute, for sound is dispersed and lost in the great gorge. We too were speechless. Weariness and irritation had no place here. Time ceased to exist. The world with its load of tragedy and triviality fell away. What was a lifetime or a century or even a millennium here where thousands of billions of years have recorded the passing mutations for science to read and decipher!

For an instant, in that mystic hour of sunset, I touched the fringe of the infinite. All the human turmoil and suffering of the present was swallowed in the ageless past and the far future, when life, as we know it, will vanish into oblivion, leaving only a fossil trace in the rock of time. And perhaps, in the void, the echo of some human voice will linger on after man, with all his sound and fury, is dust, when thought is the sole language and love the only power.

As twilight filled the Canyon the rocky sanctuaries of the ancients blurred and melted and the ranges across the great silent rift darkened against the sky. A night-jar – or a bat – winged past us and broke the spell. We shivered as we returned to the car, for night on the wilderness plateau is cold. Nocturnal animals were stirring, and in the trees an owl hooted. The dusk was palpable, a chill violet substance cut by our headlights.

It is estimated that seven thousand tourists pass through Grand Canyon Village in a day. Historians, philosophers, scientists, naturalists and many others come to the high lonely wilderness plateau among the deserts and mountains of Northern Arizona. They come for many reasons – as students, as pilgrims in search of a great spiritual experience, or out of interest or curiosity. It is a long way to come – even for most Americans.

The Canyon is not the result of any single cataclysm. If it were, it would have little to tell save one dramatic tale. It has evolved, as life has, down the ages and it has recorded every phase of its long story. It is the world's most formidable example of erosion. The long fierce Colorado River, bearing sand and silt, rocks and boulders, cut the first gradual cleft in the earth's slowly rising crust as it raced from the high northern mountains on its journey to the Gulf of California. Melting mountain snows, torrential rains, landslides, and tributaries wore away its banks down millions of years, steadily widening, deepening and lengthening a vast fissure 278 miles long and a labyrinth of smaller canyons.

From the blazing desert floor to the high cool plateau the Canyon walls and peaks escalate in natural steps and gradients, each with its own climate and the fauna and flora of its level. Rattlesnakes and gila monsters crawl in the hot desert dust among weird succulents, and black archaean rocks – the oldest known to geologists – while up on the South Rim the gentle deer browse among the evergreens, and raccoons and squirrels scamper along ledges where the Alpine flowers nod in the breeze. On the higher North Rim, deep in snow and impassable for many months of the year, arctic foxes and skunks and animals of snow-bound lands live in aspen woods and fir forests. Even the squirrels on each Rim are of different clans, for the animals cannot intermingle. The Canyon is the mighty moat which only the birds can span. No wild creature would attempt the long descent into the heat belt, the dangerous river crossing and precipitous ascent on the other side.

Today man, the most inquisitive and enterprising of all beasts, achieves the Canyon traverse. He follows precarious mule tracks into the depths, and Havasupai Indians, who know every inch of their desert valley, guide him. There is a bridge over the Colorado and there is Phantom Ranch, an inn with a pool for those travellers who brave the journey. It is a journey, they say, equal to a trek from Northern Mexico to Southern Canada, measured not in miles but in changes of climate, vegetation and wild life! To scientists and biologists every step of the way is rewarding. In the mosaic of brilliant pebbles on the Canyon floor, in crags and buttresses, in layers of rock, they can read messages from prehistory. There are fossils of sea plants and shells, of fish, frogs and salamanders long since extinct, and of ferns that grew milleniums after ancient seas receded. There are the cliff caves and the ruined irrigation systems of the first red men who inhabited the area thousands of years ago before the later Indian tribes came to the plateau from the deserts, before the trappers and Spanish missions brought death or God to the Canyon's Rim.

Tourism in America's National Parks is well organized. Grand Canyon Village on the South Rim, the terminus of the Sante Fe Railroad, has two hotels on the lip of the Canyon. There are trailer parks and camping sites and a luxury motel in the woods called Yavapai Lodge. The Visitors' Center gives the tourist any information he may require; there are daily lectures by Park Rangers in the little Museum with its mammoth telescopes trained on Canyon views; there are camp-fire jamborees and every afternoon the Hopi Indians dance outside the Hopi House with much ado and beating of drums. There are organized excursions and many trails to follow into the hidden places of this wondrous spot.

We left our bags and our car at Yavapai Lodge and strolled through the darkening pineland paths to the Bright Angel Restaurant where we ate our dinner above the starlit abyss. The restaurant was crowded; there were cases of souvenirs in the hall, Indian trinkets of turquoise and silver, woven cloth, basketwork and leatherwork. We were sleepy after the long day, overwhelmed by the awesome magnitude of our surroundings. For the first time we felt that we had indeed 'come a long way'. Moreover, we both realized that we had not allowed ourselves long enough here and that a tight schedule of bookings ahead would not permit us to extend our stay of three days.

After dinner we put on our coats and went onto the terrace. We sat on the parapet with the gulf yawning below, its fantastic peaks rising from the fathomless sea of night, their heads faintly touched with starlight.

'Imagine the first white man to discover this – like Livingstone and the Victoria Falls.'

'It was centuries before Livingstone,' said Elspeth. 'Yet, to the Canyon, that first white face was yesterday.'

'Yesterday' was the year 1540. The Spanish conquest of Mexico was complete. That cruel, ruthless and remarkable General, Hernando Cortes, had destroyed the power of Montezuma II, the Aztec Emperor, by uniting his enemies against him; the treasures of the Aztec civilization were loot for Spain and the heathen population were souls to be saved; the Army and the Church had taken possession. By 1539 the Franciscan Friar, Marcos de Niza, was exploring Arizona, reconnoitring the wealth of its Indian *pueblos* and a trail for future missions, and in the following year Coronado, the great Spanish explorer of the American south-west, sent a party north to search for gold and silver in the mountains. Don Lopez de Cardenas, the leader, and his little band of soldiers crossed the wilderness plateau only to find themselves, hungry and exhausted, on the brink of the 'Great Gorge' beyond which they could not go. It must have seemed to them that they had arrived at the world's end – an impassable rift.

Three hundred years went by. The Franciscan Missions had become the beads of a rosary over the face of the land, but when Mexico fought and won her War of Independence against Spain their influence was broken. Mexico's less successful war with America followed and Arizona was one of the territories ceded to the United States in the uneasy peace of 1848. But settlement in the newly gained south-west was slowed down by the Civil War and it was not until 1869 that the Grand Canyon was seriously explored. In that year Major John Wesley Powell, a one-armed Civil War hero, took his boats a thousand miles down the Colorado Rapids. 'Every waking hour passed in the Grand Canyon has been one of toil. Ever before us has been an unknown danger, heavier than immediate peril,' he wrote.

Since then adventurers and scientists have been lured by the 'Great Gorge'. At the turn of the century tourism was already established and in 1904 the Sante Fe railway crawled to the South Rim. President Theodore Roosevelt visited the Canyon and described it as 'The one great sight every American should see.' He declared it a National Monument and in 1919 an Act of Congress made Grand Canyon National Park a reality.

I have no doubt that there were thousands of other visitors at the Canyon when we were there, for the hotels and trailer parks were full, but somehow the immensity of the place absorbed them into its profound peace. Yavapai Lodge in its woods was strangely quiet. I fell asleep instantly and was wakened in the morning by soft leaf-filtered sunshine and muted bird-calls.

After breakfast at the Bright Angel we sat on the South Rim in the morning light. Other people drifted here and there quietly, enjoying the majestic ever-changing glory of the scene. Swallows darted and swooped over the abyss with twittering abandon.

'They're green!' I said. 'Not blue.'

'There's blue if you want it!'

Elspeth indicated a jay in the shrubs on the lip of the Canyon. Or perhaps it was a Western bluebird. I wished we had an ornithologist with us. Robins and woodpeckers I recognized, and high overhead buzzards wheeled slowly.

'There's somebody I don't know!' I pointed to the ledge. 'So pretty, but who is he?'

Elspeth had her camera out, and a little girl sitting near me on the wall, said:

'That's a chipmunk. Don't you know chipmunks?'

'I come from South Africa,' I said. 'I know elephants, giraffes, rhinos, hippos and lions, but not chipmunks.'

He was tiny and grey with bright eyes and a bushy tail, no bigger than a large rat, and presently his girl friend joined him. They had the quick movement of squirrels, but less jerky, and they were not at all timid. They were used to the well-meaning humans who came to sit on the low stone wall and who often brought bread or nuts to feed the birds and little animals. Down in the Canyon we could see a string of mules descending the narrow paths and ledges to the desert floor. We watched them enviously.

'Once I could never have resisted that! Now I couldn't look at it.'

'Know your limitations!' said Elspeth gently.

'I do – but I don't accept them gladly.'

We spent our time more prosaically, discovering viewpoints each more magnificent than the last, listening to the short informative Rangers' talks on the Canyon's evolution, its life zones past and present.

Down on the desert floor about two hundred Havasupai farm their subtropical valley, tan leather, make baskets and guide visitors. Up on the Rim about four thousand Hopis live in their cliff-top *pueblos* (communal dwellings) much as their ancestors did in the days when the first pale-face appeared in their wilderness. But the biggest of all the American Indian Reservations are those of some 80,000 Navajos spreading over 15,000 square miles from the Canyon into the surrounding deserts.

We said farewell to Grand Canyon National Park at its eastern entrance, stopping to look our last at that mighty abyss from the Watchtower at Desert View. Far below us the Canyon flattened out into the boundless parchment waste of the Painted Desert, streaked and daubed with lemon and lavender, sage and glowing coral, broken by breast-shaped hills and angular ridges with the snow-capped San Francisco Peaks rising 12,670 feet above the plain.

It was no wonder, I thought, that the American astronauts would train for their final moon-probe in this terrain of plains and ranges, craters and crevasses steeped in solitude and grandeur, dwarfing man to the insignificance of a transient alien. The essence of the Canyon is this strange sense of timelessness, not blank but eloquent with the message of its great wound. Erosion has been nature's archeologist, excavating the past, layer by layer, down the ages and through prehistory to the genesis of earth herself.

On the Canyon's lip we had learned that we were nothing – less than a grain of dust or a note of music in the wastes of time. We were humbled and exalted in the face of a great truth.

Our destination for the night was Flagstaff, an attractive holiday resort in the heart of Arizona's best preserved Indian ruins and within easy access to the ski-runs of the San Francisco Peaks.

We followed the Little Canyon route to Cameron in the Navajo territory of the Painted Desert, where we stopped for lunch and petrol. Even here, out in the blue, petrol was cheap. When we told the young man in charge of the pump that we'd have to pay nearly three dollars for four gallons in England he made a show of fainting.

'Gee! How do you people live over there? It's a wonder you aren't all on bicycles!'

We had lunch in a restaurant like a miniature mud fortress. There was a shady patio and I would have liked a beer, but beer, combined with the somnolent desert heat, would hardly have been conducive to attentive driving and it was my turn at the wheel. Across the way was the trading post which reminded me of the general stores you'd find in any South African Bantu reserve. The same hot sleepy atmosphere with folk sitting outside in the verandah shade, oblivious of time, only these people were less dark-skinned and their inky hair was straight and coarse, framing flat Mongolian features, and, instead of blankets and beads, they wore velvet blouses, full skirts and silver and turquoise ornaments. Inside the store you could buy anything from a pin to a saddle, and, as in South Africa, the shoppers never hurried, though they knew what they wanted. The place was pervaded by a curious musty smell of incense, tobacco, hot human beings and heavy clothes that had never known the wash tub.

We made several detours that afternoon to see various *pueblos*, the primitive mud tenements of the medieval Indians who had once inhabited these foothills. How simple and unimpressive was the mark they had left upon their land compared with the churches and castles of their contemporary builders in Europe! And, while they lived here in peace, their life-rhythm broken only by acts of God – volcanic eruptions and the terrible drought that ultimately drove them south – those distant dangerous Europeans were preparing for the great trans-Atlantic voyages of exploration that were to lead to the white conquest of the whole American Continent.

Flagstaff was cool, green and pretty, and we stayed at one of the many motels that line the highway. Take your choice. They all supply travellers' luxuries as if these were necessities. Face tissues in the bathroom, cool drinks in slot machines on the corner of the verandah by the crushed ice refrigerator from which you help yourself, television in every room. Next day was our last on the road. We were due at Phoenix that evening, ready to fly to New Orleans the following morning.

Flagstaff to Phoenix was a drive full of interest. We set off through the beautiful Oak Creek Canyon, a narrow valley threaded by a fast clear little river. Except for its towering walls of rose-red rock just visible between the young leaves of oaks and chestnuts and the darker foliage of firs, it might have been England even unto the lilac blooming in the garden of an anglers' inn. We left the car and took a forest path to the river's bank and strolled along it past an artificial pool where freshly caught trout swam, unconscious of their doom.

'Wouldn't Ronnie and Daphne love this!' said Elspeth, whose friends are always meandering about in the back of her mind, waiting for some small association to bring them forward. 'It's their sort of river – and trout for breakfast!'

As we went farther along the path we saw a notice board on a shelflike part of the bank.

'This section reserved for the physically handicapped.'

Elspeth pointed to a little stone wall. 'To prevent wheel-chairs going over the edge. Rather touching.'

There were no fishermen that day. Not a soul was at the water's edge. At a sylvan bend I paused.

'Shall we stay here an hour or two and just enjoy all this? Relax and reflect.'

'Why not, it's glorious. The Grand Canyon was too stupendous, it made one restless. Here one can belong and think.'

She walked on and left me. I sat on a flat boulder at the edge of the stream. The woods smelt cool and fresh, the young leaves, laced by clear gold sunlight, danced, and the stream chuckled. A little bird sang a solo, all trills, that was part of a woodland symphony. I reflected that my friend could always surprise me. I had not thought of the Grand Canyon as being 'too stupendous' or of feeling 'restless' in its presence, but suddenly I knew what she meant. It absorbed individuals into itself. One was engulfed and drowned, no longer a separate personality. I had succumbed willingly. Perhaps she had resisted. Awe and a sense of total insignificance don't necessarily make for a comfortable frame of mind. Here one could indeed 'belong'. Here was the familiar charm of glade and leaf-mould, of running water, shining pebbles, a myriad shifting lights and shadows and the living gleam of trout to lure the gentle liar who whiles away the summer hours with rod and line, sitting on a river bank, wearing an ancient hat, its band stuck with fragile tempting flies.

As we travelled south the trees thinned and nature's red rock towers became more formidable, and presently, in the hot Verde Valley, we turned into Beaver Creek to Montezuma's Castle, a most astonishing example of the medieval cliff-dwellers' *pueblo*.

This five-storeyed communal dwelling with twenty rooms, that once accommodated some two hundred people, was carved high out of the coral and pearly-pink limestone cliff. It was approached by hairpin steps and little ladders, and birds flew gaily in and out of the rooms without walls. The lovely Arizona sycamores shaded the valley and wild flowers bloomed at the foot of the cliff. The red-skinned people who had lived in this safe easily-defended *pueblo* perched above their fields were a sedentary agricultural community and their collective home was their fortress. The name, Montezuma's Castle, is only connected with Mexico's Aztec Emperor because it was originally believed that at one stage the *pueblo* was occupied by refugees fleeing north from the Spanish conquest.

The daily lives of this vanished tribe are depicted in the small museum near the *pueblo* and also the flora and fauna of the area. I was fascinated by a gila monster and a sordid-looking brown rattlesnake, while Elspeth studied the plants and their properties.

'This yellow daisy we've admired all the way – it's a creosote bush and they used its resin as gum. And these thin flexible yucca leaves served as thread, and the juniper bark made torches. This was their home-grown tobacco and they ate mealies.'

Their bows and arrows and their stone implements intrigued us, so did their cotton cloth, their turquoise and shell ornaments and their red clay pottery. We were reluctant to move on.

Once the Verde Valley and the creeks were behind us we made swift time along Highway 64 through a flowering desert of rosy rocks and clumps of tall yellow bushes in happy contrast to aloes of all sorts with their deformed limbs and spiky thorns sprouting clusters of weird unlovely blooms.

'They've got some tough place names around here!' said Elspeth. 'What about this one? Dead Man's Wash!'

We had already passed Bloody Basin Road, Horsethief Basin, Black Canyon and Squaw Valley.

'Just to give you an idea what used to go on,' I said.

'Cowboys and Indians – the land of the cattle rustler and the stage-coach – part of the Wild West.'

She was right enough, for Arizona was, in fact, one of the last States to enter the Union and only achieved her full Statehood in 1912.

The blazing afternoon sun was low when we reached the agricultural outskirts of Phoenix, the capital, a spreading modern city with ranch-type homes in residential garden areas that seemed like part of an oasis in the golden desert glare. There was a swimming-pool at the Sky Riders' Hotel near the airport where we stayed the night, for summer temperatures top the century day after day, but the winter climate is ideal and many visitors go to Phoenix in search of health in the dry bright desert air, sunny by day and cold at night. The city is cosmopolitan with a high proportion of Mexicans, for it is only two hundred miles from the Mexican border.

We had a swim before dinner and turned in early. The lonely world of the Grand Canyon seemed incredibly distant and dreamlike. It really might have been the moon.

11a The Mojave Desert – the mountains in the background have been
shaped by wind erosion

11b A ghost town in Nevada

12a The French Quarter in New Orleans

12b Washington from the air

CHAPTER TWENTY

The Deep South

The Hertz Motors Phoenix Representative, pretty and smiling in her smart uniform, took over our dusty car at the airport and checked the mileage.

'Twelve hundred miles, and the gas to be charged in London with the bill. Did you enjoy your journey?'

Elspeth gave her the duplicates of the petrol coupons we had been using.

'Loved it. We only wish we could have gone farther and taken longer.'

Soon we were deep in conversation about America, Australia, England and South Africa. Whatever business we had to do, whether it was getting our air tickets, checking baggage or even paying our hotel bill, involved a friendly chat. Everybody was amiable and nobody was in a hurry. We were intrigued by the names of the airlines marked up on a big board. Apache, Frontier, Western, Bonanza, America, Continental and Transworld. At Dallas, Texas, we were to change from our American jet into a Delta.

From the air we looked down upon the draught-board of Phoenix, chequered by agriculture. The city was young and modern and prided itself upon its contemporary appearance and outlook. Yet I found myself recalling the controversial case of the Phoenix housewife, attractive dark-eyed Sherry Finkbine, whose picture had made the front page of the world's news when she had tried and failed to get a legal abortion in the State of Arizona. She was one of the few American expectant mothers who had taken the drug thalidomide and, with thousands of tragic examples of limbless thalidomide infants being born in Europe, she had determined not to risk bringing another cruelly crippled child into a world difficult enough for the physically sound. She and her husband had flown to Sweden where good sense prevailed and the operation was performed and Sherry was told that her child would indeed have been one of the victims of the drug. Since then she has added a fine normal baby girl to her family.

Soon the prairies of Texas were gold beneath us, the home territory of the famous Texas King Ranch which has such a flourishing offshoot in north Western Australia. But more valuable than cattle and grain is Texas oil. From the day oil was struck at Spindletop in 1901 the power and importance of Texas was assured. The giant had been born with all his mighty potentialities for good and evil.

We alighted on Love Field, Dallas, in the ruthless glare of noonday. The thermometer stood at ninety-five in the shade. We had an hour to wait and we spent most of the time in the observation-room.

We were aware of a new atmosphere here, something we had not yet encountered. The voices over the loudspeaker sounded warm and lazy.

'The Southern drawl – light brown velvet. And those hats!'

I followed Elspeth's admiring gaze to the straw 'pork pies' and 'ten gallon' Stetsons worn by tall rangy Texans with a swagger to their walk. A great many coloured people were among the crowds meeting and seeing off friends, or simply watching the come and go of the planes through the plate glass wall of the observation-room, as we were doing. The women were heavily made up, jaunty and defiant in tight-fitting dresses and stiletto heels. The men looked surly. I fancied too that a sinister aura still clung about the name of Dallas – the shadow of murder, the memory of noon on Friday, November 22nd, 1963.

Months had passed since then, yet the most tragic, dramatic and world-shattering assassination in history had gone curiously unexplained and unavenged.

President John F. Kennedy, brave, forceful, brilliant and much-loved, was assassinated in this Southern city on a goodwill tour. His motorcade was passing through the crowded streets of Dallas at noon on that crisp sunny November day when he was shot in an open car with his wife, Jacqueline, beside him, accompanied by Governor and Mrs Connally. The hidden sniper's bullet struck President Kennedy in the head and the same fusillade wounded Governor Connally. Jackie Kennedy cried, 'Oh, no! Oh, no!' and cradled the bloodied head of her dying husband as he was rushed to Parklands Hospital. Within an hour the United States had lost a young dynamic President whose sincere desire for world peace had inspired hope in countless millions all over the globe. The world reeled in shock and horror. It mourned a saviour and it mourned a man – the husband of a beautiful woman, whose dignity and control in the face of disaster were to command universal admiration, and the father of two little children, six-year-old Caroline and three-year-old John, who were both to celebrate their birthdays in the following tragic week.

Lee H. Oswald, an ex-Communist, ex-U.S. Marine, was arrested the same day, and forty-eight hours later he too was shot. His murderer, Jack Ruby, drew a gun and killed him at Police Headquarters in full view of the police and millions of television viewers when he was about to be transferred from Police Headquarters to prison. Ruby was apprehended and alleged to be 'unbalanced'. Little more was heard of the case and the world was left to draw its own extremely varied conclusions.

The second act of the Kennedy tragedy was performed here on Love Field in the huge White House Boeing 707 in which President Kennedy had flown 75,682 miles. An hour after his death, his successor, the fifty-five-year-old Texan Vice-President, Lyndon B. Johnson, was sworn in by United States District Judge Sarah T. Hughes in the presence of as many of the White House representatives as could crowd into the big drawing-room of the Boeing. Among them was Jackie Kennedy, dazed and dry-eyed, while Judge Sarah Hughes wept as she administered the oath. Immediately after the ceremony the great plane took off for Washington, bearing the living and the illustrious dead.

America's President Johnson was born and bred in Texas. His ancestors fought Indians and Mexicans, and the place he loves most is his ranch in the hill country of his home State. Like Kennedy, he served in the U.S. Navy during the war, and afterwards devoted himself entirely to politics. There is nothing

he doesn't know about that tough unscrupulous game. But the
task ahead of him transcends politics. It is a heavy burden de-
manding experience and inspiration. In this dangerous nuclear
age the world looks to America's President to keep the peace.

When we resumed our journey I noticed a small reminder of
ancient conquests – the influence of Spain to the west and France
to the east of the frontier State of Texas. The brown paper bag
protruding from the pouch of the seat in front of me, like a stiff
inanimate baby marsupial, announced its purpose in three languages. 'For motion sickness. Pour mal de mer, Para el mareo.
After use fold toward you. Despriés de uso doble hacia usted.'
Soon New Orleans and the Mississippi were beneath us.

Though all America was exciting to Elspeth and me, this was
the part of our transcontinental journey that we had expected
would most belong to the realm of romance and fiction, of 'Show
Boat' and Negro spirituals, but there were sombre overtones in
the picture, for New Orleans cannot shake off the dark shadows
of her past or the menace of her present.

On the afternoon of our arrival we walked down Canal Street
to the banks of the wide grey-green Mississippi River with its
paddle-steamers, barges, flat-boats and miles of warehouses. This
'Ole Man River' carried its cargoes of furs, hides, lumber, sugar,
bananas, rice and cotton from the high snows of Central America
to the Gulf of Mexico. The last lap of its journey through the
Southern States is hot and steamy, past swamps where the cotton-
mouths crawl and the tattered fringe of Spanish moss festoons
the live oaks like widow's weeds. Willows weep in the labyrinth
of *bayous* – fresh water creeks and salt sea inlets – that criss-cross
the Mississippi basin. Cypress marshes, that once bred yellow
fever, have now been drained to create the beauty of Lake Pont-
chartrain.

Towards the end of May the cool breeze of the Gulf of Mexico
tires by the time it reaches New Orleans, and we found the heat
and humidity trying, but the city is well adapted to its climate.
Offices, shops, hotels, many private houses and even cars are
air-conditioned, and the men look cool in Palm Beach suits and
the women in cottons. They are very cosmopolitan. In the Vieux

Carré we heard Italian, French and Spanish spoken as freely as English.

How charming that old French quarter is! A long ago architectural jewel reset among the skyscrapers of young America. Outside the white houses, with their exquisite wrought-iron grilles and balconies, old-fashioned carriages with sleepy horses wait to take visitors clop-clopping through the narrow sunny streets to world renowned restaurants and antique shops. Here the Creoles held sway in the days when those proud descendants of the first settlers from France and Spain ruled the city in an aristocratic *cabala*. Now they too are in the Crucible, being rendered down to make good Americans of the future.

New Orleans is not really an old city by European standards – about two and a half centuries – but she is old in experience. Adventure, war, high delight and deep suffering have marked her tempestuous history. She lies on the old Spanish trail between California and Florida, and was named by the French Governor of Louisiana after the Duke of Orleans. She was born of Europe's famous mercantile system, which granted Royal Charters to trading companies in many distant territories, thus forming the basis of settlements and colonies. John Law's famous Trading Company had received its charter from France, and in 1722 this marshy spot on the Mississippi, sixty miles north of the Gulf of Mexico, became the capital of Louisiana. What a 'capital' it was then! Some five hundred inhabitants housed in cypress cabins separated from one another by swampy pools swarming with reptiles! A few years later things looked up. The Jesuits arrived, so did Capuchin monks and Ursuline nuns, and, better still, a cargo of 'good girls' to make good wives to the settlers. The industrious Jesuits cultivated the soil. They grew myrtle for wax, oranges, sugar-cane, figs and indigo, but when New Orleans was ceded to Spain in 1762 – much to the fury of the inhabitants – the Jesuits were sent packing and their excellent plantations were confiscated in the name of the King of Spain.

At the beginning of the nineteenth century Louisiana was restored to France, only to be immediately occupied by America under the terms of the Louisiana Purchase. France was a useful ally to America in her War against England, though France's own star was waning. So, in 1815, the year of Waterloo, it happened that the last battle of the American War of Independence was fought in New Orleans. General Andrew Jackson and his American forces defeated the English under the command of General Packenham.

But even then, peace was a word with little more meaning than it has today. Indian attacks, skirmishes with smugglers and pirates, epidemics of cholera and yellow fever, floods, fire, the arrival of slaves and of mulattoes from the West Indies, and of enterprising German, Italian, French, Irish and English settlers kept the rapidly growing port in a ferment for the next few decades. In the Civil War it became a Confederate stronghold and was once again the scene of battle when it was captured and occupied by Northern Union Forces in 1862. The victorious Republican Congress then decreed that the Southern States must be regarded as conquered territory, reconstructed and admitted to the Union. The period of 'reconstruction' was total chaos, and many American sagas like *Gone with the Wind* have told the terrible tale. All Negroes were emancipated, enfranchised and secured in employment, while white men were virtually deprived of the ballot by the restrictions placed upon its exercise. The citizens of New Orleans formed a 'White League' to restore white supremacy. Thus the seeds of future discord were well and truly sown.

The tables keep turning. Today the Negroes have the franchise but many subtle obstacles prevent them from exercising their right. Undeterred, the Federal machine of integration quickens its pace and enforces its intentions.

Friends of Peter and Pam flew from Mobile in the adjoining State of Alabama to meet Elspeth, and we did the fashionable things. Breakfast at Brennan's in the Vieux Carré – at eleven o'clock, with wonderful eggs and waffles and a 'hair of the dog' while tall palms cast their shade on the patio's creeper-covered walls – and lunch at Antoine's, the unique restaurant that has passed from father to son through generations. Its atmosphere is Edwardian and the walls of its many private rooms, used for special dinner parties, are papered with the photographs of the high and mighty. All the most famous faces of close on a century are there, expressing their signed approval of Monsieur Antoine's art – Kings and Queens, Eastern potentates, writers and artists of renown, stars of stage and screen and of course the gilded members of the international set which trails its restless glitter through our time as Las Vegas flaunts its neon-lighted Strip in the waste of the silent desert.

We took a streetcar to Audubon Park and rattled and clanged along the wide avenues of the Garden District where the spacious old colonial mansions with high pillared porches are set back in tropical gardens ablaze with flowering shrubs and shaded by splendid magnolias in full bloom. Once these were the city homes of wealthy plantation owners with slaves to do their bidding, now most of them are converted into hotels or clubs or are used for non-residential purposes.

But a few private homes still exist in the beautiful Garden District and maintain the standard of hospitality and gracious living that was the traditional hallmark of the South. Such a home belonged to Judge John Minor Wisdom and his wife, Bonny, the friends Bob Murray had telephoned about us that Sunday afternoon in San Francisco.

The evening we dined with them was memorable. From the moment the Negro butler ushered us into the lofty drawing-room with tall French windows opening on to a magnolia-screened patio, it seemed to me that we stepped into the past – a past that held nostalgic echoes of a way of life fast vanishing here, and also in my own home province, the wine-growing Cape. In the Cape you may find it still, but it is a survival – and we all know it – just as it is in the Deep South where the old customs are going with the wind of change.

Long gilt-framed French mirrors reflected the diffused light of crystal chandeliers and the quick flash of a cocktail shaker as our hostess mixed a dry martini and our host talked to us, smiling and relaxed. I thought he looked very young for a man of so many responsibilities. Judge Wisdom, a Southerner, was a Judge of the Federal Court of Appeals in New Orleans, where it was his formidable duty to ensure the enforcement of the integration laws of the United States – laws repugnant to most whites in the Southern States, where racial segregation is deeply ingrained.

Twelve of us went into the spacious dining-room with silver candelabra gleaming on the polished table, the candle-flames steady in the air-conditioned room. A coloured maid served a dinner worthy of Antoine himself, and the butler filled our glasses with the wines of France. Those who served were dignified and expressionless, and I wondered if they too were apprehensive about the long hot summer of discontent that held the South in its feverish grip.

We were joined later by Kit, the daughter of the house, who had been out with the Pony Club and was still in her riding clothes. She was a slim lovely girl who had been Queen of the Mardi Gras celebrations, an honour which carries much the same distinction as being the 'deb of the year' in a London season. Kit had all the Southern passion for horses and had studied equine history from its earliest beginnings. We hated leaving that hospitable house and it was long after midnight when we returned to our hotel.

But happy as our evening had been, we could not fail to be aware of the tension of the times. A troubled frown had creased the Judge's forehead when I had asked him if the practice as well as the principle of integration could be peacefully accomplished.

'There will be bloodshed and violence,' he said frankly, 'but ultimately we will succeed.'

'It's South Africa's problem in reverse,' I said to Elspeth, afterwards. 'Here the Federal Government causes strife by forcing racial integration on the people, and at home our Government imposes rigid apartheid, which causes trouble too. It's a running fight either way, with roots deep in prejudice.'

'And with flowers of hate and fear. Nice thought!'

When she had gone to her room I stood at my window, staring down at the lights of New Orleans. The brightest loom hung over Bourbon Street with its cabarets and its streetcar named Desire. Where did it carry its passengers? There were many answers. Desire has a thousand forms. Desire for freedom, for dignity, for the chance to grow. I thought of Kit and her generation that is so full of courage and the will to help the underdog. Seek the reformers among the students! It is ever thus. Even now seven hundred students from various northern universities were preparing to spend their long vacation on the 'Mississippi Summer Project'. They were ready to risk their lives in helping Negroes win a better education and their legal right to be registered as voters. Already three students had disappeared in Central Mississippi, and their comrades knew that murder was not too big a crime to daunt fanatic racists. (The young men, two white and their Negro companion, had indeed been killed.)

The long dormant Ku Klux Klan was active again in the South. The hooded figures, symbolic of white superiority, had first appeared a century ago, after the Civil War, creating their own terrible law of lynch and whip. Now, in protest against the Civil Rights Bill then going through Congress, the Klan, under the leadership of Imperial Wizard Robert Shelton, was once more on the warpath with all its mumbo-jumbo methods of intimidation. The fiery crosses were burning on the hillsides and in the fields of the Old South, beacons of fear, threats of death.

That night in New Orleans I experienced the same strange *frisson* that I had known in Christianborg Castle in Accra many years before. Christianborg – now a residence of Kwame Nkrumah – had been, down the centuries, a fortress, a castle and a prison, the Gold Coast depot for slaves from the hinterland awaiting transportation to the New World. In the darkest hour of a night like this I had stood on the battlements above the sea. It was the hour when the wind drops and the tide turns and all is still save the thump of the surf against the dungeon walls, and it seemed to me that the moan of the waves was the lament of captives who would never see their homes again, nor the light of day till the slave ships carried them across the ocean to unknown fetters and unknown toil.

For many the banks of the Mississippi had been journey's end. The ghosts that lamented at Christianborg walked here too.

In *A Nation of Immigrants*, the book on which President Kennedy was engaged at the time of his assassination, he wrote of the American Crucible:

> Only in the case of the Negro has the melting pot failed to bring a minority into the full stream of American life. Today we are belatedly, but resolutely, engaged in ending this

condition of national exclusion and shame and abolishing forever the concept of second-class citizenship in the United States . . .

Equality in America has never meant literal equality of condition or capacity; there will always be inequalities in character and ability in any society. Equality has meant rather that, in the words of the Declaration of Independence, 'all men are created equal . . . (and) are endowed by their Creator with certain unalienable rights'; it has meant that in a democratic society there should be no inequalities in opportunities or in freedoms.

Out of a total population of 200 million the United States has 20 million Negroes, a restless minority, its theoretical equality hamstrung in fact by poverty and prejudice. Throughout the land, from Hollywood to the Deep South, the melting-pot was simmering with the dark frustrated ingredient so difficult to assimilate, a strong ingredient that will one day inevitably colour and flavour the whole brew.

At present the Negroes form one tenth of the population, but it is estimated that the black women bear 40 per cent more children than whites and that by 1972 the proportion will be one eighth, and that, in many great American cities, Negroes will be in the majority.

The dark tide is flowing fast. It is important now, even frightening, but does it matter in the sea of time? On the lip of the Grand Canyon I had ceased for a moment to think in decades. The spell of that mood was still upon me. The great waters that cover the face of the earth flow into one another without restraint, each ocean subject to its own climate and storms with its own prevailing winds and currents. These currents may be hot or cold, breeding the life of tropic coral reefs or Arctic ice-floes; their influence is as powerful on land as it is at sea, affecting every growing thing, from plants to people. Is it impossible for the races of the world to exist together in tolerance, to overlap and merge, to influence one another and yet retain their own individual character in a greater or lesser degree; to be drops in the mighty ocean of humankind?

Abraham Lincoln and John Kennedy, both victims of an

assassin's gun a century apart, shared the same ideal – that every person, regardless of creed or colour, should be given the opportunity to develop to the limit of his or her capacity. It doesn't really seem too much to ask, either in the United States, or South Africa, or anywhere else on earth.

CHAPTER TWENTY-ONE

Virginia, the Honeysuckle Trail

Our flight to Charlottesville, where our friend, Frances Hoare-Smith, was to meet us, was both beautiful and boompety-boomp.

Charlottesville is half-way between New Orleans and New York. When we left the Mississippi we looked down on Georgia with its peaches, and South and North Carolina with their tobacco plantations, and soon we were flying across the Great Smoky Mountains that merge into the Appalachian Range to form a forested barrier between the coastal valleys and the interior. Westward lay the Atlantic and the islands first explored in 1584 by two of Sir Walter Raleigh's naval captains, who sailed north from the Gulf of Mexico up the coast of what is now North Carolina and landed on the islands of Wokokon and Roanoak, bestowing the name of Virginia upon the entire region (much larger than the present State) and taking possession of it in the name of Elizabeth, the 'Virgin Queen'. Europe was always doing this. Somebody stepped ashore in a new continent and simply planted a flag and 'took possession' in the name of his country, regardless of the fact that the territory was already populated. Heathens just didn't count!

Captain Barlowe's reports to Sir Walter Raleigh make entrancing reading today (in Hakluyt's *Voyages*) and must certainly have rejoiced the heart of the gallant courtier-sailor for whom they were originally intended. The sea around Virginia teemed with fish and the islands with 'Deer, Conies, Hares and Fowl . . . in incredible abundance'. The woods were glorious with 'the highest and reddest Cedars of the world; Pines, Cypress, Sassafras, (and) the Lentisk, or the tree that beareth the Mastick, the tree that beareth the rind of black Cinnomon . . . and many other of excellent smell and quality'. Of the natives he wrote:

The next day there came unto us divers boats, and in one of them the King's brother, accompanied with forty or fifty men, very handsome and goodly people, and in their behaviour as mannerly and civil as any in Europe. . . . A day or two after this we fell to trading with them, exchanging some things that we had for Chamois, Buff, and Deer skins.

The 'things' exchanged for the furs were mostly tin dishes which the King indicated would make fine breastplates against enemy arrows.

On the strength of Captain Barlowe's glowing accounts, Raleigh decided to establish a trading-post which could also serve as a foothold against intrusion by Spain and would form the nucleus of a colony. He sent an expedition consisting of seven ships under the command of Sir Richard Grenville, carrying supplies, and colonists to the tune of a hundred men and seventeen women. One wonders how these individuals were persuaded to embark upon such a hazardous enterprise. By skilful propaganda – or a touch of duress? Perhaps a combination of the two, just as sailors were pressed into service against considerable opposition but hoped (when they came to!) that they might have the good fortune to share in plenty of loot.

The early Virginian expeditions all followed a classic pattern. The future colonists were dumped in their distant dangerous territory under the leadership of someone deputed to be 'Governor', with ample provisions and basic supplies for a certain period, during which they were advised to fish, cultivate tobacco and other crops, to trade, and to appease the 'savages'. They were promised that ships would return in due course with further supplies including 'good women'. Then a Spanish or a French war would intervene, there'd be no ships to spare and the settlers would be left to fend for themselves and the devil take the hindermost – which he seldom failed to do. Another invariable snag was the mood-swing of the natives. When they found that those who had come to trade and gone away, swearing eternal friendship, had returned with guns to share their country, they not unnaturally ceased to be 'civil' and became hostile. It was a very old story.

Before long the little settlement was in serious trouble with the Indians and was only rescued by that exciting and efficient sea-hawk, Sir Frances Drake, who happened to pass that way, home-ward-bound, after one of his highly successful voyages in search of Spanish treasure ships. When he realized the desperate plight of the colonists he took them on board. Loaded down with Spanish loot and disillusioned British pioneers, he sailed into Portsmouth harbour in the summer of 1586. Meanwhile Sir Richard Grenville had been as good as his word – though several months overdue – and had arrived in Virginia with more supplies and settlers. The fact that the colony had evaporated in the mean-time was disturbing, but Grenville was a man of positive purpose. It is recorded that 'he determined to leave some men behind to retain possession of the Country, whereupon he landed fifteen men on the Isle of Roanoak, furnished plentifully with all manner of provision for two years, and so departed for England'. Two years! Did the men draw lots for the privilege of retaining 'posses-sion of the Country'? And how did the poor wretches feel when they stood on shore and watched the wind fill the shrouds of the departing barque? So long as she was there with her guns and her fighting men they were safe. What now? She'd be back in two years – or three, or four – but where would they be then? The answer to that question was provided by a member of another expedition dispatched by the persistent Raleigh in the following year.

. . . we found none of them, nor any sign that they had been there, saving only the bones of one of those fifteen, which the Savages had slain long before.

The three and twentieth of July, the Governor with divers of his company walked to the North end of the Island, where Master Ralph Lane (Governor of the first colony) had his fort, with sundry necessary and decent dwelling houses, made by his men about it the year before. . . . When we came thither, we found the fort razed down . . . overgrown with Melons of divers sorts, and Deer feeding on those melons; so we re-turned to our company, without hope of ever seeing any of the fifteen men living.

They learned later from a friendly Indian that the fifteen had been killed by the tribe. Hardly a propitious welcome for the new colonists! It was 1587 and the war with Spain was approaching its climax. The Armada sailed in 1588 and every English ship was needed to destroy the might of Spanish sea power. The colonists left in Virginia were the forgotten men. A few abortive attempts were made to see how they were getting on, but it was not till 1607 that yet another and better equipped expedition was landed at Jamestown in the name of the London Company with a charter to trade and settle. Meanwhile the unfortunate Roanoak colonists had met with the same ugly fate as the fifteen. All, save seven, had been massacred.

The new Company, depressed but not daunted, planted tobacco and did its best, but after four years of Indian wars, sickness and famine, the settlers persuaded Captain Christopher Newport, who had arrived with still more colonists, that the enterprise was doomed. He agreed to take them home. And just then, as in a tale of adventure, the well-stocked ships of Lord de la Ware, who had been appointed Governor-in-Chief, appeared at the mouth of the James River and everybody was persuaded to give the project another trial. Ten years later the first Negro slaves were imported to the plantations, the tobacco industry grew in importance and a sound Government was established. A new civilization had been firmly implanted in Virginia.

In 1620 the Puritans settled in New England and forty years later the Quakers colonized Pennsylvania. Britain's American colonies grew and strengthened between the coast and the line of French forts barring the way inland. Their raw materials and industries prospered, but they were disunited and independent, fighting the Indians continually, and the French off and on, till the British conquest of Canada broke the power of France in North America. From that time onwards Britain began to exasperate her trans-Atlantic colonists. Unreasonable tariffs and taxes inflamed other quarrels, and by 1775 George III and Parliament between them did what the Indians had failed to do – united the colonies against a common foe. It was sad that the foe should have been the Mother Country. The War of Independence lasted seven years, and France and Spain helped the colonists. Virginia was the heart of that war, just as she was later to be the heart of the four-year Civil War between North and South.

It could be England! I thought, as we came out of the clouds over the mountains and looked upon the soft well-watered hills and vales of Virginia, the scattered farms among great trees, and horses and cattle grazing in green pastures. When we stepped out of the plane at Charlottesville airport the summer afternoon was sweet with the scent of honeysuckle, and there, on the grassy verge of the runway, stood Frances.

Three years had elapsed since last I had seen Frances, whose English naval husband, Captain Gerald M. Hoare-Smith, had died in the beautiful heatherland country of George in the Cape of Good Hope, where they had made their home after the war. The last time she and I had met had been on board the ship that was to take her back to America – alone. My husband had been with me that day. Now, as we greeted each other, the tears of many poignant memories stung our eyes. But soon we were laughing and talking, covering up emotions, catching up on news.

'It's about thirty miles to Keswick,' she said. 'Through an English type of countryside. It's horse-breeding country. One of the Keswick Stud foals fetched eighty-five thousand dollars at the Saratoga Yearling Market in New York State.'

'Those blissful cattle!' Elspeth was enchanted by the Herefords and Ayrshires, and I was fascinated by glimpses of stately mansions set back in parks and gardens.

'Some are still privately owned,' said Frances. 'Others have been converted. For instance, my Club, which is also a Golf and Sports Club, is a very fine example of what a southern home used to be like in the spacious days.'

Honeysuckle rampaged over high banks patched with the delicate pink and white of laurel and the deeper glow of wild azaleas.

'The scent – it's heaven!' I inhaled it with delight.

'The honeysuckle trail,' said Elspeth. We had followed many 'trails' in our American travels.

'It's a weed here,' said Frances. 'A strong one – all over the place. Now, about Cloverfields where I live. It's an eighteenth-

century farm homestead – like so many that you have at the Cape –
but it's a country guesthouse now. It belongs to Mrs Rafferty
and Mrs Jocelyn, two sisters, members of the original family
who received the title deeds from George II in 1730. They've
known me since my childhood, and in that house I'm still Frances
Nolting, and Miss Frances to the coloured cookie, just as you,
Joy, were always Miss Joy in your mother's home.'

She turned into a long avenue of oaks in the full splendour of
their summer foliage, and the moment Cloverfields came into
view I understood why she had always loved the Cape and felt at
ease in its old homesteads of this same period. They too have
dignity and grace and a welcoming atmosphere.

Cloverfields was a big colonial clapboard house with the
traditional high-pillared porch front and back. Its white wood-
work was dappled with the shade of graceful Kentucky locust
trees, limes, poplars, oaks, willows, and dogwood that in spring
is starred with pink and white flowers.

Mrs Rafferty and her sister came down the steps to greet us
with such warmth and spontaneous Irish charm that we felt at
home immediately. It was very easy to see that, in this place, the
years 'Frances Nolting' had spent out of Virginia with her English
Naval Officer husband must have appeared to her old friends like
a strange interruption that had enriched and altered the course
of her life for a time – something almost mythical that only a
sudden break in her deep voice or a certain sadness in her eyes
could bring into sharp clear focus for a minute.

Frances had a suite on the ground floor and, since two of the
residents were away on holiday, Elspeth and I were allowed to
occupy their rooms. Our windows framed the wonderful trees
full of songbirds – even the wrens trilled like nightingales – and
between the leaves we glimpsed meadows abloom with little
flowers, and the attractive clapboard and log cabins and cottages
occupied by various relations of our hostesses – sons, daughters,
nephews, nieces and grandchildren – all with one thing in
common, a passionate Irish love of horses and dogs. One son-in-
law was a master of foxhounds; a Madonna-faced daughter was
responsible for walking adorable hound puppies; everybody of
a reasonable age (neither too old nor too young for his or her

knees to grip the horse's flanks) rode with the Hunt; and Frances, who had no family of her own, shared the interests and friendship of this vital human tide that surged in and out of Cloverfields.

On the evening of our arrival we had drinks on the lawn under the trees in front of the house.

'So that you can meet the others,' said Frances.

'The others' came and went in the dusky half-light of that balmy evening, and later we dined with our fellow guests at the long refectory table where Mrs Rafferty and Mrs Jocelyn took turns to preside over the generous meals of the South.

After dinner we sat out of doors and talked far into the night. Fireflies danced among the leaves, and the hounds from the cottage across the woods bayed to the great red moon rising above a gap in the trees. Honeysuckle drenched the soft air, intoxicating and nostalgic. Like the lilac in Oak Creek Canyon it spoke of the little island whose brilliant, grasping, eccentric Queen had given Virginia its name in the golden age of her reign.

A coloured maid brought me coffee and toast in bed next morning and I felt more than ever at home. I could hear Mrs Jocelyn on the back porch giving orders to her farm-hands. The poultry and domestic animals were her concern. Both she and her sister had seen the last of seventy but they were ageless – far too busy to get old.

Of course Frances took us to the stud farm.

'They have to see Kelsey Stud,' said Mrs Rafferty. It was inconceivable to her that we should miss horseflesh at its most aristocratic.

The owner was away but a friend took us round, and we gazed at colts frisking fetlock-deep in lush paddocks, separated by the pretty white plank fences of the countryside. The main stables were in a huge 'barn'. Never have I seen such superb equine accommodation. Gentle, spirited eyes looked meltingly into ours from luxurious stalls, and we walked round the great elliptical arena on a broad sawdust track. A valuable mare in labour moaned like a human being, and we left her to her birth-pangs while we went back to the homestead. At its core was the owner's bedroom, a pine cabin reminiscent of an earlier age, a homely pearl embedded in a large elegant eighteenth-century shell.

One day we went up into the wooded Blue Ridge Mountains along the hundred mile Skyline Drive overlooking the Shenandoah Valley that was such a bloody battlefield in the Civil War. We saw deer in the glades, but no bears or bobcats came ambling out of the ancient hemlock groves or indigenous forests. Ravens, buzzards and vultures planed overhead while the smaller birds went about their summer business in the trees. Long ago this had been the hunting ground of Indian trappers, but the first white explorer of the uncharted range was John Lederer, sent by Virginia's Governor, Sir William Berkeley, at the end of the seventeenth century. He found only wolves, bears, deer and birds. No other signs of life. Later the settlers pushed their frontiers forward into the mountain valleys and glens and made a living out of barktan and timber.

In our short time at Cloverfields Frances managed to show us a great deal, besides visiting the homes of her friends and swimming in their pools. The University of Virginia at Charlottesville was very dear to her heart. Her father had been a distinguished architect and her appreciation of its beautiful and unusual features was almost professional. It had been designed by America's famous President, Thomas Jefferson, the Virginian who followed George Washington.

Thomas Jefferson was more than an architect of classic houses and academic buildings; he was a statesman and a student of government, and it was he who drafted the American Declaration of Independence with its never-to-be-forgotten manifesto.

> We hold these truths to be self-evident, that all men are created equal, that they are endowed by their Creator with certain unalienable Rights, that among these are Life, Liberty and the pursuit of Happiness.

The manifesto was intended to assert the equality of the rebellious American colonists with their rulers in England. It was not concerned with Negro slaves. That was another and a greater revolution, which came much later and swept Europe first and America last. When it did, its impact provoked her long sad Civil War, and it was then that Abraham Lincoln stretched Jefferson's American creed to embrace all mankind.

Thomas Jefferson's home, Monticello, on a high hilltop above Charlottesville, is today maintained as a memorial to him. From this three-storeyed domed mansion in its lovely gardens and plantations we looked down upon the University of Virginia as he had done in the days when he trained his telescope on the site and watched every stage of its building and progress. He died at Monticello a few years later in the bosom of his family at the age of eighty-three. It was 1826, and the great rotunda that is the library and dominating feature of Thomas Jefferson's 'academic village' had just been completed. He had seen the creation of a place of reflection and inspiration, a place of green vistas, of gardens cloistered by mellow brick serpentine walls, of classic pavilions and colonnaded dormitories built around this central rotunda. In his era there were 218 students; today there are five thousand, and tomorrow a growing proportion of them will be Negroes. He had not envisaged that!

We were to have broken our flight from Charlottesville to New York at Washington for twenty-four hours sight-seeing. But we were easily persuaded that it would be impossible to do Washington justice in so short a time and that it would be better to stay on at Cloverfields and go direct to New York. So we rested at the end of our honeysuckle trail, lazy and contented, slowly beginning to assimilate some of our experiences and impressions of the United States that had offered us so many aspects of her complex and immensely varied scene and character.

'One learns a little bit of history here and there in one's travels,' I said to Frances, 'a wider understanding. No wonder there was a time when your country didn't want to know about Europe's wars. She's practically never stopped fighting her own!'

'And still does – on far-away fronts.'

'The world's too small these days and America's too big. Where Europe's concerned, it's the flow-back.'

Long ago Europe had conquered the American continent, now the United States is all-powerful in Europe. The 'nation of immigrants' has the blood of every European country in her veins; she is unique in the world and in our time.

We left Virginia refreshed and relaxed. As we flew over that gentle State, which has suffered the martyrdom of war with such courage, I opened a book of Walt Whitman's poems and prose. Some of his original manuscripts are housed in the rotunda of the University of Virginia, the land which stole his heart. I turned to the words he had written a century ago when he served as a medical aide to the wounded soldiers of the Civil War.

Dilapidated, fenceless, and trodden with war as Virginia is, wherever I move across her surface, I find myself rous'd to surprise and admiration. . . . The soil is yet far above the average of any of the northern states. And how full the breadth of scenery, everywhere distant mountains, everywhere convenient rivers. Even yet prodigal in forest woods, and surely eligible for all the fruits, orchards and flowers. The skies and atmosphere most luscious . . . I should say very healthy . . . a rich elastic quality, by night and by day. The sun rejoices in his strength . . . the nights are often unsurpassable. Last night (Feb. 8,) I saw the first of the new moon, the outlined old moon clear along with it; the sky and air so clear, such transparent hues of colour, it seem'd to me I had never really seen the new moon before. It was the thinnest cut crescent possible. It hung delicately just above the sulky shadow of the Blue mountains. Ah, if it might prove an omen and good prophecy for this unhappy State.

That silver winter sickle had indeed been 'an omen and good prophecy'! I closed the book and thought of the grand old ladies whose hospitality we had received; of the hounds baying to the full moon on an 'unsurpassable' night of fireflies and 'atmosphere most luscious'; of the moaning of a mare bringing forth a winner; of the great sheltering trees, and of the scent of wild honeysuckle that, for me, will always evoke the soft Virginian scene.

CHAPTER TWENTY-TWO

'Hi, New York!'

We were to change planes at Washington, and we regretted that all we would see of this beautiful city was a bird's eye view. But Virginia had seduced us. The afternoon was heavenly, clear and springlike, and there it lay beside the blue Potomac River, spreading tidily inland in a well ordered pattern of parks, lakes, gardens and buildings, a worthy seat of the United States Government. The great dome of the Capitol brooded majestically over the White House and the City, almost sanctimoniously, like St Paul's in London, St Peter's in Rome, or St Sophia in Istanbul.

Beside me, Elspeth took a mirror from her handbag, examined her reflection critically, and ran a comb through her hair.

'Another airport,' she said. 'Then one more, and that'll be the lot.'

We stepped out into the sun, and I groaned.

'Now for the long trek!'

It seemed a mile from the runway to the Central Hall, where we checked our tickets on to New York and vowed once again never to squeeze excess weight into our handgrips. I no longer wondered why St Christopher was the patron saint of travellers. His burden had grown heavier and heavier the further he carried it: so did our handgrips at innumerable airports. We walked another mile or two along a tunnel to the observation lounge. It was worth it. The Capitol dominated the horizon and the river gleamed on the boundary of the airfield. Gulls galore presented their small problem to the stiff-winged giants of the air and I wondered how many were sucked and plucked in a day. Feathers against iron. Arrows against guns. Man's weapons and inventions grew deadlier and more potent with every decade. That was President Johnson's problem – over there, in the White House.

When this city came into being a century and a half ago, after the Declaration of Independence, it would have been impossible to foresee our nuclear age. Even Jules Verne didn't get quite that far.

It has occurred to me that cities expressly designed to be the capitals of aspiring countries possess the cool cerebral quality of Athena, patron and founder of the world's most precious city, Athens. Athena sprang, fully armed, from the brain of her father, Zeus, ready, at birth, to assume all the honours and responsibilities of her senior status as Goddess of Wisdom. Capitals like Washington, Ankara, Canberra and Brasilia share this same feature. The long period of infancy, childhood and adolescence has been by-passed by a single builder's leap into maturity. They are as old as their first buildings. They represent the regal crown of a nation. The heart you must seek elsewhere. North, south, east or west, you will find America's heart – a strong pulsating heart that has grown with a nation's lifetime of struggle, suffering and success. Washington is the head. It commemorates the name of the man most responsible for his country's unity and independence.

George Washington, born in 1732 and destined to be a General, a statesman and first President of the United States, was, like his successor, Thomas Jefferson, a Virginian. He too had plantations and slaves; and he married a rich wife who brought him more of both. He ran his plantations judiciously and treated his slaves with humanity and kindliness; he was an athlete, a swordsman and a wrestler, keen on fox-hunting and horse-breaking. He enjoyed his military career and, as a young recruit, wrote to his brother: 'I have heard the bullets whistle; and believe me, there is something charming in the sound . . .' Defeat was a word he recognized only when it applied to his enemies. The Union of the States was his noble conception and with the might of arms and pen – Jefferson's pen – he brought it into being. As President he was aloof and formal, and some complained that he behaved as if he were 'a king'. Yet he had won the day for democracy – that word which is so fat with good intentions. As for equality: like truth, it must be sought at the bottom of a well.

'That's our flight being called,' said Elspeth. 'We'd better get weaving; it's a long trail to the runway!'

The last airliner of our world tour was an enormous jet from Miami, Florida. It was packed to capacity and there was no hope of a window seat. So my first glimpse of New York was of a dense and complex design of closely built areas spreading for many miles from Manhattan Island across the Hudson bridges. It was much interrupted by the bobbing heads of other passengers.

The Hudson River was charted early in the seventeenth century by an English navigator, Henry Hudson, flying the Dutch flag and seeking the fabled north-west passage. But he had to report that the river led neither to the Pacific nor to China and the Indies. Some years later Peter Minuit, first Director General of the Dutch West India Company, brought off the smartest deal of all time and purchased Manhattan Island from the Indians for twenty-four dollars and a handful of trinkets! His countrymen colonized the port and named it New Amsterdam, but in 1664 the British seized it and re-christened it New York. The fortunes of war and treaties of peace between Britain and the Netherlands tossed it back to Holland and back again to Britain, who lost it finally to her rebellious colonists. It was there that George Washington was inaugurated first President of the United States of America.

We landed at John F. Kennedy Airport some sixteen miles out of New York, and, after the usual long march, an affable and fine-looking Negro in charge of baggage found us a taxi and put us on our way. We told the driver we were strangers and he immediately constituted himself our guide. Kennedy Airport was being redeveloped, he told us. We had landed in the old unimpressive part.

'Where's Idlewild?' I asked. 'I've always heard of Idlewild.'

'Lady,' he said patiently. 'You've just come from there.'

'But that was Kennedy.'

'Same thing. They changed the name.'

'What a pity! Idlewild is such a lovely name.'

'So's Cape Canaveral. They changed that too. It's Cape Kennedy now. When the President was killed the whole nation was in shock. They just kept naming and renaming things for Kennedy. Old and new, anything at all. Now, *there's* the World Fair! Looks good. You'll be going to that.'

We stared at bizarre pavilions and pleasure grounds, and

Elspeth murmured to me: 'That's not for me. Not another world tour – not yet.'

Away ahead the famous skyline came into view, suddenly revealed by a bend in the road, a masterpiece unveiled, a picture long familiar from films and photographs, yet totally unexpected. Like the Grand Canyon, it caught you off guard. The Canyon was the ageless creation of nature and New York was the contemporary zenith of man's architectural genius.

In the sultry lemon-gold of that June evening the unbelievable towers and spires leaped up into the sky like tapering tongues of flame, ethereal, touched with magic. I saw a legend written against the sky and heard its music – the Wagnerian strains of Gotterdämmerung. Valhalla in the last blaze of glory, before the twilight of the gods, might have looked like this; the Valkyries rode the firmament again, their strange steeds springing from the rocket base of Cape Kennedy, their destination nowhere.

'There on your right,' said the taxi driver, 'that's Harlem.'

The great wedge-shaped Negro ghetto, over fifty blocks long, stretches along the waterfront into the heart of Manhattan Island right up to the fringe of Central Park. Some 250,000 people live in the squalid overcrowded tenements, more than ninety per cent of them Negroes and the rest Puerto Ricans and poor whites. It is the dark side of New York, only a few miles from the world's telescope, the United Nations Building.

'Can you take us into Harlem?' I asked. 'It would be interesting—'

'Could be too interesting! I wouldn't go in there for any money. Harlem's a bad place these days and the black man's in a bad mood. If a coloured man calls my cab I don't see him.'

'Why's that?'

'I been stuck up twice. That's twice too many.'

'What d'you mean – stuck up?'

'A gun in my back while they wait for me to hand over my money. And they don't wait long! They're killers in there.'

He jerked his head in the direction of the high blocks with shabby washing fluttering above dingy streets. I found it hard to believe. This wasn't the Deep South with a long history of slavery and humiliation. This was the North, where all men were equal and the White House could be any man's goal, regardless of creed or colour. In theory anyway.

The trees of Central Park were in the young leaf of early summer, and we looked for miles down an avenue a hundred feet wide.

'Fifth Avenue,' said our driver with nonchalant pride. 'All the way from Central Park to Washington Square. Straight avenues, straight streets across them, blocks between. You can always find your way in Manhattan.'

I had expected the skyscrapers to be claustrophobic, pressing down upon the streets, darkening them, dwarfing humans into ants. Instead New York City is a place of airy beauty, the summits of escalating towers stepping gracefully back to allow the free flow of light and air.

About 13 million people live in and around Manhattan, a polyglot population containing a high percentage of Italians. We saw no Western fancy costumes here; the prevailing impression was of well-tailored clerical grey.

We drew up at the St Regis between Fifth Avenue and Madison Avenue. We scarcely had time to pay our driver before the next occupants were piling into his cab. As in London, the demand for taxis is greater than the supply.

Our hotel was luxurious and not too big. An elaborately adorned elevator whisked us up to the seventeenth floor. I dared to go to my window among the roof-tops and spires. It wasn't even high – until you looked down. The carpet was as soft as a Virginian meadow.

My telephone rang. It was Bill Berger, my literary agent, who was coming round later to make my acquaintance. So far we had met only on paper.

'How will I know you?' I asked.

'That's all right. I'll know *you*.'

He was tall with iron-grey hair and an olive-green dinner jacket, and next day I discovered that he had a riverside apartment and office, and the only cat I have ever met prepared to do a trick and 'sham dead' at the word of command. She was a fine beast and probably rode broomsticks on moonlight nights. Shamming dead was the rent she paid for the full ownership of Bill's apartment.

I was welcomed and entertained by my American publishers; and kind friends took us to exotic restaurants, and to their clubs that might easily have been in London, so sedately Edwardian were the furnishings, so English the assumption that the best was just good enough. But those extra dry, excessively potent martinis enjoyed by the members were not in the least English! We went to 'Barefoot in the Park', an essentially New York play, very funny and rather unsophisticated. We goggled at the lights of Broadway and Times Square, but reckoned they didn't really have much on Shaftesbury Avenue and Leicester Square.

'One's always a bit over-impressed by the other man's city,' I said.

'Wait till you see Grand Central Station,' said Elspeth. 'That's going to impress us no end.'

It impressed us so much next day with its bright functional dignity, and we were so busy comparing it with drab old Waterloo, that we almost missed our train to New Haven, Connecticut, where we spent the day with Elspeth's friends, Mr and Mrs John Moffitt, who had a lovely home in that city of woods and gardens, parks and vistas. But the real core of New Haven is Yale University which centres round the elaborate tower of Wrexham Memorial Quadrangle, the replica of Wrexham Church in Wales, where Elihu Yale is buried. Elihu Yale, citizen of Boston and one time Governor of Fort St George, Madras, was the first great benefactor of the newly founded University. In those days – 1718 – the American colonies had not yet broken away from England, and it seemed to me that the older parts of Yale, mellowed, gothic and shaded by great trees, were reminiscent of Oxford, the matriarch of all English-speaking universities.

We had booked seats in the observation car of our train back to New York and we sat comfortably in swivel armchairs and watched the pretty water-front with yacht clubs and holiday homes and a wealth of flowering trees, and then we plunged into one of the many long tunnels that connect New York with the mainland or other adjacent islands. New York City is compressed into the length of Manhattan Island and the only ways in or out of it are under or over the river that girdles it. Bridges, tunnels, subways and ferries convey the City's millions to and from their daily work.

I found it difficult to believe that this rich important port, probably the biggest in the world, with its huge population speaking every conceivable and inconceivable language and all thinking American, had been born at the same time as my home town. Cape Town too is a key point in the trade routes of the globe, and, like New York, it was brought into being by Dutch mercantile enterprise, but there the likeness ends. The Dutch East India Company sent Jan van Riebeeck as first Governor of the Cape of Good Hope in 1652, while his contemporary, Peter Stuyvesant, was ruling New Netherland for the Dutch West India Company. New Amsterdam (soon to be re-christened New York when the English flag was raised in 1664 – without bloodshed) was Stuyvesant's seat of Government. He it was who established the first municipal government for the city he was destined to relinquish to the British much against his will. He had fought the Portuguese at Curaçao and lost a leg, so he stumped around with a peg-leg decorated with silver bands. He was recalled to Holland after the surrender of New Amsterdam, but the New World was in his blood and he returned to Manhattan, where he owned a farm called the Bouwerie, from which the present Bowery takes its name. He died there in 1672 and was buried in a simple chapel. In 1799 that lovely church, St Mark's, was erected on the site of his burial place.

Of course we found time to go shopping. Elspeth knew exactly what she wanted, while I wandered aimlessly through showrooms filled with temptation. Round the corner of Bonwit Teller's we ran into a queue stretching miles down Fifth Avenue. It was orderly and we wondered what it could be. New York is not a city of queues like London.

'An exhibition of the late President Kennedy's favourite possessions,' said a policeman.

We didn't join that queue. We went our own ways and met that evening in Elspeth's room, which looked onto a charming little roof-garden. She had a friend with an antique shop down there somewhere, and she had lunched that day in Wall Street with another friend while I had been occupied with my literary engagements.

'I can't tell you what it was like,' she said. 'Paul's office is on the forty-seventh floor of the Chase Manhattan Building. One wall is all window – the river wall. He was at his desk when I was shown in and, when he stood up, he might have been standing in space! I didn't dare walk forward. I crept round the wall, touching it, terrified – but terrified!'

She had mastered her terror, however, and was rewarded by seeing the world's first atomic merchant ship, the 22,000-ton *Savannah*, come up river to her berth with escorting vessels and a true noisy New York welcome.

'The noise and excitement! Tugs hooting and barking, liners blowing their fog-horns in salute, fire-boats putting up such a spray we could scarcely see the ship at times – and was she beautiful! Snow white, flagged all over, and they say she can go round the world without refuelling. Practically perpetual motion.'

She broke off when a bellhop brought in an armful of parcels.

'I can't wait to show you my shoes!' She opened the shoe-boxes and produced the longest neatest narrowest most elegant shoes I had ever beheld.

'Triple A's. Where else in the world do they care about women with narrow feet? We have to go slopping around in boats. And in here is the suit from Bergdorf Goodman.'

'Oatmeal,' I said. 'Very simply tailored.'

'How did you guess?' She laughed as she unknotted the string with those long almond nails. 'And I suppose you went out and bought yourself a blue dress.'

I had to admit it. 'But it's a very good blue. Not quite navy.'

'You don't have to tell me.'

The Bergdorf Goodman suit was lovely and very expensive and just right for my friend's triple A figure. But, really, in New York, which is the centre of the American clothing trade, you can buy the most attractive dresses and costumes at very reasonable prices. American clothes are different. They have gay and springlike touches, and every stenographer can look like a million dollars – and most of them do.

'What's in that box?'

'Jane's foundation. No wonder she wanted me to get it for her here. Their undies are marvellous. Cosmetics too. They really consider women in America.'

'You can tell that from the cartoons – even if you've never been here. The women are always a little taller than their husbands and they get their own way and the last word. It's a woman's world. And now I must go and put on my new blue dress. It has a coat with a lime green and cherry lining. I think you'll approve.'

Her eyes danced, and she left that unanswered. She had to change too.

'Our last evening,' she said. 'I wish we had longer here. Can you imagine Central Park with snow underfoot and all these dream spires dripping icicles – Grandmother's diamond earrings! It must be glorious in winter.'

Her infatuation for America reached its peak in New York. It was Elspeth's Mecca. She worshipped happily at the trans-Atlantic shrine, which she had approached in humility – if not barefoot, then 'slopping around in boats' (actually Elspeth has never 'slopped' in anything in the whole of her life) – and I knew that when she went on board the *Queen Elizabeth* next morning in her new suit and shoes she would feel as good as any *hadji* wearing the ceremonial *yashmak* after the great pilgrimage to Islam's holy city.

CHAPTER TWENTY-THREE

'So Long, America!'

On our last evening, Bill, my literary agent, invited a few friends to his apartment to meet me. Among them was the editor of a famous magazine for women.

'What's the theme of your next novel?' she asked.

'I don't know yet.'

'Why not the colour bar?'

'Not as a main theme. Only in so far as it impinges on the everyday life of people like you or me. In South Africa that amounts to a strong secondary theme – often highly dramatic.'

'Why not as a primary theme?' she persisted.

'For a good many reasons. Too much of the intimate detail of a black homelife would obviously lie outside my personal experience. One would need to *live* in a black home to understand it fully. Then, too, I don't regard the colour bar as fundamental – like love or hate or jealousy or the aloneness of people. It's a prejudice rather than a basic emotion.'

'But this prejudice – this barrier of colour – surely that's basic!'

'I believe it's transient. I think it'll come and go like the persecution of the Jews, and only certain people will practise it. It's one of many forms of intolerance.'

'Intolerance doesn't die.'

'It goes out of fashion. The world is outgrowing discrimination in all its aspects. Racial equality, in particular, is a world trend, and the stronger because it's largely born of white guilt.'

'Like the emancipation of slaves.'

'I'd say so.'

She was a tall young woman with sincere spiritual eyes and untidy auburn hair. She tossed back her coppery mane and gave me a very straight look.

'Your government wouldn't subscribe to that.'

I laughed. 'We aren't brain-washed. A lot of us do our own thinking.'

'What makes you say this colour prejudice isn't basic?'

'Because its roots lie in pigmentation, environment and inferior education. The first will be diluted by miscegenation when the second two are improved – especially here, where the emphasis is on integration at every level. The emancipation of women was far more complex. There, the difference was as fundamental as it could possibly be. There's still a chronic battle over equal pay for equal work, and there's a perpetual argument about the effect on a home when the mother is a career woman. That's what I call a basic problem.'

Bill topped up her Bourbon on the rocks, and the cat jumped into my lap and purred loudly.

She frowned. 'That's half of Harlem's problem. The women work, the men loaf because they can't get jobs, and the children run wild. A big proportion are illegitimate, anyway. No wonder they hunt in packs.'

'I've read about that in your papers. The Blood Brothers – teenage killers trained to use knives, razor-blades and deadly judo grips – like guerillas. They lie in wait in the subways and rape and murder whites. Why – when the White House is so determined to see them right?'

'It's a symptom. It stems from poverty and unemployment; slum conditions; narcotics – ten per cent of Harlem's population are needle addicts – while the teenagers smoke reefers the way we used to try out cigarettes when we were kids. You talked about education. A Negro school will have about forty to a class and the teacher spends the lesson keeping order instead of instructing the pupils. It's estimated that Negro school-leavers are a couple of years behind their white contemporaries, so what chance have they got of horning in on skilled work? The women can get better jobs and better pay. Only when every school is integrated and the blacks share the same education as the whites will you get some foundation for equality of opportunity. And that means a social revolution.'

'Isn't that what your Civil Rights Law is supposed to produce –

something approximating to Britain's long bloodless social revolution?'

'Prejudice checks our reforms.'

'It can't stop them. Only sixty years ago women medical students weren't allowed into dissecting rooms; they were stoned in the streets outside Edinburgh University. Nobody despises a woman doctor these days on the grounds that she's the wrong sex for her job. It'll be the same with your blacks – easier in the long run because social integration will lead to intermarriage. A snuff-coloured nation.'

She accepted the idea with a philosophical shrug.

'What would happen if you tried integration in South Africa?'

'We're a white minority. We'd lose our country in less than ten years and find ourselves with no place to go. We're not English, Portuguese, Belgian or French with a homeland to run to if we're kicked out of Africa.'

'What's the solution?'

'There are no simple solutions for us. Our Government recognizes and develops certain territories as Bantu homelands – rather like you have your Indian Reservations. But with a difference. Your Indians are Americans. The Bantustans will be autonymous states, foreign Frankensteins standing round our borders.'

'What's the future of that?'

'I'm no crystal-gazer.'

'Look into the bottom of your empty glass. What do you see?'

'I see my country shrinking into a small white sock on the foot of a huge black continent – an important naval base on the Eastern sea route, strategically valuable as a vital stronghold against Communism in Africa and the East. I see our leaders learning sense and treating the black foreigners in the Republic with the same courtesy they accord any other foreigner—'

'Uhu – that's looking mighty far ahead!' She threw me a cynical smile that widened into gaiety. 'We talk as if fate allowed situations to develop quietly and naturally towards their logical conclusions. Long before they can do that some shattering event intervenes and everything blows its top.'

If she had read her own empty glass that evening could she have seen into the following long hot summer! The racial riots of Harlem, the death lists of Los Angeles and Chicago, or the tragic Act of God that added to the torture of the Deep South with the Mississippi floods; the mass burials of Louisiana's dead, and the dreaded alligators and snakes surrounding her river homes like the forces of evil incarnate?

I refused to let Bill drown the picture in the bottom of my glass, and the cat spilt off my lap as I rose to go. She stretched, yawned and went out – in search of her broomstick no doubt. Night had fallen and the witching hour was at hand.

When I got back to my room at the St Regis I scribbled the gist of that conversation into my writer's note-book. As I put it away the police sirens screamed. Their sinister wail was as much a voice of the night as the roar of a hunting lioness in my own distant country.

I went to the window, wondering what the emergency was. Could be anything. But now, in this summer of fear and dis-content, it was probably a white victim bleeding to death in some deserted tunnel. City police had been doubled, their cars guarded every six hundred feet of certain subways, the Jewish community of a section of Brooklyn had established its own vigilantes throughout the hours when 'the streets were dark with more than night'; but violence did not sleep.

The sirens died away, and once again I yielded to the magical beauty of New York. The green floodlit dome of the Waldorf, the fragile lace minaret of General Electric and the star-seeking spire of the Empire State Building rose from the shadowed floor of Manhattan with ineffable grace. Like the buttes and pinnacles of Arizona's Grand Canyon, they were sacred places; shrines of Mammon, of big business and high finance. Not far off was the twentieth-century Tower of Babel, the United Nations Building. There were many climates in the Grand Canyon of Manhattan, many life zones, from the poisonous reptiles in the depths to the gentle deer on the heights.

Even the stars above the city's loom were not all of God's making. Somewhere up there was Telstar; and particles of man's scientific ingenuity whirled round and round among the constella-tions of space. Human beings strive upward, always up. It seemed to me that America's creed was written across the firmament in the script of New York's aspiring silhouette – 'the sky's the limit!'

The great liners lay in their berths along the Hudson River like horses in their stalls, nosing the embankment. The *Queen Elizabeth* was the biggest and most imposing of them all – a seasoned senior, presiding over her section of the docks with regal self-assurance, regardless of that proud white warning of the shape of things to come, the nuclear *Savannah*.

'One's right in the middle of Manhattan,' I said. 'Those sailors in the rigging look as if they're climbing the skyscrapers!'

'Who'd be a sailor or a steeplejack?'

We were in the observation lounge for'ard.

'She's incredibly high – this ship!'

'And incredibly long. But I expect we'll soon get our bearings.'

Elspeth was very knowledgeable about the *Queen Elizabeth*. She had been briefed by Peter and Pam, who had made the crossing scores of times.

'We have breakfast in bed about eleven tomorrow,' she went on. 'Lunch whenever we like, dinner any time at all – caviare or smoked salmon, crêpes suzettes, anything we want – and we see the very latest pictures at the cinema. There's bingo and dancing and a cabaret, and the band plays in the Verandah Grill till sun-up – if there's anyone left to dance. How about that?'

'Too good to be true.'

But those splendid phantoms – Peter and Pam – who had guided us across the American Continent did not fail us now. Everything was all they had cracked it up to be, and Elspeth knew her way around that monster vessel as if she had travelled in Queens all her life instead of for the first time. We went shopping, of course, because Bond Street was on board. 'Twin sets and cosmetics – not to be missed,' she quoted Pam. 'And we dress up. Everybody dresses up to the nines.'

She was right about that too, although there were no glamorous film stars on board as we had hoped there might be.

It was thrilling when our leviathan began to get under way,

moving out into the River, pushed and pulled by her busy escorting tugs. It was cold with the threat of rain, and waves beat stormily against the island base of the Statue of Liberty, France's gift to America. The great figure with the torch looked lonely and brave and noble, the symbol of a nation that wants to honour its high ideals. The open sea was grey and choppy and I thought of the little ships that had brought the first English settlers to the shores of North America so long ago.

We went down to the smoking-room and ordered drinks from the barman who always looked after Peter and Pam. We felt that we had known him for years.

'You know something,' I said to Elspeth, when he had brought us olives and almonds and gone to take another order. 'It's an awfully long time since we've heard the English language as she's spoken in her own country!'

I discovered later that the deck steward had served with my husband in H.M.S. *Warspite* during the war. When he talked of the Navy in the windy sunshine out on deck, a great slice of my life, long dormant, woke with a host of living memories. Young adventurous sea-gypsy travels; haunting anxious wartime years; the sharp zest of brief reunions, and poignant partings with the future obscure and danger on every side. I was glad when my husband's old shipmate sought me out and placed my chair in some sheltered corner – 'so you can be alone to scribble in that big note-book of yours' – but more often than not, when he left me, I'd sit with my hands idle in my lap and my eyes closed, oblivious of the huge liner bearing me across the North Atlantic, seeing only the lean grey warships that had been my rivals, my pride and the greater part of my destiny.

The place he had found for me was quiet and out of the wind.

'This is where Sir Winston Churchill used to like his chair,' he said with affectionate reverence. 'You must see his life on the pictures. We'll be showing it this trip – "The Finest Hours", it's called.'

So that too quickened the past and left me raw. Elspeth and I had heard those great fighting speeches in the Battle of London when we had shared her agony and her triumph. Afterwards, when the film was over, we recalled that the *Queen Elizabeth* had

been a troopship in the years when the U-boats hunted in packs
to savage the convoys and the lone troopers. Like Churchill
himself, this ship was old and proud, an asset in peace and a
menace in war.

Her staff worked round the clock to give the passengers a good
time. Every morning the *Ocean Bulletin*, North Atlantic edition,
published on board, was pushed under the cabin door and with
it 'Today's Programme', which offered entertainment for everybody, day and night. Then at last we were docking in Southamp-
ton, and the boat train was speeding through the wooded English
countryside with bluebells radiant on the banks and may foaming,
pink and white, in the hedgerows. I had forgotten the wonder of
copper beeches and the dark majesty of spruce.

At Waterloo we parted, Elspeth to go home to her Chelsea
flat, while I took a taxi to the South Kensington mews cottage I
had taken again for the summer.

The tulips in Hyde Park stood to attention in battalions of
regimental colour; the great chestnuts spread their candles of
salmon and cream, and willows leaned over the Serpentine where
waterfowl floated sedately beneath a canopy of noisy gulls. Odd
looking couples strolled across the grass – bearded beatniks in
leather jackets and girls in tights with long straight hair raining
down their faces and over their eyes. Dogs chased each other and
fought and frisked while humans went their own sweet way, as
they do in England. My heart lifted. London – with her crescents
and leafy squares, her mansions and cottages, her parks and old
London River – was still the dearest city of them all!

I paid off my taxi outside the bright red door and the driver
carried my cases up the seventeen narrow steps to the top of the
stairs. Rona, Glen's step-sister, who owned the cottage, was
waiting to welcome me and stay the night before returning to
her husband and their home in the country. The window-boxes
spilled over with geraniums and forget-me-nots; a hand from a
window farther down the Mews scattered crumbs for the pigeons
and sparrows who descended onto the cobbles with a whirr of
wings. A little golden dachshund made a feint at them and
scattered them momentarily. Rona's elderly purblind poodle was
curled up in her basket in the kitchen while a Chihuahua,

trembling with taut excitement, stood in the open doorway at the foot of the stairs.

'Nothing has changed!'

'Not even him,' Rona shooed the tense suitor off the doorstep, and shut him out. 'He's the sex maniac of the Mews, that Mexican!'

She looked round at the lovely flowers that filled the cottage.

'I've run out of vases. You're lucky to have so many friends.'

'How well I know it! Is Mrs Barnes coming tomorrow?'

Rona nodded and smiled. 'As usual.'

The cottage wouldn't have been the same without Mrs Barnes. She'd bring me my coffee and toast tomorrow morning, and a grapefruit which she'd buy on the way from Fulham to South Kensington. We'd laugh and talk, and it would be good to see each other again.

A pile of letters lay on the writing desk with the proofs of my new novel, *The Man in the Mews*, begun in this cottage last summer and finished in Australia. All that could wait till next day. Tonight Rona and I would talk our heads off.

The church-bells chimed, and the long English twilight flowed gently into the room. The telephone rang.

'There'll be a lot of that,' laughed Rona.

I went to it, happy, knowing I'd hear the voice of one of my friends. The great continents and oceans were forgotten; only this little island mattered now, and this cottage of many memories. Piet and Glen had lived here when first they were married, while Piet was a medical student at Guy's. I could almost see the big Russian blue cat who had adopted them – the cat who came in out of the cold and made his home at their fireside.

My ghosts were everywhere, and I was glad of them.

CHAPTER TWENTY-FOUR

Land of Their Origin

I had my car in London, and towards the end of July I drove north to see old friends and my husband's sisters, Winifred in Worcestershire and Dorothy and her husband, Professor Norman Capon, in Wales.

The drive from London was sheer delight. I was alone but well content to fall under the familiar spell of a countryside infinitely varied, safe and cosy, enclosed by hedges and the horizons of an island not too large and not too small. The wider horizons lie in the English imagination, in the minds of sailors and of the young men and women who have always braved the unknown in search of greater opportunity for themselves and their children.

Oxford, where Piet had been at a preparatory school during the early years of the war, was relaxed in the lazy reflective glow of the long summer vacation. The Cotswold villages rested sleepily behind their mossy stone walls or contemplated their ancient rural images in quiet waterways; the Vale of Evesham was as lovely as its name, rich and fruitful; there were swans in the reaches of the River Severn. In Worcestershire the hay was harvested in neat bales and the hops were high on their trellises, and every now and again a gap in a hedge revealed the rolling landscape where cows grazed in meadows powdered with daisies and slashed with the hot yellow of mustard.

Mine was a sentimental journey to the sixteenth-century cottage, sheltered by orchards and girdled by a stream, where my sister-in-law, Marion, had created an enchanted enclave, a cottage garden that was pure rustic England, its essence unchanged from the reign of the first Elizabeth to the second.

There Marion had 'painted' her seasonal pictures – 'I *see* it,

247

Joy-Joy! I paint it in my mind and it happens!' She had called forth her flowers, coaxing reluctant spring through the white wintry earth, making of summer a magic so spontaneous that one held one's breath to behold it, and of autumn a treasure of copper and gold. Winter had been the long fallow Sunday of rest. Nothing was forced in her garden, nothing grew out of its natural order. She and the Creator of all things bright and beautiful were in perfect accord. Her corner of Eden was a sanctuary for birds and beasts, for the trout in the horseshoe bend of her border stream, or for the troubled heart of a friend in need. She no longer toiled joyfully – though often painfully – in her garden through the long evenings of summer twilight. She rested in a hallowed pasture where the birds sang in the surrounding orchards between the green grass and the pearly sky. But her garden, tended by her sister, Winifred, remained a thing of rare and cherished beauty, and the little crucifix over the cottage doorway was still a talisman against all evil.

I spent a few days nearby in a small black and white Elizabethan inn anchored in a sea of fragrant roses. Then Winifred and I drove on into Wales by way of Shrewsbury on the Severn and Llangollen on the Dee.

The Welsh town of Llangollen was in gay regalia for the Eisteddfod contests and celebrations. Groups of folk singers and dancers from many countries strolled along the river bank, wearing their colourful national costumes, and the Welsh, in their full skirts and black steeple hats with goffered white frills under the brims, were like folk from the age when wizards and witches chanted incantations and cast spells. We wound up the Horseshoe Pass where the shaggy little sheep came to our picnic spot to share our lunch. Ruined abbeys and castles dotted the mountainous scene. Most impressive of them all is the great medieval mass of Ruthin Castle, now a luxury hotel, where Winifred and I stayed for the few days of our family reunion with Norman and Dorothy Capon.

In the market square of the old hilltop town of Ruthin the local aged sat on benches in the pale primrose light and smoked their pipes, occasionally mumbling to one another in a language that made soft gibberish to my ears.

My brother-in-law smiled. 'What d'you expect? You're in Wales and Welsh is the language of the people.'

We stood looking down upon a fertile undulating scene of green fields and woods.

'Good pasturage for our sheep,' said Norman. 'But not much like the Outback stations you've told us about!'

'No. But it could be Virginia. It's not surprising that the first Virginians fell in love with their new land. Even uncultivated, it must have looked like home. But they weren't fighting each other like the Welsh and the English, they were soon at war with the Indians.'

'And later with each other,' Norman reminded me. 'The human animal is a predatory quarrelsome beast by nature. He spends his life grabbing and mating and fighting.'

Virginia was often in my mind that summer holiday. The dust of Elihu Yale was part of a Welsh churchyard; and later, when I said goodbye to my husband's family and went to friends in Gloucestershire, the long roots of that trans-Atlantic State caught up with me again.

I broke my journey for a few hours to wander round Berkeley Castle at the mouth of the Severn. Like Ruthin Castle it had been a moated fortress guarding the Welsh marches, but it was even older, dating right back to Edward the Confessor and the Norman Conquest. Its massive cliff-like walls and ramparts of Cotswold stone, the colour of dried rose-petals, gloomed over its lawns and lake and the shining river that bounded land so often torn by war. Centuries of history haunt its baronial hall, its galleries and rooms. King Edward II was murdered in the King's Gallery and Sir Francis Drake had frequently stayed in a room which bears his name. Among the family portraits of famous Berkeleys who had fought their country's battles on land and sea was one of Sir William Berkeley, that arrogant nobleman who was appointed Governor of Virginia in 1641. His was a proud and forceful face, bold and fiery. For a time, while Oliver Cromwell wielded power at home, Sir William Berkeley, a staunch loyalist, had retired to his plantation, but after the Restoration he had returned to his post.

He had lived like a despot in Virginia, autocratic and intolerant, persecuting the Puritans, exploring the country, fighting the Indians and the French and oppressing his opponents, till finally he found himself with a rebellion on his hands. So ruthless were his methods of quelling it that even his patron, Charles II, could not countenance them, and he was recalled in 1677. He died that same year in Twickenham. His brother, John, first Lord Berkeley of Stratton, was one of the proprietors of the Carolina Plantations.

Thus it has been down the centuries in Britain. Her sons and daughters, from the highest to the humblest, have sailed to the distant lands of her dominions and colonies, where, by and large, their influence has been for good. Human beings – explorers, administrators, merchants, missionaries, labourers, and even convicts – have been Britain's most significant exports. Her colonists have been her greatest contribution to world progress and the advancement of backward races. Inevitably, exploitation and colonization often went hand in hand, like the good and evil in our schizophrenic world. They can only be weighed against each other in the scales of time, and by that test Britain has come out well. Her island cannot support its population, and throughout her history, she has been compelled to expand. Now a strange thing is happening. Her black chickens are coming back from the ends of the earth to roost in the overcrowded country and cold climate of their foster mother. She can offer them a new high standard of living.

That summer I became aware of a growing hostility against these cuckoos in the matriarchal nest – even unto such un-British manifestations as fiery crosses burning on the doors of Jamaican and Pakistani immigrants. Yet here, as in America, successive governments had tried to persuade and compel the integration and absorption of the dark Commonwealth tide flowing so strongly towards the home island. Britons are reasonable people – insular abroad, perhaps, but tolerant at home – and their prejudice has a rational basis. It is not so much a matter of complexion as of the fact that they fear the newcomers will cause a slump in social and economic standards. Their way of life is different. It is still natural for coloured immigrants to live in swarms and to produce numerous children and some of them take readily to easy-money rackets – to traffic in women and drugs, to intimidation of a strong-armed brand. Violence lies near the surface in the Negro temperament. It is hot and ebullient, in tune with nature's cruel and profligate forces. Nature, left to herself, produces life with prolific speed and squanders it callously. The same applies to that child of nature, the Negro, not yet inhibited by centuries of artificial social restraints.

Thus coloured immigrants came to live in overcrowded neighbourhoods which, once respectable, deteriorated into ghettoes, and the Rachmans and their fellow gangsters grew fat on these conditions. Britain is not a vast country like America, Australia or South Africa with great vacuums for industrious settlers to fill. She can absorb so many and no more; thus it is little wonder that cities already beyond saturation point should show concern. Emotions are roused too for other reasons. Male immigrants outnumber female, and white boys find themselves competing with coloured immigrants for their girl friends. Nothing could be more fundamental or inflammable than this sex rivalry. In the animal kingdom any new intrusive herd invading a home territory to mate with the females or threaten the grazing is asking for trouble. The human animal reacts to the same stimuli in the same way. He demonstrates, and then he fights.

The 'mods' and 'rockers' too were adding their contributions to the disturbances of the English summer. Let a 'mod' steal a 'rocker's' girl and the insult would be settled with a knife-thrust. These white teenage packs, hungry for excitement and publicity, made themselves aggressively important by taking their private gang warfare to public holiday resorts. It was as if new barbaric forces had suddenly been unleashed, naked and exhibitionist. Even the screaming teenage girls, yielding hysterically to the tom-tom beat and witch-doctor wail of pop singers with strange names, seemed to be part of some primitive fertility rite finding a new weird outlet in civilized society. They were the ones who made the headlines as they were carried, 'sent' and tranced, moaning, foaming, or shrieking, from performances that in a savage community would be conducted with the tribal secrecy of initiation ceremonies.

But the great majority of young people command my unstinted

admiration. Their lives are not easy in an age of new freedoms which hustle and corner them into relationships for which they are not ready. The girls spring from childhood into maturity at one leap; the romantic dreams of adolescence are transformed into clumsy realities, and they often have to grope their way through a tangle of confused and lacerated emotions into the only real security a woman wants. Marriage, a home and a family. Having achieved that, how self reliant and sensible these young couples are! They run their homes and bear their babies with the minimum of fuss and the maximum of philosophic good sense. Standards and attitudes have changed, but youth remains essentially sound.

When I left my friends in Gloucestershire I drove back to London by way of Stratford-on-Avon, where the white swans grace the river with privileged pride.

In Perth, Western Australia, the city of the Black Swan, there is, at the University, a replica of Shakespeare's earliest theatre, where his plays are performed as they were in his own day – except, of course, that young actors no longer have to take the part of female characters. In Stratford, Shakespeare's Memorial Theatre is strictly twentieth century.

England's theatre is diffused today, no longer concentrated in London. The Shakespeare season, the Edinburgh Festival, the National Theatre at Chichester and the avid demands of the screen all milk off the best producers and theatrical talent, so that the London theatre, which once offered so many sumptuous courses, is now meagre fare. Among the few theatres playing to capacity was the Lyric with 'Robert and Elizabeth', the story of Robert Browning's stormy courtship of Elizabeth Barrett, set to music. The lovers were played by two Australians, Keith Michell and June Bronhill.

Keith Michell came from Adelaide and June Bronhill from Broken Hill in New South Wales.

When I read her name on the programme, I turned to Elspeth who was with me.

'Do you remember Beth Gall telling us about June Bronhill? She used to sing at concerts in Broken Hill and the people were sure she had what it takes to make a real first-class singer. They raised fifteen hundred quid to send her to England.'

'Yes,' whispered Elspeth. 'And she took the stage name of Bronhill – short for Broken Hill.'

She hadn't failed the city that had proved its faith in her. We recalled the unfailing generosity of the Outback – the people who always helped one another. We too were proud of the stars of 'Robert and Elizabeth'.

The leaves of the plane trees danced along the Embankment before the wind; chrysanthemums appeared in the flower-shops; women calmed down after the brief lunacy of the summer sales; Wimbledon was cold; Ascot was drowned; Cowes took the rough with the smooth; and Goodwood, between the great estates of noble Dukes, was the friendliest race meeting of the year; and so the London season went its customary way into early autumn, when wilting debs and exhausted mamas took hard-earned vacations. August settled into an Indian summer. Beech leaves, bright as sovereigns, rich as rubies and sere as parchment, lingered on the parent trees, bracken tarnished slowly, and the fickle sun shone with sweet fidelity day after perfect day.

Elspeth and I made plans to return to Australia in 1966.

'And next time it has to be New Zealand too!' she said. 'Now you must write your book.'

'How can I settle down to work after nearly eight months on the spree?'

'You'll enjoy it. It'll be fun digesting our travels, living them over again, sharing them. You can start work on board ship on your way home.'

A few days later the red front door of the mews cottage closed behind me for the last time. The window boxes were ragged now, the geraniums leggy and tired, the forget-me-nots shedding their petals. A chill little breeze snuffed its way over the cobbles between the pretty houses. The Indian summer was at an end and soon the grey days would stretch their damp fingers over the London scene.

But when I landed in Cape Town a fortnight later spring's carpet covered the land. Namaqualand daisies and brilliant *vygies* splashed their dazzling colour everywhere; arums creamed the fields; water hyacinths scented the *vleis*; the oaks were in young green leaf and the vineyards budded in valleys where blossom surged and the tall pale poplars stood guard between one paddock and the next. The sea – jade, purple and sparkling sapphire – scalloped the shore, and the white dunes gleamed in the sun.

I walked up the easy mountain paths of Kirstenbosch wild gardens. Sugar-birds swooped and flirted among the proteas in courtship displays and sunbirds hovered like tiny singing jewels. The heather hummed softly with harmless bees, its scent intoxicating in the sparkling air. Silver trees burnished the slopes, and, far below, the Flats, yellow with wattle, spread away to the mist-blue ranges between the coast and the hinterland.

The waterfall roared in Skeleton Gorge, and the torrent, swollen with recent rain, foamed over the boulders in laughing cascades.

There, on the mountainside, that glistening spring day, who could possibly doubt that the world is a proud and wonderful place!

Cape of Good Hope
October 1965

H